BOMBER BARONS

By the same author:

Calshot, 1913–61
The Flying Elephants
Mosquito at War
Hurricane at War
Airmen of World War One
Sunderland at War
Hampden Special
Beaufighter at War
Path Finders at War
Albert Ball, VC
For Valour – The Air VCs
Sopwith Camel – King of Combat
History of the RAF, 1912–78
Guns in the Sky – The Air Gunners
Coastal Command at War
Spitfire
Fighter Command 1936–68
Surviving Aircraft of World War Two
Age of the Biplane
Bomber Group at War
Air War over Europe, 1939–45
Desert Air Force at War (co-author)
Encyclopaedia of British Military Aircraft
Lancaster
Hurricane
Wellington at War
Images of Air War, 1939–45

Edited:

Bomber Pilot 1916–18
Fighter Pilot on the Western Front
Wings over the Somme
Fall of an Eagle – Udet

BOMBER BARONS

CHAZ BOWYER

LEO COOPER

First published in 1983 by
William Kimber & Co. Limited

Published in this format in 2001 by
LEO COOPER
an imprint of Pen & Sword Books Limited
47 Church Street
Barnsley, South Yorkshire
S70 2AS

A CIP record for this book is
available from the British Library

ISBN 0 85052 802 X

Printed in England by CPI UK

DEDICATION

To the greatest Bomber Baron of them all :
Marshal of the RAF Sir Arthur Travers Harris Bt,
GCB, OBE, AFC, LLD – 'Butch'.

Contents

Introduction

Comparisons are always invidious, particularly in the contexts of human courage and endeavour. To attempt to define courage alone involves myriad variables of circumstance, opportunity, ability, and individual motive and determination. It follows, therefore, that in any overall view of the aerial warfare of 1939–45, for example, to single out specific roles as being more important than others is to pursue a rutted, biassed outlook on recording history. If, for instance, the chosen criterion was the acreage of media exploitation and fulsome plaudits given to the deeds of fighter pilots – a continuing near-obsessive facet of 'research' which I personally term the 'ace cult' – then any objective reader would be presented with an entirely false, unbalanced picture of the aerial conflict of World War Two, and for that matter of its earlier counterpart of 1914–18. I would be the last to minimise in any manner the vital and enormous contribution to the air war made by fighter, maritime, reconnaissance, or other air and ground crews throughout 1939–45. Nevertheless, it should be firmly recognised that the *prime* weapon of aerial offensive warfare had to be the bomber. Only the bomber forces *could* have a true overall strategic impact and influence on the course and eventual outcome of the war, albeit necessarily closely interlocked with all other air arms within their air forces for protection, close support, intelligence, *et al.*

The aerial bombing offensive against (mainly) Germany and Italy by Royal Air Force Bomber Command during the years 1939–45 has been the subject of many published works in the years since that fateful conflict. Some have been academic studies by learned authors, some – relatively few – have been autobiographical, offering an individual participant's view of the offensive from a singular view-point, while certain more recent tomes have emerged as merely sensation-seeking diatribes by journalists and novelists plainly jumping on the aviation history wagon. Nearly all have made oracular judgments of the ultimate effectiveness of RAF Bomber Command's offensive; indeed, a few appear to have set out simply to 'prove' how

13

*in*efficient and purposeless that offensive was in the final analysis, thereby – albeit unwittingly on occasion – denigrating the actions of the crews who participated, and by inference the men themselves. To judge any particular generation's morals, actions, or behavioural standards by the mores of later (or earlier) generations is not only illogical, but can only produce a misleading and distorted set of conclusions.

My purpose in this book is not to pontificate about any final analysis of the RAF's bombing offensive during 1939–45, but simply to bring together within the limited parameters of one pair of covers descriptions of a tiny handful of the sort of men who were tasked with implementing that aerial assault at the 'sharp end'. For all the machinations of the chairborne strategists and hierarchies, it fell to the ordinary bomber crews to fly into enemy-held skies by night and by day to pursue that offensive – and to place *their* young lives in dire jeopardy *each* time they set out on an operational sortie.

While the wartime lay public quickly became familiar with names and deeds of a host of fighter pilots, only rarely did a bomber 'boy's' name appear in headlines; two prime exceptions to such anonymity were Wing Commander Guy Gibson, vc, dso, dfc, and Group Captain Leonard Cheshire, vc, om, dso, dfc, whose truly outstanding flying careers were widely broadcast both during and since the war years. Within RAF circles, however, many men with comparably notable careers achieved unsought, and unpublicised, high reputations among their peers on the bomber grapevine as superlative examples of those undefinable qualities of rare courage and instinctive leadership; individuals who unconsciously inspired total confidence and trust in all with whom they flew to war.

Such men became familiarly dubbed 'bomber barons' by their contemporaries – the cream of Bomber Command in the eyes of their fellow fliers. Those barons varied widely in character and background, seldom conforming to any lay image of the hero of romantic fiction; indeed, not all were necessarily popular in the social context. Nor was there any specific standard of sortie totals, or multi-decorations, to identify a baron. Many rose to senior rank, with three-figure operations' tallies; others died as junior officers or senior NCOs before their true potential had been realised or achieved. Yet all had in common a spirit of dedication – to their 'job' and, especially, to their crews; a spirit often termed 'press-on' in RAF parlance, though each man would have vehemently denied such a label.

My selection of barons herein is patently a personal one, but I would emphasise to the reader that I might equally have featured the careers of many other bomber men who worthily earned the soubriquet baron, each of whom would provide a comparably vivid example of those supreme qualities to be found among so many men of the bombers. As will be seen, many made the ultimate sacrifice in pursuit of their self-imposed codes of duty, honour, and 'brotherhood' – let their example *never* be forgotten.

CHAZ BOWYER
Norwich, 2001

CHAPTER ONE

Background

Any assiduous student of aviation history can piece together a factual history of RAF Bomber Command by reference to a host of published material, official documents and records, private sources, etc. Pure statistics, though invaluable to the dedicated historian and researcher, remain merely an exercise in mathematics and long hours of faithful re-recording unless they have some purpose. In the specific context of this book, however, the unadorned facts behind Bomber Command's aerial assault on the Axis powers during 1939–45 will provide not only an authentic backdrop to the bombers' efforts, but will illustrate only too starkly the conditions with which those crews had to contend, thereby offering an accurate perspective to the actions and accomplishments made, individually and collectively. In particular, the scale of their overall sacrifices, suffering and prowess will become plainly evident.

At the outbreak of war with Nazi Germany in September 1939, RAF Bomber Command was little more than three years old as a distinct formation within the structure of the Royal Air Force. As such the Command came into official existence as a separate entity on 14 July 1936 with its headquarters at Uxbridge, commanded initially by Air Chief Marshal Sir John Steel, who was succeeded in his appointment in September 1937 by Air Chief Marshal Sir Edgar Ludlow-Hewitt. Originally, the Command comprised three groups of regular-service RAF units, totalling 32 squadrons, plus No 6 Group, consisting of twelve squadrons of the Auxiliary Air Force and Special Reserve. At that date, without exception, every squadron was equipped with biplane bomber designs, but in the same year the Air Ministry issued to tender various specifications calling for twin- and four-engined monoplane bomber projects for future RAF use.

With the highest priorities for expansion and financial allotment at that period being awarded to the Royal Navy, then RAF Home Defence organisations, Bomber Command's actual expansion and re-equipment with more modern aircraft was relatively slow, at first, but the introduction of several modern bombers to firstline squadrons – as represented by such designs as Vickers Wellingtons, Armstrong Whitworth Whitleys, Handley Page Hampdens, Bristol Blenheims, and Fairey Battles – soon increased in mounting pace before 1939. By September 1939 the Command's strength showed an overall total of 53 squadrons, spread among six groups, though only 33 of these were classified as operational; the remainder being Group Pool (Training) or Reserve units working up to operational fitness, or acting simply as training sources for advanced air crew trainees prior to the latter joining operational squadrons.

On 2 September 1939 the Command's operational strength in Britain was abruptly decreased when the ten squadrons of Fairey Battles comprising No. 1 Group flew across the Channel to France to provide on-the-spot tactical support to the British Expeditionary Force (BEF); while No. 2 Group's seven Blenheim squadrons were on standby to join the Battles later – a move soon postponed and, by December, cancelled.

This depletion of UK-based bomber strength meant that Bomber Command at the outset could only call on 23 *operational* squadrons – some 370 aircraft – to instigate any form of aerial offensive against Germany. Even these units were equipped with Whitleys, Hampdens, Wellingtons or Blenheims; all twin-engined medium range designs with limited bomb load capacities and equally limited capability for penetrating German skies to any significant depth. Other restrictions upon the Command's potential striking powers were many. Political havering and indecision during the opening months of the war resulted in severe parameters being imposed upon Bomber Command in respect of the type of objective it could actually attack. Initially, no bombs were permitted to be dropped on to German soil, and only German naval targets could be assaulted – though, curiously, these did not include dockyards.

Nevertheless, RAF bombers penetrated German skies on the first night of war, 3/4 September, when ten Whitleys 'bombarded' Hamburg, Bremen and part of the industrial Ruhr area – with six million (13 tons) of propaganda leaflets! On 4 September a force of fifteen Blenheims set out actually to bomb German warships reported at Wilhelmshaven and the Schillig Roads, while a separate gaggle of Wellingtons attempted to attack shipping at Brunsbüttel. The Blenheim raid devolved into a near disaster. Five aircraft could not even find their target and returned to base; five others were shot down trying to bomb the *Admiral Scheer*, while a high percentage of bombs dropped failed to detonate or achieve any damage. The Wellingtons lost two aircraft to German defences; one to flak and the other to a Messerschmitt Bf 109 from II/JG77 – the first RAF aircraft destroyed by the Luftwaffe fighter force during World War Two.

If such results seemed inevitable to die-hard military authorities, they were merely part of the overall operational picture of the period. Primarily, the bombers had carried out their raids in broad daylight *without* any form of fighter escort; a policy of potential disaster inherited from World War One which complacently maintained that a closely-formated bomber force could by its combined defensive firepower ward off any enemy fighter opposition. This policy continued to be adhered to by Bomber Command chiefs for many months, despite such overt examples of its folly as a raid by 24 Wellingtons against Wilhelmshaven on 18 December 1939. At 18,000 feet, in a clear blue sky, the immaculate formation was swamped by a succession of Luftwaffe fighters. Twelve Wellingtons were shot down, and three others crashed on return to England – a casualty *rate* of almost 63 per cent.

Such fiascos were no fault of the air crews involved, unless a natural over-reliance on inculcated, rigid, peacetime RAF training and tactics could be blamed. The bombers they flew were badly equipped for the war conditions in which they were expected to operate. Internal heating for crew comfort, and hence efficiency, was virtually non-existent. Oxygen systems were unreliable. Defensive firepower was inadequate. Navigational aids were outdated. Aircraft radios were obsolete Standard bombloads, comprised mainly of obsolete General Purpose (GP) bombs of 250 lb and 500 lb designs were, in the main, impotent against thick-skinned or armoured targets, creating little worthwhile damage. Fuel tanks were unprotected against bullet or shell intrusion.

By early 1940 Bomber Command had begun to direct its main assaults against German targets by night. Though this ploy offered better, natural protection to unescorted bombers, it also exacerbated the myriad deficiencies of crews and equipment. In particular, the lack of internal heating, either for the crew or their technical equipment, nullified many sorties. The winter temperatures of 1939–40, by night especially, coated outer surfaces with ice and frost, while below-zero levels internally froze controls, instruments, etc., and provided instant ice-burns should any crew member thoughtlessly remove a glove and touch metal. Hydraulic systems froze solid, as did oxygen lines, bomb-release circuitry, wireless sets. Each sortie became virtually a raw contest of human endurance against some of nature's more deadly facets.

The overall character of Bomber Command operational procedure at that time was somewhat piecemeal. Briefing of crews tended to be casual affairs, omitting specific timings of sortie-starts, arrivals over target, etc. – these 'details' being mainly left for individual crews to decide. The actual sorties too were highly individual, each crew and aircraft being on its own once airborne and on course for Germany. Usually, only Command Headquarters really knew the actual total numbers of aircraft despatched each night; at squadron level the crews were often only aware of their own unit's participation. This seeming lack of sensible co-ordination of bomber forces was not entirely due to any loose administration or communication twixt HQ and squadron; the plain fact was that Bomber Command simply had totally inadequate numerical strength in aircraft in 1939–40 to attempt any form of inter-laced bomber stream or massed formation for the nightly air offensive.

The operational bomber crews of the early years – in the main regular-serving, ex-peacetime men – were given no specific number of sorties to accomplish before being rested from firstline operational flying; the concept of limited-sorties' tours for bomber crews had yet to be introduced. It meant in practice that many crews on squadrons in September 1939 were still flying operational trips to Germany in late 1940 and early 1941; albeit at a more 'leisurely' frequency than was to be the case in later years. Yet if the pace of operations during the first twelve months appeared relatively slow or sparse, the toll of air crews and aircraft indicated the increasing dangers. In those twelve months 1,381 air crew men were killed, 419 became prisoners of war, and 269 were wounded – all on operations. A further 383 died on non-operational activities and 217 were injured/wounded. In summary, nearly 2,700 bomber men 'removed' from the firstline squadrons – a figure equivalent to more than the entire operational crew strength of the Command on the outbreak of war. During the same period the crews had released a gross total of 6,766 tons of bombs on enemy objectives; had despatched totals of 9,001 sorties by night and 3,040 by day; and had lost 342 aircraft 'missing' alone – 175 of these by day – apart from an even greater quantity of aircraft written off in crashes and other accidents. Of the aircraft officially listed missing, less than fifty had been claimed by German nightfighters; the bulk fell to the anti-aircraft (flak) guns, day fighters, or technical troubles.

Yet what was actually achieved for such sacrifice? In truth, very little. The gross bomb tonnage dropped had been relatively small and spread over a myriad of objectives, none of which had suffered significant damage. The chief bugbear for the crews was simply their inability to navigate *accurately* to any designated target by night, lacking the radar navigation and bombing aids which had yet to be introduced;

indeed, the crews' prime aid for navigation-cum-target-location then was merely a full moon ! The extent of this failure to find targets was reflected in the opinion of Air Chief Marshal Sir Richard Peirse on succeeding to control of Bomber Command in October 1940, who stated that only one out of five bombers despatched on operations even *found* their briefed objectives – and even this twenty per cent made actual bombing errors from five to 100 miles away from the actual target.

To blame the crews for this would have been quite wrong. Most were inexperienced in nightflying, let alone night bombing – the pre-war trained crews had seldom even practised take-offs and landings by night with a full bomb load until the war came. Their aircraft and instrumentation aids were in the main unsuited or obsolescent for bombing distant targets 'in anger'. Moreover, the higher 'policy' for Bomber Command then lacked positive direction or aim. While such diversions as the tactical bombing of invasion barges *et al*, during the 1940 Battle of Britain had been vitally necessary, such dispersion of effort merely diluted any possibility of mounting a true strategic bombing offensive against Germany. The successive AOC-in-Cs of Bomber Command in the period 1939–42, four in all, received a steady flow of priority directives, outlining prime objectives, these being changed almost from month to month at one stage by either the Air Staff or, occasionally, by imperative personal orders from the Prime Minister, Winston Churchill.

The year 1941 brought little overall change in the broad picture of bomber operations. New squadrons were slowly formed, new bomber designs commenced their operational careers, including the first of the long-awaited four-engined heavy bombers, Short Stirling and Handley Page Halifax, alongside the twin-engined Avro Manchester and De Havilland Mosquito. Even the American Boeing B-17 'Flying Fortress' made its operational debut in Europe, wearing RAF livery with No 90 Squadron, in July. Of these, however, only the all-wood constructed Mosquito could be claimed to be successful from the outset; all other new aircraft had dismal initial sorties abounding with technical teething troubles and no small casualty rates.

In addition, fresh, bigger bombs came into firstline usage, while in August 1941 the highly secret GEE radar aid to navigation and target location had its first Service trial over enemy territory; and in December a blind-bombing device coded 'Trinity' (a crude form of the later-termed Oboe radar device) was tested over Brest. In December, too, came deliveries of the first three examples of the revamped Manchester

– now titled Lancaster – to No 44 Squadron, harbingers of the main heavy bomber equipment of Bomber Command in the near future.

For the crews, the year had seen an escalating intensity in operational efforts with totals of 27,101 sorties by night and 3,507 by day; though inevitably their losses mounted too – 701 aircraft by night, 213 by day, and at least 300 more aircraft which crashed on return and were write-offs. These losses represented some 4,000 and more human casualties killed, wounded, prisoners of war, or just classified as 'missing'. Of the night losses, 421 had been justifiably claimed by Luftwaffe nightfighters (compared with only 42 in 1940), despite the relatively weak strength of the *Nachtjäger* at that time. Convinced of an early victory in his recent invasion of Russia, Hitler refused to acknowledge any urgency for building an adequate Reich defence force against the RAF's bombing incursions; this left the nightfighter units with little more than 250 fighters in total, only half of which could be counted as ready for action at any given moment. Each of these were simply day fighters with few modifications or special equipment for their highly specialised role, making their successes all the more remarkable.

The year 1941 was also a crucial one for the very existence of Bomber Command as a 'separate' strategic offensive formation. The increasing successes of Germany's U-boats in their predacious attacks on Allied merchant shipping supply lines in the Atlantic had resulted in clamorous demands from the Royal Navy and RAF Coastal Command for many bombers to be transferred to convoy protection and anti-submarine duties – a petition backed in some degree by Winston Churchill. The seeming failure of Bomber Command to inflict any significant impact on Germany's will to wage war weakened the Command's protestations for maintaining its independence. This situation was still fermenting when, on 23 February 1942, Air Vice-Marshal Arthur Harris succeeded to the appointment of AOC-in-C, Bomber Command, a position he was destined to occupy until the end of the European war.

On occupying his chair, Harris inherited a Command comprised of 58 squadrons, though seven of these were non-operational for various reasons; a gross tally of little more than 600 operationally-fit aircraft on any given night, of which less than 100 were four-engined heavy bombers for long-range penetration. Before Harris could tackle the questions of increasing the Command's strength and striking power, he decided to quash the continuing clamour for diversifying – and thereby diluting – his bombers to other roles. To accomplish this he ordered a trio of densely concentrated attacks on three key German cities,

Cologne, Essen and Bremen, each of which was to be undertaken by a force of '1,000 bombers' – a figure unprecedented in bomber annals. The first of these occurred on the night of 30/31 May 1942 against Cologne, when 1,046 bombers and 88 'intruder' aircraft set out initially and devastated the German cathedral city. Losses of bombers amounted to 44, plus seven others which crashed on return; less than five per cent of the overall raiders. His magic figure of '1,000 bombers' had only been accomplished by scraping the barrel of training units, etc., but the massive propaganda effect of Harris's virtual confidence trick effectively smothered all opposition to retaining Bomber Command *per se*.

The long-recognised inability of the bulk of bomber crews to navigate to and accurately locate designated targets by night began to be resolved slowly with the introduction of various radar and radio aids in 1942, but also led to the creation of the Path Finder Force (PFF) in August 1942; four selected squadrons (initially) tasked with the future role of spearheading all major bomber attacks to locate accurately, then 'mark' targets for the main force crews. By the autumn of the year the steady flow of Lancasters, Halifaxes and Stirlings from the factories to firstline squadrons, supplemented by the introduction of American-designed Bostons, Venturas, and the excellent ubiquitous DH Mosquito, augured well for the Command's strike ability in 1943; exemplified by a force of 94 Lancasters which flew a daring daylight assault against Le Creusot on 17 October, followed by another daylight raid against Milan by 74 Lancasters on 24 October. Nevertheless, the year had been a particularly difficult one for Harris's crews; the night raiders alone losing 1,291 aircraft 'missing' – roughly the equivalent of fifty complete bomber squadrons – more than half of these falling victims to German nightfighters which by then had begun using various radar-interception aids in linked co-ordination with ground radar controller stations. Moreover, more than 1,000 other night bombers had returned to England in battle-damaged condition, often crashing and/or carrying injured men.

By 3 September 1942, the third anniversary of the outbreak of war with Germany, and virtually the halfway point of the entire conflict, RAF Bomber Command air crew casualties on actual operations had mounted to totals of 11,366 killed, 2,814 prisoners of war, and 1,655 wounded/injured; while a further 2,539 had been killed and 1,538 wounded (injured in varying degree) on non-operational flying – primarily during some stage of training. Statistically speaking, almost exactly 20,000 air crew men killed, crippled, or in the hands of the enemy. In the same three years the Command had despatched a gross total of 86,800 individual sorties by day and night; thus the human casualty rate *could* be said to have been one 'life' for every four sorties flown.

By 1942 each bomber air crew member knew that, on joining an operational squadron, he was required to complete a tour of thirty sorties over enemy-occupied territories before he could be rested from frontline flying, usually with a posting to some aspect of instructional duties; though volunteers for the PFF were expected to complete at least forty-five trips as a first tour. Strictly speaking, any one-tour man could be recalled after six months' rest for a second tour of operations, after which he could be declared permanently non-operational for the rest of his wartime service unless he *voluntarily* undertook even further operations.

A simple analysis of official bomber air crew casualties for the period 1939–42 alone indicates clearly that the chances for any man even to survive one operational tour was little better than one in three. The odds against surviving a second tour grew slimmer on each subsequent sortie – increased experience offered greater hope of avoiding the 'Grim Reaper's scythe', but was never a guarantee against being 'chopped'. Throughout the whole war approximately 125,000 air crew men served at some stage in Bomber Command, and of those who survived a first tour of operations nearly 7,000 *volunteered* for a second tour, while many hundreds continued onto a third – such was the spirit and dedication of the bomber 'boys'.

Without any implied invidious comparison of the crews who flew operations during the first two years of the war – theirs was basically a battle of desperation for the very survival of Britain itself – it can hardly be denied that from about mid-1941 the overall nature of the RAF's bombing operations took on a much grimmer tone. The almost gentlemanly mode and approach to sorties evident in the earliest months of the air war had swiftly dissipated as casualties and aircraft losses climbed steeply. By 1942 the crews were in no doubt of the hazards awaiting them on every sortie, each trip becoming a tense ordeal of physical and spiritual endurance. By then an operational sortie in a heavy bomber lasted from six to nine hours on rough average. Thus, a full tour of sorties amounted to perhaps 300 flying hours or less for each individual crew member. To the layman it might seem little enough time out of a man's normally expected 'three score years and ten' lifetime. Yet how many men can say that they spent some twelve days of their life in *constant* danger of death or horrific mutilation *every* second, *every* minute of those few days? Even so, such figures only account for the actual flying hours involved; to these must be added the many more hours, days and nights of – at times – intolerable strain imposed on each man prior and subsequent to every sortie.

Each night's operations commenced for the crews by mid-morning when targets, and therefore bomb loads, fuel capacities, and a hundred other details, were decided and notified to both air and ground crews. Final checks on the technical state of each facet of the aircraft culminated in a night-flying test (NFT) by its crew who promptly notified their ground staff of any 'snags' for immediate rectification. Final briefings of the air crews involved each man in last-minute 'polishing' of his esoteric equipment, while out on the dispersal sites the 'erks' (ground maintenance) sweated hard as they loaded bomb bays, filled fuel tanks, checked yet again every detail of 'their' aircraft. Throughout these seemingly long preparatory hours the tension inside each air crew member inexorably mounted in anticipation – only the totally insensitive or unimaginative knew no fear – until the moment of relative relief when he finally walked, cycled, or more usually climbed aboard a truck to take him out to his aircraft for the actual trip.

Once at dispersal 'final-final' checks were made around the 'kite', after which the skipper 'signed' for the bomber in the Form 700 proffered by the ground crew 'Chiefy'. A last cigarette, perhaps a ritual 'wetting the tail wheel' for luck, then climb aboard and settle into take-off positions. Once settled, the crew might still have to wait – would it be a last-minute 'scrub'? Each minute of waiting for the 'off' increased the knot-tight feeling deep in the gut.

Finally getting the 'green' to go, the take-off run began at the end of the runway. *Every* take-off in a maxi-loaded bomber was always dangerous; encased in a light-metal machine carrying up to 10,000 lb of explosives, thousands of pounds of highly inflammable petrol and oils. A burst tyre, engine failure, loss of pressure, or one second's lack of total concentration could spell instant disaster. Once safely airborne and on course for the objective, the outward leg meant crossing the North Sea's coldly inviting waters before reaching an enemy coastline usually pre-alerted along its line of flak defences, with the ever-present Luftwaffe nightfighter force in probable ambush locations just beyond.

The flight across enemy-occupied lands meant running a hair-thin gauntlet of flak, fighters, searchlights which intensified as the bomber made its final approach to the designated target. Once committed to the ultimate bombing run, a pilot *had* to fly straight and level up to the bomb-release point – no evading the holocaust of lights and shells reaching up to destroy him; perhaps minutes or seconds during which the bomber was a sitting duck for predicted flak guns aided by radar. Once the bombs had gone, a further few seconds of steady course to obtain an aiming point photo, then a full-boost turn and climb out of the hell of probing lights and necklaced streams of multi-coloured tracers and shells.

The return flight was no less anxious – three, four, or five hours of watching instruments for the first sign of any faltering in engines or controls. Too often the aircraft bore flak and/or cannon shell damage – shattered tails, riddled fuselages, hydraulic lines to flaps, elevators, undercarriages ruptured, or one engine feathered and trailing a steady line of oil. One or more crew men could have suffered wounds during fighter attacks, some might be lying on the fuselage floor, having made their last flight. Every mile of the trip home could bring further hazards from flak or fighters, while unforecast weather conditions might add complications to an already fraught situation.

Once clear of the enemy coast the crew still needed to cross that damned North Sea – already a graveyard for hundreds of previous crews who hadn't 'made it'. With that obstacle behind them, the crew still needed to locate their base airfield, or – if badly damaged and/or carrying wounded or dead men – the nearest aerodrome to accept them in an emergency. Once over base, they might still be diverted to another airfield due to blocked runways by preceding bombers which had crashed, or, more often, dense fog nullifying visibility near the ground. Even as a bomber came in to land it might become a victim of marauding German fighter intruders seeking scalps from the weary returning bomber streams. Touchdown could still be 'dicey' – unsuspected flak damage to the undercarriage could turn a perfect let-down into an horrendous ground-loop, belly-crash, or complete disintegration; all or any such arrivals were highly likely to terminate in an explosion of pierced fuel tanks.

De-briefed and back in their respective messes relaxing over their post-ops fresh egg and bacon meal, the crews might slowly begin to recall isolated incidents of the trip. That near-miss near-collision with a burning Lancaster totally out of control . . . the 4,000 lb 'Cookie' which plunged down from a higher kite and missed the rear gun turret by inches . . . the ugly snout of a Messerschmitt 110 coming head-on at incredible closing speed, its nose cone alive with orange flashes as it opened up with its cannons, then skimmed straight over the cockpit only feet away . . . the blinding gout of flames as another Lanc received a direct hit . . . the Halifax going down on its last return to earth illuminated by half a dozen searchlights, and the poor sod who'd baled out but got his chute caught on the tail fin . . . their 18-year-old mid-upper gunner's body laid out on the rest bunk, with half his head shot away. . . . And they'd have to go again tomorrow night – 'once more unto the breach'. . . .

It was a pattern for all-bomber sorties until the end of the war; an endurance test of mind and muscle, of nerves, of guts . . . and, in a few cases, of sanity. Occasionally, an air crew member broke under the constant strain and refused to carry on; he could take no more. In such cases, depending very much on the understanding (or lack of it) of his commanding officer, the man was either sent on immediate leave in the hope that he'd 'recover', or, too often, he was posted away immediately to some backwater unit, stripped of all rank, and had his documents annotated 'LMF' – Lack of Moral Fibre, the official euphemism for 'yellow' or coward. That young men, often no more than boys, should be so labelled and permanently stigmatised – often by *non*-flying senior officers – may or may not have been justified in the 'interests of discipline'; officialdom's view was that such cases needed to be removed from the operational scene as quickly as possible in case the 'culprit' contaminated other air crews; the difference between controlled and uncontrolled fear was a razor's edge.

Objectively, there were compensations in being operational air crew if one compares their war with that of the fighting infantryman or sea-borne sailor. Minimum rank for air crews was Sergeant, with reasonably rapid promotion to Flight Sergeant, Warrant Officer, or a commission in prospect. Pay, relatively, was good, and between operational flights air crews were domiciled in 'civilised' accommodation on many airfields, particularly the pre-war permanent type of RAF station, with all the amenities of a mess at their disposal. If actual operations exemplified the Service call for devotion to duty, at least the non-operational aspects of air crew life were attractive for any Serviceman, particularly when it came to relations with the opposite sex, to a majority of whom any man wearing an air crew brevet (especially commissioned officers . . .) carried an aura of glamour.

It was, in truth, a form of living and fighting marked by extreme contrasts almost daily. At one moment one might be high over Berlin, grimly sweating out the flak barrage – a few hours later swapping insults gleefully with close friends in the warmth and comforts of a mess bar, planning an outing next evening with the current 'popsie' from the local town or village. If the adrenalin ran fast, off *or* on ops, and life's prospects seemed distinctly brief on occasion, then most could at least lead a short life and a merry one while they could. Perhaps the very youth of most air crew men, and its associated peak of human resiliency and swift adaptability, were the true rock foundation for ultimate survival.

The years 1943–44 saw Bomber Command roused from its preceding sleeping giant status and begin truly to implement its original *raison d'être* as the long arm of Allied strategic offensive striking power against the Third Reich. By March 1943 Command strength stood at a total of sixty-five squadrons in total, thirty-seven of which were operating four-engined heavy bombers, and by the end of the year could muster some 1,600 aircraft, mainly Lancasters and Halifaxes in the 'heavy' class overall, though average nightly availability total, i.e. fully serviceable operational machines was close to 1,000 aircraft. In March 1943 'Butch' Harris launched his Battle of the Ruhr with a 400-plus bomber attack on Essen utilising the newish radar device Oboe; while on 16/17 May Wing Commander Guy Gibson led his newly-created 617 Squadron in the famed 'Dam-busting' operation against the Möhne, Eder and Sorpe dams of Germany. On the night of 24/25 July Harris despatched the first of a series of 'knockout' blows against the city of Hamburg in Operation Gomorrah, reducing that city to a smoking ruin; while on 17/18 August Group Captain John Searby acted as 'Master of Ceremonies' for a specially requested raid on Peenemünde, home of German V-weapons research and development, by almost 600 aircraft.

New navigation and bombing aids began to be used operationally throughout the year, as were a variety of new bombs and pyrotechnics. These included such devices as G–H blind-bombing radar sets, Airborne Cigar (a disruptive radio transmitter to erode German fighter control-ling); while in the 'ironmongery' department the 12,000 lb High Capacity (HC) HE monster bomb was first dropped in anger by Lancasters of 617 Squadron on 15/16 September against the notorious Dortmund–Ems Canal target. In November, commencing on the night of 18/19 November, Bomber Command initiated the so-termed Battle of Berlin, which was to continue until late March 1944 – a battle in which sixteen major raids involved more than 9,000 individual sorties. The cost of the Berlin battle was high – 492 aircraft 'missing', and 954 other aircraft 'damaged' (nearly 100 of these being written-off in crashes on return to the UK).

A measure of Bomber Command's operational escalation in effort from April 1943 to March 1944 inclusive was revealed in its losses: 2,703 aircraft, or almost exactly 19,000 air crew men who failed to return, the rough equivalent of 130 complete Lancaster squadrons, or more than the total strength in squadrons available to Arthur Harris in April 1943. The chief cause of such a tally of casualties was the greatly strengthened Luftwaffe nightfighter force guarding the Reich's night sky. During just five months, from November 1943 to March 1944, the *Nachtjäger* were officially credited with slightly more than 1,000 confirmed victories – a figure remarkably close to known RAF losses to fighter attacks, and probably a slight underestimation.

On the night of 30/31 March 1944 the *Nachtjäger* accomplished the peak of their successes when they were responsible for bringing down 79 of the 94 bombers lost in a raid on Nuremburg, apart from probably contributing towards the damage to others which led to eleven more bombers crashing back in England on return. Such high 'scoring' was achieved by various methods, including infiltrating any main force bomber stream and picking off victims as opportunity arose; while the favoured mode of attacking an RAF bomber was from below and astern, firing their cannons into wing fuel tanks and engines, rather than into fuselages with the attendant risk of detonating full bomb loads at close range. Such stab-in-the-belly tactics meant that many bomber crews perished in a holocaust of petrol explosions without ever knowing what hit them, but such was the nature of air 'combat' by night over Germany.

From mid-April 1944 overall direction of Allied strategic aerial offensive was placed under the control of the Supreme Commander, Allied Expeditionary Force, General 'Ike' Eisenhower, in preparation for the imminent Allied invasion of Europe. It meant that for the immediate future Bomber Command had to switch its main efforts from Germany to France, in order to implement the Transportation Plan – the disruption of all modes of transportation from the Channel coastline to the central interior areas of France. In some seven weeks leading up to 6 June – the invasion date – Bomber Command's heavies dropped more than 42,000 tons of bombs on such objectives, reducing the internal French transport system to a shambles.

This shift of emphasis had a bonus effect on bomber casualties inasmuch as the bulk of Luftwaffe defence forces were by then concentrated in defence of the Reich itself. Of a total of 21,226 sorties flown in late April and May 1944, 488 aircraft were listed as 'missing' – far less than might have occurred had the pace of the preceding year's assault on Germany been maintained, though in itself a tragic enough tally of death. The planned bombing of the French lines of communication and transportation culminated initially on the eve of the actual invasion, when, among others, 1,136 heavy bombers blasted ten major German coastal batteries immediately adjacent to the proposed invasion landing beaches, dropping 5,267 tons of high explosives bombs and effectively nullifying the threat.

Once the invasion forces were ashore and firmly established, the bombers became part of the close-support air forces supplying tactical aid to the ground armies by bombing all or any German forces and installations along the fighting frontline and its immediate reserve areas; but a large proportion of Harris's command was able to return to its prime strategic bombing role by joining again the USAAF's 8th Air Force in destroying Germany's vital oil resources. Though oil production and refining facilities had been a primary target for Allied bombers almost from the outset of the war, it was only since May 1944 that those bomber forces had been capable of a true strategic offensive in significant weight against Axis oil targets.

In June 1944 the combined attacks of RAF Bomber Command and the American 8th and 15th Air Forces caused a loss of virtually ninety per cent of Germany's fuel production within just three weeks' operations by day and night. Luftwaffe nightfighter strength during the latter months of 1944 steadily increased numerically, rising to a peak paper quantity of 1,355 aircraft, of which about 1,000 could correctly be termed operationally available at a moment's call. Yet, paradoxically, Bomber Command's loss rate steadily declined during the same period. On 14 October, for example, 1,063 heavy bombers attacked Duisburg in daylight and lost just fifteen aircraft to the defences; while that same night 1,005 bombers returned to Duisburg and suffered the loss of only six aircraft. The month of December 1944 saw Bomber Command despatch a gross total of 15,333 aircraft into German skies and incur the loss of 135 machines – a casualty *rate* below one per cent.

Such 'acceptable' casualty rates were due almost solely to the vast supremacy of the Allied air forces now in European skies, combined with the rapidly deteriorating effective use and state of the Luftwaffe and its diminishing fuel and facilities. Massive bomber formations were now attacking German cities, airfields, factories, etc. by day and night with near-impunity, and this pressure was maintained until the final weeks of the European conflict. The last heavy bomber operations by Bomber Command were flown on 25 April 1945 when three separate raids, totalling almost 1,000 aircraft, bombed among other targets Hitler's private mountain retreat at Berchtesgaden; while the final Command operations were flown on the night of 2/3 May by almost 350 Mosquitos.

The operational strength of RAF Bomber Command as the war

culminated can be judged by its composition in late March 1945. On 2 March the Command's order of battle showed a total of 98 firstline or bomber support squadrons, equipped with an overall total of 2,254 aircraft. Of these, the dominant aircraft was the Avro Lancaster, with 56 squadrons equipped with the type; while the other principal four-engined design in use still, the Handley Page Halifax, equipped seventeen firstline units apart from other flights or formations. Such figures did not include the enormous back-up training and other duties' organisation.

In bald statistics, throughout the whole war in Europe against Germany, Bomber Command crews had flown a total of 364,514 individual sorties by night and day – more than eighty per cent of these by night. Aircraft losses – i.e. classified as 'missing' or 'failed to return' – amounted to 8,325; though at least 16,000 others had been categorised as 'damaged' in varying degree from 'repairable' to 'written off charge'. Total bombs dropped – all types – totted up a figure of 955,044 tons, though this is almost certainly an underestimate due to indeterminate records for certain periods of the early war years.

Impressive as such statistics may seem, the foregoing tallies relate almost wholly to inanimate items – aircraft, bombs, *et al*. The true cost of the bomber offensive was in its human sacrifices. From 3 September 1939 to 8 May 1945, Bomber Command suffered the losses of 47,268 air crew members killed and 4,200 more wounded and/or crippled on actual operations; apart from a further 8,305 men killed in non-operational flying aspects of training or non-flying accidents. Collectively, this roll of honour represented some seventy per cent of the *total* RAF personnel killed throughout the war in *every* theatre of operations. Of the Command's overall casualties in men, almost forty per cent had been air crew members from Commonwealth or other 'non-British' origins. Of these men who gave their lives, the Royal Australian Air Force lost 3,412; the Royal Canadian Air Force 8,209; the Royal New Zealand Air Force 1,433; while 48 others came from other countries outside the United Kingdom. If self-sacrifice was the price of victory and freedom, the young air crews of Bomber Command had paid the bill with grievous generosity. Indeed, it would be hard to find a comparably proportionate record of losses in any equivalent formation in any other fighting service.

Of those air crews no finer or more appropriate tribute can be found than that paid by Arthur 'Butch' Harris, the man who was ultimately responsible for sending so many of them into the hell of operations night after night :

There are no words with which I can do justice to the air crew who fought under my command. There is no parallel in warfare to such courage and determination in the face of danger over so prolonged a period . . . it was, moreover, a clear and highly conscious courage, by which the risk was taken with calm forethought . . . it was, further-more, the courage of the small hours, of men virtually alone, for at his battle-station the airman is virtually alone. It was the courage of men with long-drawn apprehensions of daily 'going over the top'. Such devotion must never be forgotten !*

* *Bomber Offensive* by A. T. Harris : Collins, 1947.

CHAPTER TWO

Nick Knilans

At 5 pm on 26 November 1943 the first of sixteen Lancasters from
619 Squadron took off from Woodhall Spa, each loaded with a
4,000 lb HC 'Cookie' blast bomb nestling among some 3,000 lb of
incendiaries in the bomb bays. The target was primarily Berlin, but
twelve of the Lancasters had been briefed to drop their loads on
Frankfurt en route as a feint diversion attack, hopefully to draw the
Luftwaffe defence fighters away from the main bomber stream's path
to the Big City. In the case of Lancaster III, ED859, 'V-Victor' the
feint was rather too successful. As it approached Frankfurt at 20,000
feet a Junkers Ju 88 bore in from dead astern, closed to 150 yards,
then raked the bomber with a hail of cannon shells. Four more times
it closed with its intended victim, its fire shattering the port inner
engine and destroying the port tail elevator, before the Lancaster's
air gunners finally shot it down in flames. Even as the doomed Ju 88
plunged to earth, a second German, a Messerschmitt Bf 110, attacked
the corkscrewing bomber from the port beam. As it passed closely
over the Lancaster, it ran straight through a burst of fire from the
gunners, jinked away to starboard, then disappeared into the blackness.

The damaged bomber steadily lost height as its pilot fought for
control, finally levelling out at some 13,000 feet. Taking stock of
his situation, the pilot decided to press on to Berlin on his remaining
three good engines – another 200-plus miles to go to target. Reaching
the city, he lowered his seat to avoid being blinded by the dozens of
searchlights weaving around him, then put the crippled aircraft
into a shallow dive to start his bombing run. Running the fierce flak
barrage, he saw cascades of incendiaries and 'Cookies' raining down
from the main force well above him, while to one side he caught
a glimpse of another bomber jettisoning its entire bomb load only
seconds before it exploded in an horrific gout of flame. Concentrating
on his instruments, the Lancaster captain made his bomb run through
the inferno and emerged apparently unscathed. Setting course for

home he found his aircraft was still slowly losing height and he eventually crossed the Dutch coast at merely 2,000 feet altitude.

On arrival over his base airfield, however, he found that his problems were not over – a thick blanket of ground fog precluded landing there and he was diverted to Spilsby. Here, still with only three good engines, and a punctured main tyre, he finally landed safely. Of his companion skippers on that sortie, nine had made landings at other airfields, one of these crashing in the fog and killing his crew, while Lancaster 'S-Sugar', with ruptured fuel tanks from the Berlin flak, managed to reach the mouth of the Humber before running out of petrol and baling out. Eventually, twelve hours after actual take-off, the skipper of battle-scarred 'V-Victor' tumbled thankfully into his own bed. It had been 'just one more op' – his seventeenth of his first operational tour.

His name was Hubert Clarence Knilans – 'Nick' to all – and he was an American citizen serving with the RAF, wearing the uniform and rank of Pilot Officer, RCAF. The dicey trip to Berlin that night brought him the award of a DSO, but by October 1944 – 34 operational sorties later – when he had finally finished with operational flying, Nick Knilans had added a British DFC, two American DFCs, five Air Medals, and a dozen campaign or active service medals. Born on 27 December 1917 in Delevan, Wisconsin, Nick Knilans came from a family with Irish roots; his great-grandfather, Daniel Knilands, had emigrated from Tyrone to the USA in 1848, and his grandfather had fought in the American civil war. Growing up on his father's farm during the depression years of the 1930s, Knilans was nurtured on hard work and lean rewards, and on leaving high school, he worked the farm. In April 1941, however, he was drafted for military service, then immediately granted deferment to continue helping his father on the family farm. Since he had no wish either to be deferred, or to join the US Army, he sought a way of achieving his ambition to become a pilot. At that period the US air services required any pilot candidate to have a college degree as a prerequisite, thereby nullifying any hope in that direction, so Knilans packed a small bag, withdrew his meagre savings from the local bank, and after telling his family he was taking a few days vacation in Chicago, set out for Canada in October 1941, hoping to enlist for pilot training in the RCAF.

Arriving at the Canadian border without a cent left in his pocket, Knilans was accepted by the RCAF and officially enlisted on 25 October in Windsor, Ontario. In Canada he received training up to 'wings' standard, was promoted to Sergeant, then shipped to Britain to complete his training in Scotland and at 1660 Conversion Unit, Swinderby. At the latter unit he flew Manchesters and the bomber type he was to fly operationally, the Avro Lancaster. Soon his first posting came through – No. 619 Squadron, based at Woodhall Spa, Lincolnshire. Here he was to spend the following eighteen months, completing two operational tours with two different units, both flying Lancasters. Allotted to 619's B Flight, Knilans flew his first operational sortie as second pilot to the flight commander, Squadron Leader Scorer, in Lancaster EE111, 'S'; a bombing and 'nickelling' trip to Cologne, along with fifteen other Lancasters from the squadron. Scorer's crew were veterans, including Flight Lieutenant J. A. Howard, DFC, the squadron gunnery officer in the rear turret, whose alertness saved them from the attentions of a Messerschmitt Bf 109 just as the Lancaster had completed its bombing run. Three nights later Knilans was second dickey to Flight Lieutenant S. E. J. Jones in Lancaster EE106, bound for Turin.

As they neared the Alps, a burst of yellow-streaking cannon shells came up over the port wing. Both air gunners immediately opened up at an enemy fighter stalking the Lancaster, registered hits and watched it explode. When they reached Turin, the 7,000 lb high explosive bomb load was dropped from 14,500 feet and the bomber set course for southern France, crossing part of the Bay of Biscay at less than fifty feet height – to escape German radar – and eventually regaining base after a trip lasting almost eleven hours.

Having been blooded on two second dickey trips, Knilans was allotted his 'own' Lancaster, JA898, and left Woodhall Spa on the evening of 24 July 1943 with his own crew, and a bomb load of 11,500 lb destined for release over Hamburg; his crew's first sortie 'in anger'. Once over German soil, Nick's bomb aimer, Joe Tate, slung out bundles of Window (anti-radar silver foil strips) with gusto, then guided Knilans over Hamburg city on a good bomb-run.

Arriving over base again, Knilans let down for landing but, due to a faulty altimeter, almost nosed into the ground. His port wing dipped into a gravel pit, hit a sand bar, then at full boost staggered upwards, barely above stalling speed. Slashing its way through the tops of a tree grove, the Lancaster almost decapitated several airmen's wooden huts at the edge of the copse before finally gaining a little height. Circuiting cautiously, Knilans ignored his altimeter, relying on his own vision, and brought the aircraft safely down. As he shut down engines in his dispersal hardstanding, he glanced at the altimeter

– it was registering 960 feet altitude! Once outside the aircraft, Nick inspected the port wing engines – both had their propellers neatly curled at every tip. The time was 0435 hrs on 25 July. By 0900 hrs Knilans and his crew were back in the briefing room for their next sortie – the Krupps Works at Essen – that same evening.

Piloting Lancaster EE116 this time, Knilans and his crew left base at 2226 hrs carrying 11,000 lb of bombs, heading for the 'Happy Valley' at Essen. Though only on his fourth sortie, Nick Knilans was already learning the crucial lesson of survival, and on the approach to Essen he slowed down to let the first bomber wave absorb the flak fury directly above the target. Then, spotting one unfortunate Lancaster to port being firmly coned by the circling searchlights, he edged towards it hoping to slip by the victim while all the lights were concentrating upon the other man. Sliding under the trapped bomber a few hundred feet lower, Knilans could see hundreds of flak shells reaching for the coned bomber.

Suddenly that bomber dived towards Knilans, bringing the flak and searchlight beams with it, and Knilan's aircraft shuddered under the impact of several hits, before the other Lancaster passed below, then exploded. Nick's 18-year-old flight engineer, Ken Ryall, reported, 'Starboard inner overheating. I'm feathering it'. Knilans had already trained Ken to feather any bad engine immediately – over-heated engines catch fire quickly. Changing throttle settings and trim tabs to compensate the loss of engine power, Nick eased the Lancaster into its bombing run. Orders normally required a 60-seconds' rock-steady, straight and level run-in to drop the load, then a further straight and level follow-on for taking a photograph of the bomb strike. Such a run, undeviating through the heart of the flak, was probably the most dangerous, and nerve-racking, section of the sortie. Knilans had no illusions about it – he decided to give his bomb aimer thirty seconds only for the run-in, and less for the photo; as he remarked later, 'High-flying photo-recce planes could take better pictures by daylight, and the less time spent in this part of the sky the better for survival. The higher-up officers had their war to fight, but I had mine! . . .'.

The trip back to base with only three engines was uneventful. On checking for damage later, Knilans found that a shell had passed clean through the main petrol tank without exploding, leaving holes big enough to fit his leg in; while one steel sliver had sliced the glycol lines to the engine radiator, hence the reported overheating.

Knilans' first sortie as captain of his own crew and aircraft on 24/25 July had been as one of the phalanx of 791 bombers despatched by

Bomber Command to begin Operation Gomorrah – the intended 'taking out' of the city of Hamburg; and it was to Hamburg that Knilans returned on the night of 27/28 July, in Lancaster ED977, one of 787 aircraft initially sent, to 'brew up' the holocaust of fire and destruction already instigated. By then Hamburg was virtually in its death throes, and Knilans afterwards described the scene which greeted him :

'We began to see a glow on the horizon some 100 miles from Hamburg. It grew to a tremendous sea of fire lighting ground and sky for miles around. The seething flames were rearing upwards several hundred feet to merge into a column of smoke. This fiery column rose up to 20,000 feet.'

He made his bomb run, then a German fighter was spotted climbing towards him 'like a shark coming up from the depths'. 'The smoke column was nearby. I turned into it. I had my oxygen mask on but the smoke began to make my eyes water. I turned some more, still inside the smoke, before coming out into the clear sky again. The bandit was gone. The trip home and the landing were uneventful.'

He was to return to Hamburg on the night of 2/3 August, his sixth 'op', and the final blow of Gomorrah. Piloting JA848, he took off in a heavy, gusting rainstorm – 'like flying into a bottle of ink' – and on reaching Hamburg found the still-burning city covered by a massive thunderhead. Having his position plotted quickly, Knilans made a timed run to target, plunging into the heart of the glowering storm clouds. No sooner into cloud than he felt the Lancaster forced into a dive by an immense down-draught, with the crazily-dancing blue streaks of St Elmo's Fire flowing over the windshield and wings. Rime ice began forming on wings and propellers, breaking away to hammer the fuselage like frozen flak.

At 14,000 feet Knilans gave the order to drop bombs, hit an up-draught and promptly pushed his control column fully forward with fully applied starboard rudder. The Lancaster shot upwards again, emerging from the clouds at 21,000 feet with the starboard wing nearly vertical. Flying south of Bremen before turning for the home run, Knilans and his gunners warded off a half-hearted attack by a nightfighter along the way but reached base without further problems. Afterwards, a flak shell hole was found in the starboard elevator, just two feet from the rear turret.

Three more sorties during August – to Mannheim, Milan and Munchen Gladbach – were interrupted by a short instructional course on instrument flying for Knilans, after which he was commissioned as a Pilot Officer and given a short 'kitting-up' leave. On the night of 22 September he returned to operations by bombing Hanover, then attacked Mannheim two nights later, and returned to Hanover on 27/28 September, his twelfth sortie. Knilans was not superstitious but had pause for thought after his next – the 'unlucky thirteenth' – to Hagen on 1/2 October. Meeting 10/10ths cloud over the target, he bombed on the cloud-marker target indicators and turned for home, only to be told that the starboard inner engine had lost oil pressure. The flight engineer feathered the engine, while Knilans prepared to tackle the forecast heavy rain and thunderstorms ahead on the return flight. Surviving the rain, lightning, and strong winds which battered the Lancaster, Nick eventually reached base. Next day his ground crew 'Chiefy' (Flight Sergeant) quietly showed Knilans an RAF 4 lb incendiary bomb which had penetrated the starboard inner engine nacelle, severed oil and petrol feed pipes, but failed to ignite . . . patently a 'present' from a higher altitude bomber over the target.

On the night of 3 October Nick and his crew were in good humour. The rear gunner, Gerry Jackson, had been presented with a newborn son by his young wife in Dumfries, Scotland the previous day; moreover, the whole crew were due for a nine days' leave next morning. Climbing in to JB131, 'T-Tommy', they left base at 1844 hrs and set course for Holland on the first leg of a raid against Kassel. Two and a half hours later, as Knilans made his turn for the second leg to fly between Munster and Hamm, his wireless operator reported a blip on his Monica radar set but thought it might be another Lancaster some 300 yards further back and lower. Knilans rolled his aircraft to starboard to let his gunners get a better view, but as he straightened out again a stream of tracer cannon shells and bullets came up through the port wing, just two feet from Nick's head, while other cannon shells thudded into the fuselage.

Instinctively diving hard away, Knilans yelled to his gunners, 'Where is he now?' Only the mid-upper gunner, Roy Learmouth, replied, telling his skipper that his perspex had been shattered and splinters had hit him in the eyes. From the rear turret came only silence. The first burst had exploded inside Jackson's turret, killing him outright. Other damage included the port inner engine, which had to be feathered, and (as Nick found later) the tail assembly and port main wheel had suffered.

Though now without any defences against further fighter assaults, Knilans decided to complete the sortie. Reaching Kassel, he duly bombed it, then worked his way into the part-protection of the main bomber stream for the return journey. On the way home one of his crew confirmed damage to the port main wheel tyre, so Nick decided against landing quickly at Manston – a grass airfield which might produce a ground-loop on landing, hence possible disaster – and instead flew back to Woodhall Spa. Here, with no little skill and sheer muscle power, Knilans managed to land with one wheel and three engines without crashing. As soon as he clambered out of the Lancaster, Knilans went to the tail turret which had yet to be opened. Prising the jammed sliding doors apart, Nick extracted the body of his dead gunner and put him in the nearby ambulance. Gerry Jackson now would never see the face of his newborn son. . . .

After two more sorties, Nick Knilans was informed by the squadron commander that he was to be transferred to the USAAF immediately. Given ten days' leave in which to arrange the paper formalities at the USAAF 8th Air Force's Headquarters, Nick then became officially detached to the RAF for operations. His return to 619 Squadron in the uniform of a 1st Lieutenant, USAAF, meant being subjected to much good-humoured ribaldry, but Nick had expressed his firm resolve to see his war out with the RAF, not the USAAF, as long as he flew in the European theatre of operations.

There were, of course, some distinct advantages to being a 'Yank in the RAF'. American fliers received a 50% bonus of their basic pay added on for flying duties – which meant Nick now drew salary equal to the Group Captain RAF commanding his base station. On the other hand, under USAAF regulations, he could not be promoted to higher rank while still with the RAF. Nor could he be entitled to received the USAAF's normal officers' monthly ration of two cartons of cigarettes and a quart of liquor.

Then again, he was now eligible for both USAAF and RAF awards and decorations – an Air Medal for every five completed sorties, with an American DFC after twenty-five such trips. Though officially given these latter medals as his career progressed, in fact Knilans only ever wore the ribbon of the British DSO he was awarded with 619 Squadron. One final attraction for Nick to transferring to his native service was the 10,000 US dollars' 'insurance' granted to his next of kin, should he be killed on operations. Being officially in the Royal Canadian Air Force (RCAF) when he was transferred, he was also eligible for Canadian 'benefits' and war service medals *et al* – a mixture which amused Knilans greatly.

Returning to operations with 619 Squadron, he bombed Berlin several times during November-December 1943, but his final trip

with the unit came on 5 January 1944 when he flew ED589,
'V-Victor' to Stettin. It meant a nine-hour stint, strapped in his pilot's
seat, across Denmark, along the Baltic Sea, then down to Stettin from
the northern side. The sortie proved uneventful. Bombing his target,
Knilans reversed his outward course but descended from 20,000 feet
to less than 1,000 feet to evade the German radar. An hour after
leaving Denmark behind, Nick spotted a flare arcing up ahead of him,
turned off course, and found a dinghy with a ditched crew in it. He
circled the dinghy steadily while his wireless operator sent off their
position to the Air-Sea Rescue in England. Nick continued to circle
the ditched crew – despite the obvious danger of being homed on by
German fighters – until an ASR seaplane arrived on the scene; then
flew home as dawn was breaking.

Having completed one operational tour – and survived – Nick
now faced a decision. He could easily consider that he and his crew
had already used up their ration of luck – to the best of his knowledge,
his was the only crew on 619 to have completed a full tour to date.
Moreover, Knilans by then had grown increasingly disturbed privately
at the thought of bombing civilians in the various cities he had
'visited'; killing old men, women and children was not his idea of
waging war, and as long as the RAF stuck to its contemporary area
bombing policy, these were the most likely victims of any future
sorties. On the other hand, Nick wanted to remain on operations –
the comradeship of the crews, the positive task of carrying the war
into the heart of the Nazi empire, these were far preferable to a safe
job teaching tyros to handle a bomber at some OTU.

Knilans found a solution to his quandary – he volunteered himself
and his crew for a further tour, only this time with No. 617 Squadron.
The 'Dam-busters' at least were specialists, tackling only wholly
military targets. His crew only discovered they'd been 'volunteered'
after Nick had arranged the move, but since at that stage of the
bombing offensive any crew stood a slim chance of surviving *any* form
of war flying, they decided they would rather take their chances with
Nick.

On 8 and 9 January 1944, Knilans' former unit, 619 Squadron,
moved to Coningsby, and 617 Squadron moved in to Woodhall Spa
from Coningsby. It meant that Knilans could remain in the Petwood
Hotel Officers' Mess – 'the best damn foxhole I would ever find for
shelter'. At that period 617 Squadron was commanded by Wing
Commander Leonard Cheshire, DSO, DFC, and was carrying out pin-
point precision attacks on vital objectives. Among its crews were

several hardened veterans in bombers, including Micky Martin, the 'low-level' specialist, Dave Shannon, Les Munro, Joe McCarthy, another American, and Bill Reid, holder of a Victoria Cross. It was a somewhat élite company to be joining, but Knilans was not over-awed. He knew too well that the Grim Reaper played no favourites in his grisly selection process – veteran or tyro, all could be chopped with equal ease.

Nick's first sortie with 617 was in Lancaster ME561, 'R-Roger' to attack a ski site base of VI 'buzz-bombs' in the Pas de Calais area. This particular aircraft was to be Nick's near-permanent steed, despite its heavy controls which seemed to baffle all attempts by the ground crew to resolve the problem. His crew asked him to have the aircraft named 'The Jolly Roger', with an appropriate scantily-clad female with skull-and-crossboned pirate's hat. Knilans firmly declined; it was just not his style to take the business of war lightly.

Operational sorties with 617 Squadron in early 1944 were relatively wide-spaced in time. In February Knilans flew just two that month; to the Limoges Gnome-Rhone factory on 8/9 February, and the Antheor Viaduct on 12 February. The following month saw increased activity, however, with raids against Albert, St Etienne, Woippy, Clermont Ferrand, Bergerac, Angoulême and Lyons – mostly spot-bombing individual factories of strategic importance; while April involved a squadron total of 122 individual sorties being despatched, and some 355 tons of bombs being dropped. In May the squadron was taken off operations to rehearse a top-secret sortie to cover the imminent Allied invasion of Normandy – Operation Taxable – on which the 617 crews were to fly a pattern of precise flights, releasing Window anti-radar foil at accurately timed intervals, to simulate large shipping convoys in the Channel many miles away from the actual invasion fleet. This they achieved with total success on D-Day, 6 June 1944, a feat of precision flying and navigation. On 19 June Knilans returned to the bombing business by dropping a 12,000 lb Tallboy bomb on Watten; but next day, having set out with another Tallboy meant for Wizernes, he and the other Lancasters were recalled before reaching the target, then Nick went on leave to London.

On 12 July Leonard Cheshire was succeeded as commander of 617 Squadron by Wing Commander 'Willie' Tait, DSO, DFC, who soon began leading his unit on the continuing bombing of German sites in France. Attacking in daylight meant deliberately running through increasingly stiff and accurate flak defences around such sites, while other hazards came from other 'friendly' aircraft. On 31 July the squadron set out with Tallboys to destroy the site at Rilly La Montagne. Just as Knilans was concentrating on his instruments for the drop, his flight engineer tapped his shoulder and pointed upwards. One hundred feet higher, directly above Nick, another Lancaster had its bomb bay doors open, about to release its 12,000 lb Tallboy! Nick immediately skidded R-Roger sideways and then resumed his run. Below him another Lancaster from 617 was not so lucky, as a Tallboy struck the mid-section of ME557, S-Sugar, skippered by Bill Reid, vc. Reid's aircraft broke up – only Reid and his wireless operator, Luker, survived. Meanwhile, Knilans had his starboard outer engine hit by flak and had to feather it – ultimately making his sixth three-engine landing to date at base. On 1 August Knilans was again over France, intent on bombing Siracourt, but total cloud cover over the objective meant all aircraft returning with their bombs still aboard. It was officially the end of Knilans' second operational tour, but Nick volunteered for an additional five bombing sorties. If he survived these, he knew he would then be rested permanently.

On 4 August, still piloting R-Roger, he bombed a bridge at Étaples, while next day he lifted a Tallboy to Brest and made a direct hit on the U-boat pens there. On 6 August he bombed the submarine base at Lorient with a Tallboy, hitting the briefed aiming point, despite a flak barrage which bucked his Lancaster and scarred every bomber taking part in the raid. After a brief spell of leave, Knilans was among the eleven Lancasters detailed on 18 August to bomb U-boat pens at La Pallice with Tallboys – a particularly successful sortie. By then Knilans sensed that he was having trouble flying accurately – his subconscious seemed to be rebelling at the continuing nerve strain of operations. Nick had been flying sorties for fifteen months without a break – he decided to finish before he killed his faithful crew.

For several weeks thereafter he was detailed to fly a series of fuel consumption and all-up weight tests. One such flight involved taking off with maximum fuel possible, total bomb load, which with the Lancaster's natural weight totted up to 5,000 lb 'overload'. The main runway was blocked by a stalled Lancaster, so Nick tried to take off from the alternative, shorter runway. At barely more than stalling speed, Nick finally dragged the reluctant Lanc off the ground 100 yards beyond the end of the runway, skimmed closely over some telephone wires, 'milked up' the flaps, and finally picked up full flying speed. Engineers from the Avro company watching were astonished that anyone could take a Lancaster so over-loaded off such a short runway – and Nick privately told Willie Tait later that he wouldn't recommend doing it again either!

Though officially able to opt out of any further sorties, Knilans volunteered to participate in one more, rather special op. Piloting Lancaster LM492, he went with 617 Squadron to Russia, from where, on 15 September, he joined the attack on the *Tirpitz* lying in Alten Fjord. Returning to England, Knilans left 617 Squadron with a recommendation for a Bar to his DSO (though it was never processed) and next volunteered to fly Northrop Black Widow nightfighters with the USAAF in the Pacific theatre. The war ended before this could happen, but Nick Knilans was satisfied. He'd not only survived but had brought six of his original seven men crew through alive. He had too won his private 'war within a war', and now proceeded to carry out his wartime vow to devote his future to helping mankind in compensation for the death and destruction he had created.

For twenty-five years he was a teacher, including a two-years' stint as a Peace Corps volunteer in Nigeria, and championed the betterment of the lives of American youths with Mexican roots, apart from being a counsellor within the California prison system. He finally retired in 1978, but continues his championing of the underdog in society, especially underprivileged youth. It is a dedication to serving mankind which resulted from a private vow he made one night high over Berlin in 1943 when, fighting to control a crippled Lancaster, Nick Knilans had sworn to repay his debt to humanity.

As he figures it, he had been extraordinary lucky. He had survived more than fifty operational trips, including thirteen when his aircraft had been flak-damaged, and seven when he'd had to complete the sortie on only three engines. And of the two dozen men who'd graduated from training with him, he was the only survivor. To Nick Knilans it was a huge debt to be repaid. . . .

CHAPTER THREE

Alec Cranswick

'A quiet honest Englishman' . . . 'the perfect Englishman – quiet and retiring, but as a bomber captain in an exclusive class of his own' – just two heartfelt tributes by leading members of Bomber Command's wartime Path Finder Force to Squadron Leader Alec Panton Cranswick, DSO, DFC. Teetotal, non-smoking, with a preference for evenings listening to favourite selections from classical music, rather than the customary extrovert beery sessions in the mess, Cranswick was in all respects the antithesis of the media-boosted, popular image of the veteran bomber pilot. Yet this slim, reserved youth eventually flew a total of at least 104 operational sorties – all in bombers – then died in the cockpit of a crippled Lancaster over Villeneuve St Georges, attempting to control a doomed aircraft in order that his crew might have a slim chance to survive.

The son of an ex-Army, then RAF officer who was killed in an air accident when Alec was only eight, Cranswick was born on 7 September 1919. With an early interest in aviation, it was appropriate that Cranswick's main education was provided by St Edward's School, Oxford, an establishment founded in 1863 which in later years 'produced' such renowned pilots as Louis Strange, DSO, MC, DFC, Guy Gibson, VC, DSO, DFC, Douglas Bader, DSO, DFC, Adrian Warburton, DSO, DFC, and a number of lesser-publicised RAF personalities. On matriculating Cranswick decided against further schooling – his academic progress had been little more than average, due more to lack of interest than of intelligence – and joined the Metropolitan Police. He soon came to the conclusion that he was not best suited to any long career in the constabulary, though with a wholly characteristic refusal to quit any chosen task too readily, he persisted with his duties. In early 1939, however, the darkening shadow of Nazism across western Europe caused Cranswick to review his future, and on 24 July that year he enlisted in the RAF for training as a pilot.

After instruction at Desford, Ternhill and Bassingbourn, in June 1940 Pilot Officer A. P. Cranswick joined his first operational unit,

No. 214 Squadron, based at Stradishall, Suffolk, to fly Wellington bombers. On 18 June, as second pilot to the A Flight commander, Squadron Leader W. P. J. Thomson, Cranswick flew his first operational sortie, an attack against factories at Leverkusen, just north of Cologne. After seven more sorties as second dickey, Cranswick was promoted to captain of his own crew and aircraft in August 1940. With the crucial Battle of Britain then at its zenith, Bomber Command's priorities lay mainly in attempting to destroy the German barge fleets being assembled along the French coast intended for invasion of England, but Germany itself also figured regularly on the squadrons' battle orders, and Cranswick made his first visit in anger to the capital, Berlin, on the night of 7/8 October 1940. Hit by flak in a fuel tank over the 'Big City', Cranswick finally reached a fog-blanketed England with rapidly diminishing petrol, made an emergency landing at what proved to be a decoy airfield, and crashed, writing off his Wellington though without serious injury to any of his crew.

Further sorties to Kiel, Berlin, Bremerhaven *et al* soon brought his sorties' tally to 29 and the prospect of being rested from ops as an instructor, a thought that Cranswick and his crew did not relish. Accordingly, he volunteered himself and his crew for posting to the Middle East for further operations, and on the night of 8/9 December 1940, in Wellington R1249, he set out – only to have the pilot's hatch rip away as he took off. Remembering his heavy overload of fuel for the long flight to Malta, Cranswick decided against attempting any landing and pressed on, finally arriving on Malta early next morning.

Ostensibly, Cranswick's landing at Luqa, Malta, was merely a staging stop to Egypt, but after a few days of waiting for officialdom to offer specific orders to proceed, Cranswick was told that he and his crew were to stay on Malta, posted to No. 148 Squadron there for operations against Italian targets in Italy and North Africa, with occasional forays against enemy shipping in the Mediterranean. Initially, these sorties were against relatively soft Italian opposition, but soon after German forces moved into Sicily and the flak and fighter opposition stiffened noticeably. By the close of March 1941 Cranswick had completed 46 operational sorties, partly from Malta and some from Kabrit in the Suez Canal area, to which his squadron had been moved in March. Most of his crew returned to England but Cranswick was transferred to Takoradi, West Africa for a four to six months' detachment, ferrying aircraft to North Africa. In the event, much of that time was spent in hospital owing to bouts of malaria and scarlet fever, a period of utter boredom for Cranswick which he alleviated by reading, playing chess and delving deeply into astronomy, and writing poems.

In mid-October 1941 he finally recovered sufficiently to be returned to his old unit, 148 Squadron, still flying Wellingtons from Kabrit, and by now regularly engaged in the famous Benghazi 'Mail Run'; a long range trip entailing refuelling first at one of the several landing grounds near Fuka or El Daba en route. Three trips to Benghazi, then a raid on Crete brought Cranswick's ops' total to 50. In early November he returned to Benghazi to deliver the squadron's first 4,000 lb HC 'Cookie' blast bomb on that strategically vital port, but had to force-land in the desert on the return leg. Fortunately he was well within Allied lines and he and his crew were soon retrieved. Further sorties in support of the Eighth Army followed but by the turn of the year Cranswick had been stood down and repatriated to England. Here, on 7 April 1942, he was awarded a DFC and promoted to Flight Lieutenant; the citation for his award crediting him with 61 sorties to date.

Once home, however, Cranswick became a victim of recurring ill-health, almost to the point of a nervous breakdown; such had been the intensity of his efforts that he had overworked an already frail body. It meant many months of hospitalisation interspersed with occasional lecturing tours of various war factories under the aegis of the Ministry of Aircraft Production, to which he was officially attached temporarily.

In early December 1942, however, being considered fit again for operational flying, he was posted to No. 1659 Conversion Unit, Leeming, to learn to fly Halifaxes, where he was given a crew comprised of well-experienced men. Three weeks later he and his crew reported to No. 419 Squadron RCAF at Middleton St George, Durham. An extra member of his crew from then on was Kluva of Kentwood, a blue Alsatian bought as a puppy by Cranswick which soon accompanied its master everywhere, including flying. Given the rank of Sergeant and trade of assistant engineer, Kluva even had his own official flying log book in which Cranswick faithfully recorded Kluva's flying hours and operational sorties! Cranswick flew only five sorties with 419 Squadron, but had in the interim volunteered his crew to join Don Bennett's Path Finder Force. It was a decision not made without initial anxiety for Cranswick personally.

Throughout his operational career Alec Cranswick displayed a form of courage and determination in all things, in all situations, yet it had not been an unfeeling, unthinking courage which allowed him to return to the hazards of bombing operations again and again; rather a constant conquering of a perfectly natural fear of the odds against survival each time he set out on any raid. His highly sensitive nature rebelled always at the thought of causing death and destruction, but his detestation of the Nazi creed and inherited sense of duty gave him a constant impetus to continue, despite the ever-present prospect of death or mutilation on every sortie.

His attitude to his 'job' was summed up succinctly in a comment he'd made to his mother during an early leave period : 'I don't like what I have to do, but I think of you and my country and know I *must* carry on and do all I can. I must do what my pals who have not returned would have done. I shall try to forget the horrors we are committing.'

Such convictions helped Alec Cranswick to overcome his natural fears, and added great purpose to his flying and bombing. Unlike a high proportion of the younger, less-experienced crews, Cranswick never regarded the air war as anything other than a necessary evil; a duty requiring all the perfectionism of skill and courage he could muster to accomplish his chosen task.

Accepted for PFF operations, Alec and his crew were allocated to No. 35 Squadron in January 1943, based at Graveley and equipped with Halifaxes. As with all fresh PFF crews, they spent their first fortnight under instruction in PFF specialised tactics, methods, and scientific aids to bombing and navigation. Various new radar 'black boxes', such as H2S, were only just being introduced at this time; aids which promised greater accuracy and precision for the crews, along with recently introduced new pyrotechnic explosive stores for improvement in marking targets, etc. The bombing war was on the brink of change in most facets, and veteran crews like Cranswick's needed to be updated before being let loose in the increasingly dangerous air over Hitler's Reich. Their first PFF sortie was a relatively quiet trip to Cologne, but their next sortie was to Lorient, acting as one of the illuminator aircraft, dropping flares from some 15,000 feet to illuminate the objective for the following main force bombers.

As the bombing offensive steadily increased in scope and weight of destruction of Germany, Cranswick and his crew gradually gained further experience in their specialised roles of spearheading, marking and illuminating targets for the main bomber streams. They had their full share of hazards, such as on the night of 16 April 1943 when blazing the trail to the Pilsen Skoda Works in Czechoslovakia. En route, in the apparently clear skies, Cranswick was abruptly shaken to see a Messerschmitt Bf 110 nightfighter appear from nowhere, dead ahead and closing with breathtaking speed head-on. Instinctively pushing his control column hard forward, he *felt* the shock waves as the equally startled German pilot pulled up the nose of his aircraft and passed over the Halifax, missing an horrendous possible collision by literally inches. The vibration of its passing almost lost Cranswick his control of his bomber, but he soon recovered and pressed on to his target.

Then, having marked the aiming point, Cranswick watched the first bomb loads begin to go down on Pilsen from the main force and, his prime task accomplished, turned for the long trip back to Graveley. Within seconds his Halifax was firmly coned by several searchlights – a perfect target for the flak gunners. For the next five minutes – seemingly a lifetime to the trapped crew – Cranswick pulled every trick he knew to escape the glaring, blinding lights while flak reverberated all around him, threatening any second to claw him out of the sky. Only Cranswick's skill and stubborn determination not to give in finally succeeded in the Halifax escaping into the protective blackness outside the coning beams. As his tail gunner, Ivor Howard wrote in his log book afterwards with classic understatement; 'Shaky do!'

On the night of 20 April 1943 Cranswick took off on his 75th operational sortie – to mark Stettin – and, for once, everything seemed to go wrong. Their first mistake was to arrive too early over the objective, and they were accordingly greeted by the undivided attentions of (it seemed) the entire Stettin flak defences. Conscious of the vital need for his flares and target indicators to be dropped not only accurately but also at the planned time if the following bomber stream was to be effective, Cranswick deliberately stooged around the target area, a constant focal point for the frightening flak, until it was the right moment to drop his pyrotechnic markers.

Having done so, he finally swung out of the murderous barrage – only to realise that he was lost! The jinking and circling had baffled his navigator temporarily, a situation 'enlivened' by yet another storm of flak which came too near for comfort. Shards of red-hot steel began holing the Halifax from various angles and, in semi-desperation, Cranswick pushed his aircraft into a nose-dive at full boost. The speed built up rapidly and it took the combined strength of Alec and his flight engineer, Canadian Johnny Johnson, to eventually pull the plunging bomber out of its crazy plummeting dive. Once back on an even keel, Alec spotted the island of Sylt just ahead and thankfully headed out to sea and home.

By July 1943 Alec Cranswick had been awarded a DSO, and appointed commander of 35 Squadron's B Flight; though the latter promotion was not particularly to Cranswick's liking, in that he abhorred any form of pen-pushing, i.e. administrative duties and routine. His sole interest was flying and bombing Germany; he had no interest in any other aspects of RAF life and certainly had no craving for higher authority or Service responsibilities other than as a bomber captain. His constant pursuit of perfection in pure bombing results often called upon his deep powers of determination to succeed against any odds fate might throw into his path. On several sorties an engine failure, severe storms, dangerous icing and other dangers might have deterred lesser men, but Cranswick never gave up trying to fulfil any given task.

On 17 August 1943 – Cranswick's 87th sortie – he piloted Halifax HR926 as one of the 101 PFF aircraft detailed to provide markers for the various facets of a main force attack on Peenemünde, centre of the German rocket missiles' research and test programme. His pin-point accurate marking of his allotted 'Aiming Point E' – the barracks area on the south tip of the target – ensured ultimate success by those bombers following his specific task.

His next sortie was against Berlin on the night of 23/24 August, again in Halifax HR926, 'L-for-Leather'. It was the first of three major attacks on Berlin – the others being on 31 August and 3 September – and a total force of 727 aircraft were despatched. Of these 58 failed to return – mainly victims of the Luftwaffe's night-fighter defenders, including 35 Squadron's veteran commander Group Captain B. V. Robinson, DSO, DFC, AFC. It was Cranswick's 90th sortie, and his accuracy in marking on that occasion brought him a personal note of congratulation from Arthur Harris, AOC-in-C Bomber Command. He and his crew returned to Germany soon after, bombing Nürnberg and having one engine shattered by the flak, but flying home on the remaining three power plants and making a safe landing.

His 30th personal sortie with the PFF – his 96th overall – came on 4 October, against Frankfurt, again at the helm of 'L-for-Leather'. This trip concluded his third tour of ops and, despite his protests, he was taken off operations and posted to No. 8 (PFF) Group Headquarters at Huntingdon to fly a desk for at least six months' rest.

His appointment to a 'mahogany bomber' was dated 20 October, as one of the Operations staff officers.

While at PFF HQ Alec Cranswick met a Leading Aircraftwoman WAAF, Val Parr, who worked in the Signals Section. Over the following months their romance blossomed and eventually resulted in their marriage on 14 April 1944. By that time Cranswick's constant applications for a return to the operational scene had borne fruit, and he had been notified that he would be going to his old unit, 35 Squadron, with effect from 7 April 1944 – the same date on which all his previous promotions and indeed his DFC award had occurred. He immediately tried to gather his old crew together from their varied non-operational posts, but only managed to persuade his old tail gunner, Ivor Howard to agree.

Finally collecting a new crew together, Cranswick returned to Graveley and began crew familiarisation with 35 Squadron's latest aircraft, Avro Lancasters. They made their first Lanc flight on 27 April and continued practising until 15 May, on which date they were allocated Lancaster ND846, 'J-Johnnie'. Four nights later Cranswick made the first sortie of his fourth tour of ops, a 'soft' trip to Boulogne. Three more sorties in the next four nights finally brought his sorties' total to 100 – the century being an attack on Aachen. It was not an easy trip, carrying a load of 12,000 lb of high explosive and having to ward off determined German nightfighters en route to target, but Cranswick returned safely to write the magic figure 100 in red ink in his log book.

Though totally immersed in operations again, Cranswick now had added worries because his wife, Val, now expecting their first child, had had to go into hospital gravely ill. Taking a few days' leave, Alec flew to her side until the crisis had passed, but then had to return to his squadron. Val was still in hospital on the night of 4/5 July 1944 when Alec Cranswick and his crew set out in Lancaster ND846, TL-J, as one of sixteen aircraft from 35 Squadron leading a raid on the rail marshalling yard complex at Villeneuve St Georges, a major junction point for transportation of men and material to the German forces facing the recent Allied invasion forces in Normandy. Ostensibly a 'short trip' (compared with the more normal deep penetration sorties into Germany), it looked like a relatively routine sortie.

A possible omen of impending trouble for Cranswick came when his regular gunner, Ivor Howard, DFC, was forbidden to fly by the unit medical officer due to a heavy cold. No operational bomber crew ever liked having new members being included at short notice, and it may have bothered Cranswick that he needed to replace Howard at such brief notification. If it did bother him, he did not show it to his crew. At precisely 2316 hrs Alec gunned the Lancaster's four Merlins and began his take-off run, then climbed smoothly away into the night sky. Fixed between the hand-grips of his control column was a small photo of Val, his eleven-weeks' bride.

The master bomber for the raid that night was Squadron Leader Keith Cresswell, DSO, DFC, and the first wave of PFF marking aircraft were marshalled onto target with precise timing. Cranswick, who had initially arrived slightly early and accordingly circled outside the target area while 'marking time', now slid into his allotted slot in the programme. Diving gently from some 12,000 feet to little more than 4/5,000 feet because of unexpectedly deep cloud cover, Cranswick finally emerged from the cloud, quickly levelled the Lancaster, then settled onto a rock-steady run-in to place his war load. At such low altitude he was only too aware that he was easy meat for the German flak defences, but his job was to mark, and mark accurately – he could not evade any opposition during that crucial steady run-in. Releasing his load, Cranswick immediately received instructions from his navigator, Reg Kille, for a course to set for the return trip.

Seconds later the Lancaster was hit by a burst of flak in the rear open bomb bay, and flames leapt along the fuselage, intensified by the roaring slipstream. The bomber was crippled beyond hope and Cranswick, struggling to maintain some form of control, yelled to his crew to bale out immediately. Before any crew member could reach the escape hatch, however, the stricken Lancaster broke up, snapping free of its main spar just behind the wireless operator's cubby-hole, where the operator, Wilf Horner, was impatiently awaiting his turn to escape by parachute through the nose hatch. The break-up of the fuselage hurled Horner into space and instinctively he operated his parachute. His next dimly conscious thought was regaining some of his senses while lying on his back on a cinder track leading to a German radar post. His hands and legs were severely burned, with his right hand burned to a moulding, still clutching the D-ring of his parachute harness. But he was alive – the only survivor.

The burning segments of Lancaster ND846 fell near the French village of Reau, about ten miles from Villeneuve St Georges and the bodies of the remaining crew were transported to the village hall, then buried next day by the Germans with full military ceremony. After the war, Alec Cranswick's body was taken, along with the crew members, and re-interred in the Clichy Communal Cemetery, on the north side of Paris, in a plot cared for by the Imperial War Graves Commission.

CHAPTER FOUR

Popeye Lucas

The young New Zealander in his fresh-bought 'fifty-bob' suit sat nervously centre-front of the panel of serious-looking gentlemen in a bare room in Adastral House, London. It was the late summer of 1936, and he had come a long way for this slim chance of joining the RAF, working his passage to England on a refrigerated cargo ship, *Fordsdale*, chipping rust, swabbing decks, polishing brasswork, and pot-cleaning in the odorous galley – all for a shilling a month and 'all found'. Arriving in England with just two pounds sterling in his pocket, he'd since worked at gardening, cherry-picking and day-long harvesting while he'd waited impatiently for this interview.

Now the ordeal began. Education? Just high school, no certificates. Algebra? (What was algebra?) Why did he work his passage rather than let his father pay passage? Because he preferred to get here under his own steam. Why the RAF? Because he wanted a Service career. (It wasn't really true, he just wanted to fly. . . .) The panel muttered between themselves, then, 'We like your spirit and have decided to take a gamble on you. If you pass your medical, you'll start training right away.' The young Kiwi sailed through his medical examination – except for his dental health; he would need a dental surgeon's chit to say he was 'dentally fit for flying'. . . . Finding an ex-RAF pilot, now dental surgeon, the youngster simply told him to extract *every* tooth and fit him with a full set of dentures. This done, Fred J. Lucas enlisted in the RAF for pilot training.

Born in Dunedin on 18 August 1915, Fred Lucas was the son of an English farmer who had emigrated to New Zealand at the age of sixteen, married a local girl, and set up his own 1,000-acre farm at Tuapeka Mouth, South Otago. Here Lucas and his four brothers were raised to the dawn-to-dusk labouring routine of a farmer's life; a grinding task made even more essential during the depression years of Lucas's teenage. Then the local newspaper announced a flying competition, with first prize free tuition to 'A' Licence pilot standard. It was the trigger to Lucas's increasingly strong urge to fly. He did not win that competition but now had the 'bug', so he took his meagre savings, went

55

to Taieri and joined the Otago Aero Club. Here his instructor was Ted Olson (later, Air Commodore E. G. Olson, DSO, died May 1945).

Once fairly competent at the controls of the club's DH Gypsy Moths, Lucas applied to join the New Zealand Air Force, only to be rejected on lack of education grounds, and without even benefit of interview. Undeterred, Lucas decided to sail to England and try the RAF, setting out from Port Chalmers on 28 January 1936, just six months after his twentieth birthday.

Lucas's training initially took place at the civilian school at Sywell, but in January 1937 he went to No. 10 FTS at Ternhill, followed by advanced instruction which he completed in August 1937, was granted a commission and his wings, and was next posted to No. 10 Squadron at Dishforth, Yorkshire. With this unit Lucas – by then firmly nick-named Popeye due to his startling resemblance to that international cartoon character whenever he removed his handsome dental work – flew lumbering Whitley bombers for two years, until July 1939, in which year he married a cousin from New Zealand. On 1 July 1939, however, Lucas was one of twelve pilots posted to Marham, Norfolk, there to become one of the original members of No. 75 (NZ) Squadron. Two years previously the New Zealand government had arranged to purchase 30 Wellington bombers for the RNZAF, the first of these being planned to be flown out from England by August 1939. The first six Wellingtons were delivered between May and July 1939 to the so-termed 'New Zealand Flight', but the outbreak of war two months later nullified the whole scheme, and the New Zealand govern-ment waived their aircraft order, placing the NZ Flight's crews and Wellingtons at RAF disposal. On 4 April 1940 No. 75 Squadron RAF – at that date merely a training unit – had its name-plate transferred to become No. 75 (NZ) Squadron, based at Feltwell, to which the NZ Flight had moved on 16 February 1940.

Even before their up-grading to squadron status, however, the Kiwis had commenced operations. On 13 March 1940, Lucas took part in a general sweep recce of the North Sea, looking for German shipping, while on 27 March three Wellingtons set out to 'bomb' Hamburg with leaflets, enduring appalling weather conditions for most of their sortie. On 17 April Lucas was in one of two squadron aircraft which bombed Stavanger airfield, this time as second pilot; but his first 'op proper' (*sic*) was on 21 May when he bombed railway marshalling yards at Aachen.

Operations became intensive during June, and Lucas took a full part in the nightly forays, visiting such targets as Bremen, Hamburg,

Düsseldorf, Cologne, Emden, Kassel, Lübeck and Gotha. One of his earliest sorties was intended to be a bombing attack on Rotenburg airfield, but with ten-tenths cloud almost all the way out he flew 'by the clock' and on reaching his ETA dived through a small cloud-gap to level off at 1,500 feet over the Baltic Sea. Following the coastline, he next came upon a 'nice quiet little bay' and started across it – only to become the focal point of a fierce barrage of flak; he was over Kiel! By then Lucas was flying at only 400 feet altitude and received a thorough pasting from the flak before dumping his bomb load into the heart of Kiel and making his way to safer air.

By mid-September 1940 Popeye Lucas had completed 30 sorties and was due to be rested, but the Service grapevine had rumoured an imminent attack on Berlin and Lucas persuaded his squadron commander to let him stay and participate. In the event, he flew six more ops before the Berlin trip, which was flown on the night of 23 September. Flak opposition was particularly fierce around the German capital, but Lucas came through with a relatively unscarred Wellington and returned to base, only to be diverted to Marham because Feltwell was fogged in. At Marham Popeye managed to put his bomber down accurately along the primitive flare-path, though with one wing canted sharply due to a flak-slashed main wheel tyre. It was his 37th sortie, the end of his first tour of operations, and he was posted to a Wellington OTU at Hampstead Norris (satellite to Harwell) as an instructor. Shortly after the award of a DFC for Popeye Lucas was announced.

Lucas's first tour had been a tough one by any standards, yet once back in the officers' mess Popeye became the main instigator of many a rip-roaring session – near-impromptu parties wherein the young crews let their hair down by some fairly extrovert behaviour after a few cans of beer. Lucas's main party-piece was Operation Man Friday. Stripped of mess jacket, waistcoat, socks and shoes, he would be laid on a small table on his back, have his bare feet thoroughly blackened with a glutinous mixture of black boot polish, then be hoisted unsteadily until his feet reached the bar ceiling. Then, slowly but carefully, he would 'mark' a trail of black footprints from the entrance door to above the bar; a pastime given official approval later when Air Marshal Sir Arthur Tedder visited the mess, and wrote in the Visitors' Book : 'These foot prints to remain for all time!' If Popeye was ever the life and soul of any party, his gaiety hid the natural tension built up as sortie followed sortie; but it also helped to mask a deep personal tragedy. In 1940 his young wife Joan had returned to England after the birth of their daughter, and was living out with Lucas in Lakenheath village during the German blitz by night, when she suddenly died in her sleep.

For six months Lucas carried out his instructional duties meticulously, night and day, rising in rank to Squadron Leader by May 1941, but as soon as the end of his enforced rest was in sight he applied for a return to operations, and was posted back to his old squadron, still at Feltwell, where he was joined by Sergeants Gould, Green – both DFM-winners on their first tour with Lucas – and Fenton; his old crew wireless operator, navigator and air gunner respectively. His first sortie of his second spell of operations was to Düsseldorf on the night of 11 June 1941, taking with him as second pilot, Tim Williams – the latter's first-ever sortie.

Flying at 8,000 feet, Lucas reached his target and made his first bomb run through the flak which was nudging his aircraft off course and riddling the airframe. Not satisfied with his run, the bomb aimer told Popeye to go round again. The second run-in still didn't satisfy Green, a Nottingham lad, and again he politely requested Lucas to go round once more. By now Popeye and the rest of the crew were getting decidedly anxious, not least because every flak gun and search-light in the area seemed to be concentrating upon their aircraft only. This time Green let the bomb load go, but before Lucas could pull out of the flak a shell ripped through the fuselage, destroying the hydraulic system, and hit one engine which emitted flames, though they were soon extinguished. The loss of hydraulic pressure let the undercarriage flop down, and Popeye couldn't close the bomb bay doors. Other damage included a hole in one of the main petrol tanks, while as Lucas leaned forward to set his gyro compass a shard of flak tore through his cockpit from side to side – directly through the space occupied by Lucas's head only seconds before.

Finally leaving the flak zone, Lucas realised he was losing fuel steadily, as well as height due to the dangling bomb doors and under-carriage. By the time he reached the Dutch coast he was down to 200 feet with little prospect of improvement for the trip over the North Sea. He gave his crew the option – ditch and hope to evade capture? Or press on? The verdict was unanimous – 'Give it a go, skip'. Barely maintaining his precarious altitude, Popeye managed to reach the English coast, despite the port engine barely ticking over with its cylinder head temperature right off the clock and almost at melting point. Finally reaching base at 100 feet height, Lucas was refused permission to land due to some unexploded bombs left on the airfield by a recent Luftwaffe raid. He diverted to Newmarket, some fifteen miles away, where the Air Traffic Control held him off to let a Stirling bomber land first.

Pumping hard to ensure the undercarriage was locked down, Lucas brought the wallowing Wellington in to land in the dark, well to the right of the flarepath, floated just above the grass for what seemed ages, then touched down sweetly – just as the fuel-starved 'good' engine cut out.

As the crew lay on their parachute packs under the wings afterwards, awaiting transport back to the mess and savouring the utter peace and stillness, the second dickey, Williams, naively remarked, 'Gee! If all the trips are like this one, it won't be so bad.' Popeye Lucas's reply was unprintable!

Lucas's next sortie was a return trip to Düsseldorf, another perilous threading through fiercesome flak at 8,000 feet which led Lucas to climb to 20,000 feet for his next sortie, hoping to get above the barrage. It took patience and skill to even get his aircraft that high, moreover the temperature was zero, but he derived some comfort from watching another Wellington far below being liberally plastered by the guns. His complacency was short-lived when an appalling crash of an exploding shell sounded right underneath him. Figuring that there was no percentage in being frozen stiff *and* being shot at, Lucas promptly descended to his customary 8/9,000 feet bombing height for all future trips.

For the following five months No. 75 (NZ) Squadron tackled a wide variety of objectives in France, Germany and Italy; one of the latter sorties being to Genoa when Lucas spent nine and a half hours strapped in his bucket seat, much of that time flying blind in thick cloud and/or raging rainstorms. On 24 July the unit contributed six Wellingtons to a heavy raid against Brest, their specific target being the German capital ship *Gneisenau* harboured there. Reaching Brest in a clear sky in mid-afternoon, the Wellingtons, in neat vics-of-three formations, headed through a frightening flak barrage above the port. As they emerged from the holocaust of flak, Luftwaffe fighters were waiting for them. One Wellington, hit by several shells, had its undercarriage down and its bomb doors still open as it fell out of the formation. The hovering enemy fighters bore in for the kill. A Messerschmitt Bf 110 was too confident and was shot down by the crippled bomber's air gunner, but a Bf 109 following in delivered a killing burst, sending the bomber spinning down to destruction. Lucas, on first seeing this lame bird drop out of formation (pilot, Sergeant D. F. Streeter, a fellow-New Zealander), immediately went to its aid, but arrived too late to save it. Lucas's gunner at least extracted a modicum of revenge by destroying the Messerschmitt Bf 109 responsible for Streeter's loss.

Lucas's final operation of his second tour came on 26 November

1941, when he bombed Emden, carrying for the first time a 4,000 lb HC 'Cookie' blast bomb clutched in the semi-closed bomb bay. The trip went smoothly and Lucas returned to base without incident, where no less a person than the Crown Prince (later, King) Paul of Greece sat in on Popeye's de-briefing session. Lucas then left No. 75 (NZ) Squadron for a brief training course on Blind Approach procedures, before being posted back to Feltwell to command No. 1519 BAT Flight for a few months. In March 1942, however, he boarded the troopship *Dominion Monarch* and sailed home to New Zealand, now wearing the rosette of a Bar to his DFC for his second operational tour.

Back in his native country Lucas was appointed to command of No. 1 General Reconnaissance (GR) Squadron, RNZAF based at Whenuapai, flying Lockheed Hudsons on general coastal patrols and anti-submarine hunts. This post lasted until December 1942, when he was given command of a newly-forming unit, No. 40 Squadron, an aerial transportation unit due to be equipped with Douglas DC3s, or Dakotas as the RAF termed them. Aircraft and crews were slowly gathered together and on 13 April 1943, No. 40 Squadron made its first operational flight, a round trip to the New Hebrides, skippered, naturally, by Popeye Lucas. One week later Lucas re-married, this time to Loraine ('Lorie'), a WAAF stationed at Whenuapai employed as a transport driver.

Lucas might simply have rested on his laurels and seen out the rest of the war in his relatively comfortable tasks with 40 Squadron, but his itch to contribute something more positive to the war was summed up in a lengthy application he forwarded to headquarters. In it he pointed out that his training and experience as a night bomber pilot was being wasted '. . . driving an inter-island bus around as greengrocer to the Pacific', then offered to pay his own fare back to England, or resign his commission and go back to farming. His brash plea must have found a sympathetic reader somewhere along the official channels because on 11 November 1943 he set sail again for England aboard the *Santa Monica*, via San Francisco, then New York, and the final trans-Atlantic trip aboard the *Queen Elizabeth*. Back in London, Lucas pestered the authorities for a posting to low-level daylight operations and eventually got his way by being posted to No. 487 (NZ) Squadron at Hunsdon, Hertfordshire, a DH Mosquito unit under the aegis of the 2nd Tactical Air Force (TAF), preparing for support operations to the imminent Allied invasion of France. Teaming up with navigator P. E. Barnes – known to all as 'Tightskin', and a veteran of former Blenheim operations – Popeye soon settled in to his new role.

For six months Lucas led his flight by day and night, making high and low level air raids against transport and communications targets in France, coastal batteries, flying bomb ski sites, all by day; while the night sorties were mainly in the intruder role, attacking German airfields. In early June 1944, on his 64th sortie, he attacked some railway yards at Charleroi, Belgium, from a mere 50 feet height and had one engine shattered by ground fire. Nursing the Mosquito up to 10,000 feet, he put the aircraft nose down in a shallow dive and gave the remaining engine full boost, returning across the Channel at some 350 mph to avoid any German fighters which constantly roved the area looking for stragglers.

Just before midnight on 5 June he was returning from a patrol over Normandy when he saw below him a veritable armada of lights in the sky. He was witnessing the massed formations of towed gliders carrying the advance paratroops of the Allied invasion forces; each with its wing and tail lights fully ablaze to avoid the risk of air collision. Shortly after D-Day (6 June) 487 Squadron began air protection patrols over the Allied beach-heads, and on 11 July Popeye Lucas flew his 81st sortie of the war, thereby bringing his third tour of operations to a close.

For the following four months, with the rank of Wing Commander, Lucas was employed ferrying Lancasters from Canada to England, apart from a spell of hospitalisation for a tropical bug he'd picked up, after which he returned to New Zealand in March 1945, there to be sent to Mechanics Bay, Auckland as Station Commander; a post he remained in until August 1945 and his voluntary demobilisation from the Service.

For his first fifteen years as a 'civvy', Popeye continued to fly, establishing an air freight business despite long, weary battles with bureaucracy attempting to obviate private enterprise in such matters. Then, in 1960, Lucas became principally a hotel manager-owner high in the rolling countryside of Queenstown and Lake Wakatipu. The farmer's son had finally returned to the land.

CHAPTER FIVE

Hughie Edwards

Sunday, 6 December 1942. The Met men had forecast that the morning's light rain would give way to clear, sunlit skies over northern Europe by early afternoon. To the 94 bomber crews of Nos. 21, 88, 105, 107, 226, 464 and 487 Squadrons of No. 2 Group, Bomber Command, it meant that after several days delay due to 'scrub' weather conditions, Operation Oyster was finally on. By 1120 am 47 Venturas, 36 Bostons and ten Mosquitos were beginning their take-offs from their respective airfields in East Anglia, each gaggle quickly settling into pre-arranged formation boxes and all heading for the Essex coast and, eventually, Holland. The target was the Phillips Radio factory complex at Eindhoven, and over fifty Spitfires, Mustangs and Typhoons had been detailed for escort or support diversion roles for this raid.

Beating across the North Sea at wave-top height, two of the bombers were forced to abort due to mechanical problems, while one Ventura with engine troubles plunged into the sea. As the Dutch coast loomed into view of the leading Bostons enemy coastal batteries greeted their approach and the bombers weaved gently in evasive manoeuvres, then as they began crossing the outlying salt marshes the bombers ran full tilt into hundreds of startled wild fowl. Wings and fuselages shuddered under the impact of dozens of ducks, some suffering shattered windscreens with blood and feathers splattered around cockpits.

The leading Bostons and Mosquitos penetrated inland, meeting heavy flak over the Oosterschelde and near Schouwen, then Bergen op Zoom where the intense barrage forced the whole formation to take violent evasive action. Further inland the bombers began crossing over or near Woensdrecht airfield, from which a fierce flak barrage arose and the crews watched a host of Focke Wulf Fw 190s and Messerschmitt Bf 109s hastily scrambling to intercept the invaders. Directly over the Luftwaffe base a leading Ventura, AJ196 'C', piloted by Wing Commander F. C. Seavill, dipped its nose just ten feet and exploded into the ground, while others suffered direct cannon shell hits in engines and wings but staggered on. Then, as the Bostons and Mosquitos ahead reached Turnhout, the last turning point on the run-up to target, pairs of Fw 190s bore into attack. Two Mosquitos of the rear section led by Squadron Leader George Parry, DSO, DFC, deliberately decoyed the fighters away from the main bomber stream, then 'lost' them by superior speed, before rejoining the formation.

Within minutes Eindhoven came into view ahead and the Bostons and Mosquitos climbed swiftly to 2,000 feet to begin their bombing runs in shallow dives. The Bostons released their bomb loads first, dead-on target, to be followed by the Mosquitos whose loads were released in salvo from 1,000 feet into the smoking, exploding factory sites below. Threading their way through the inferno of rising smoke, debris and descending bombs, the Mosquitos fled to safer air, with one Mosquito, DZ371 'A' of 139 Squadron, trailing flames and smoke from a shattered engine.* Last to bomb were the Venturas, plunging through a holocaust of well-alerted flak and depositing their loads accurately into the centre of the target area.

Intent now only on getting home, the various bomber boxes dropped to tree-top altitude and made bee-lines for the Dutch coast, running a continuing gauntlet of flak, low power cables, bird-strikes, and Luftwaffe fighters; the latter continued their pursuit miles out to sea before finally turning away. Once the surviving bombers had all reached their bases, the costs were totted up. Fourteen bombers had been lost, while 23 others had the scars of damage in varying degrees. Nevertheless, the outcome of the raid was the virtual destruction of the vital factory, while although many Dutch civilian houses nearby had suffered damage, less than thirty civilians had lost their lives – a tribute to the accuracy of the overall bombing.

Leading the Mosquito formations on this raid was Hughie Idwal Edwards, holder already of a Victoria Cross and a Distinguished Flying Cross, and commander of No. 105 Squadron. The Eindhoven sortie led directly to the further award of a Distinguished Service Order only weeks later, thereby making Edwards the most-decorated Australian airman of the 1939–45 war. Born in Fremantle, Western Australia on 1 August 1914, Hughie Edwards was the son of Welsh parents who had emigrated to Australia four years before. Educated locally, Edwards worked in a shipping agent's office after leaving

---

* It ditched in the North Sea some thirty miles off Dan Helder.

school, but in 1934 he joined the Fremantle Garrison Artillery as a private soldier, then in July 1935 transferred to the RAAF for training as a pilot at Point Cook, being awarded his 'wings' in June 1936. On 21 August that same year Edwards was transferred and commissioned in the Royal Air Force, and in the following month joined No. 15 Squadron RAF at Abingdon, England, to fly Hawker Hind biplane bombers. Six months later he moved again, this time to No. 90 Squadron at Bicester, taking up the duties of squadron adjutant.

No. 90 Squadron at that time had been selected as the second RAF unit to be re-equipped with the new Bristol Blenheim I monoplane bomber, and began receiving its first examples in May 1937. Though his duties as unit adjutant meant that Edwards spent many hours sifting paper, he was expected to take a full part in all normal flying programmes undertaken by the squadron, and in March 1938 was at the controls of a Blenheim when it became uncontrollable. Forced to take to his parachute – no easy task in any Blenheim – his 'chute tangled with the aircraft radio mast and the subsequent crash left Edwards with his right leg severely injured. A main nerve had been severed and later the leg became paralysed below the knee. It meant a spell of nine months' hospitalisation, then non-flying duties until April 1940 before he was declared medically fit to fly again.

A four months' armament specialist course until August 1940 followed, but in September he crashed again, though without further serious injury. Finally, in February 1941, Edwards achieved his main wish to return to firstline flying when he was posted to No. 139 Squadron, based at Horsham St Faiths (now, Norwich Airport), Norfolk to fly Blenheim IV bombers.

His stay with 139 was brief, and on 11 May he moved to Swanton Morley to take up his new appointment as commander of No. 105 Squadron, another Blenheim IV unit. His long-frustrated ambition for operational flying may have been partly responsible for the intense determination he applied henceforth, and this facet of his character was well exemplified on 15 June 1941 when he led six Blenheims out over the North Sea, seeking enemy shipping. Sighting a convoy of eight merchant vessels a few miles from the Hague, he led his crews down to a mere fifty feet height and attacked. A fierce, accurate barrage of fire met the incoming Blenheims, but Edwards selected a 4,000-ton vessel as his target, raked its decks with machine gun bullets, then dropped his bombs from mast height penetrating the ship's

superstructure and creating great damage. His coolness and determination on this sortie in particular led to the award of a DFC on
July 1.

Three days later, on 4 July 1941, Edwards set out on his 36th
operational sortie at the helm of Blenheim IV, V6028, GB-D, from
Swanton Morley's grass airfield. The targets were the docks and
industrial factories at Bremen, and Edwards was leading a mixed
batch of nine Blenheims from his own squadron, and six more from
No. 107 Squadron, based at Great Massingham. At 0521 hrs Edwards
got airborne, briefed to arrive over Bremen at 0800 hrs, and flew
at the head of the combined formation low across the sea, crossing
into Germany a few miles south of Cuxhaven, then turning south to
Bremen at a height between 50 and 100 feet, still in formation. The
skies were brightly clear with excellent visibility – an aid to navigation
on the one hand, but leaving the Blenheims decidedly naked for any
enemy defenders, ground or air. By then three of 107 Squadron's
Blenheims had been forced to abandon the sortie, but the remainder
stayed in formation up to the edge of the target area.

Then, as had been pre-arranged at the final briefing for this Operation Wreckage, the bombers spread out in a loose line-abreast some
100/200 yards apart spread over a mile frontage, with orders to
choose individual targets of opportunity over Bremen. The objective
was ringed with barrage balloons close-hauled to 500 feet, backed
by a heavy flak 'ring of steel' – both deadly hazards for unescorted
bombers at low altitude and in broad daylight.

Reaching the outer defences, with every man now virtually on his
own, Edwards nosed his way through the forest of balloon cables,
ploughed through some telephone and telegraph wires, and jinked his
path through a frightening flak barrage for some ten minutes, collecting some twenty direct hits over the city, one shell bursting in the
mid-upper gun turret and shattering Sergeant G. Quinn's knee.
Arriving over the docks area, Edwards dropped his bombs in its
centre, then dropped to the lowest possible height until he reached the
outer city suburbs. Turning to port he circled Bremen, strafing a
stationary train en route which fired flak shells at him, then headed
towards Bremerhaven and Wilhelmshaven. Meeting more flak over
Bremerhaven, he dived to sea level and came out of Germany
near Heligoland, flying north of the Frisians for a while before turning
westwards for England. Four other Blenheims had been shot down
over Bremen, and the survivors were all battle-scarred on their return,
with three crew members wounded aboard. On 22 July the *London*

Gazette announced the supreme award of a Victoria Cross to Hughie Edwards, and a DFM and DFC apiece for his two crew men, Quinn and Pilot Officer Ramsay.

Six days after the *Gazette* citation appeared, No. 105 Squadron's Blenheims were touching down on Luqa airstrip on the besieged island of Malta, led by Hughie Edwards. For several months previously No. 2 Group's squadrons had been flying to the island on rotated detachments, tasked with anti-Axis shipping sorties in the Mediterranean in support of the Allied armies in the North African land campaign. Three days after arrival on Luqa, Edwards led six crews against a small convoy of four vessels protected by a destroyer escort some 200 miles north-east of Pantelleria, with a gaggle of Italian Fiat CR42 fighters acting as the convoy's aerial 'umbrella'. The opposition from fighters and flak proved too much, for once, and the sortie was abandoned; but the Blenheims continued their daily offensive, attacking enemy ships or blasting land targets along the Libyan coast. Such sorties usually meant attacking at near-zero altitude and the squadron lost many crews to flak, but several to collisions with ships' masts *et al.* By 11 October the squadron had returned to England, and Hughie Edwards left the unit to join a VIP lecture tour of the USA, along with such notables as Bob Tuck, 'Sailor' Malan, Harry Broadhurst, and Charles Whitworth.

On return from the American public-relations' exercise, Edwards was appointed Chief Flying Instructor at Wellesbourne Mountford in January 1942, but on 3 August 1942 he returned to the sharp end of operations when he rejoined his old unit, 105 Squadron at Horsham St Faiths as its latest commander. No. 105 Squadron had spent some nine months evaluating and operating the new De Havilland Mosquito day bomber – the 'Wooden Wonder' – and Edwards lost little time in testing the design. On 29 August, for example, while returning from a sortie in DK323 he ran head-on onto a dozen Fw 190s. As the German fighters turned for a second, stern attack, Edwards gave his engines full boost and quickly outpaced the Fw 190s, but once out of immediate danger over the sea had to stop his port engine which had suffered bullet damage. Deciding to land at Lympne, he accomplished a belly-landing without injury to himself or his navigator.

He was to remain in command of 105 until early February 1943, leading many of the unit's outstanding sorties, including the Eindhoven raid of 6 December which brought him his DSO award. On 10 February 1943, however, he received promotion to Group Captain and was appointed Station Commander of Binbrook, with control of nearby Wickenby and Grimsby.

Binbrook, a pre-war designed airfield, had been closed for several months while new concrete runways were laid, but, on 14 May 1943, the station was officially declared operational again when its latest residents arrived, No. 460 Squadron RAAF, an experienced Lancaster unit, with a high proportion of Australian air and ground crews, commanded by an Australian, Wing Commander C. E. 'Chad' Martin, DFC. Edwards' status and many administrative duties as 'Station Master' meant that officially he was not expected to participate in operations personally, but throughout his lengthy tenure of command of Binbrook he made many unofficial sorties over Germany, apart from at least fifteen legal trips when his name appeared on the battle orders. His usual ploy, when undertaking non-official trips, was to skipper fresh, inexperienced crews as they arrived to commence their first tours of operations – a gesture which installed huge confidence in the 'sprog' crews. Moreover, such sorties exemplified Edwards' constant theme to all crews that they 'must press on regardless of opposition', a creed to which he personally adhered throughout his flying career. Such apparent total lack of fear may not have appealed to many crews who were more concerned with personal survival, but was a perfectly natural facet of Edwards' character.

Continuing to inspire and, occasionally, fly with 460's crews throughout 1943–44, Edwards' final sortie with the squadron was flown on 27 November 1944 when, typically, he introduced Pilot Officer A. Whitmarsh and his sprog crew to their first taste of bombing Germany. The return leg, albeit mainly uninterrupted by enemy defences, led him over the American lines in France from where a fierce barrage was concentrated upon his Lancaster, with several hits.

Leaving Binbrook in December, he next flew to the Far East theatre of the war, becoming Group Captain Operations at Headquarters Ceylon, Kandy, but soon moved to South-East Asia Command HQ as Senior Air Staff Officer, which appointment he was to hold until the end of 1945.

Remaining in the RAF after the war, Hughie Edwards held a number of flying and staff appointments over the following eighteen years, with an award of an OBE in 1947, promotion to Air Commodore in 1958, a CB award in 1959, and an appointment as an ADC to HM The Queen in 1960. He finally retired from the RAF in

September 1963 and returned to his homeland, Australia. Here further honours were to be bestowed upon him, including a knighthood and, in 1974, elevation to Governor of West Australia.

CHAPTER SIX

Fraser Barron

As captain of aircraft, has evinced a high order of courage and skill, together with determination to strike at the enemy on every possible occasion and with the greatest destructive effect. Throughout, he has given evidence of keenness and tenacity in accomplishing his allotted tasks and on many occasions has displayed a complete disregard for his personal safety.

Thus read the citation to the award of a DFC to James Fraser Barron in the *London Gazette* dated 9 February 1943. Already wearing the ribbon of a previous DFM award, Barron was later to add a DSO and Bar to his decorations. For any man to receive four gallantry awards, apart from promotion from Sergeant to Wing Commander, all within just two years of service would appear to indicate some form of steely-eyed, square-jawed hero of popular fancy. In fact, Fraser Barron stood five feet six inches in height (if he was wearing shoes), was slightly built, handsome, modest in all things. As one of his air gunners, Harry Meades, said of Barron :

'I lived alongside, and flew with, Fraser Barron over a period of twenty months, and got to know him pretty well. He was always very quiet, meticulously neat and clean at all times, drank very little, and was a perfect gentleman always. He flew the same way – quiet, very efficient, a real pro. Flak and fighters never bothered him, he just got the job done. A very polished man, and a great credit to his country.'

Barron's country was New Zealand, where he was born in Dunedin on 9 January 1921. Educated at Waitaki Boys' High School, he later continued his studies for accountancy in night classes at Wellington Technical College. Out of the classroom Barron played a variety of sports, including rugby, cricket and tennis, with a side interest in field athletics. On leaving school he obtained employment in the Mines Department in Wellington, but on 5 October 1939 applied for training as a pilot in the RNZAF. Eventually enlisting on 2 July 1940 at Levin, one of Barron's fellow candidates was a youngster from Wanganui, Jimmy Ward, destined to be awarded a Victoria Cross little more than a year later. And indeed both boys were to continue side by side through every stage of their training *et al* until their ultimate postings to different operational squadrons in England a year later. From 29 July they received their *ab initio* pilot instruction at No. 1 EFTS, Taieri, then moved on to No. 1 SFTS, Wigram on 28 September, where on 18 January 1941 Fraser Barron was awarded his pilot's wings and promotion to Sergeant. Twelve days later he embarked on the *Aorangi* to sail to England, via Canada, arriving at Bournemouth Reception Centre on 6 March, and being posted north to No. 20 OTU, Lossiemouth, accompanied still by Ward.

At Lossiemouth Barron completed his training on Wellington bombers, crewed up, and in mid-June was posted south again, to No. 15 Squadron, based at Wyton, Huntingdonshire. 15 Squadron was only the second squadron to be equipped with the giant Short Stirling 'heavy', the first example of which had reached the unit on 11 April 1941. By the time Barron joined the unit, 15 Squadron had already been well-blooded operationally on Stirlings, flying by day or night mainly against German targets, though not without casualties, including a previous squadron commander, Wing Commander H. R. Dale, who was lost to a German nightfighter over Berlin on 10 May. He was succeeded by Wing Commander P. B. B. Ogilvie, DSO who remained in his post until January 1942 and literally led his squadron on every possible occasion.

As was the usual practice then, Barron's first sorties were flown as second pilot to a more experienced captain until, after ten such second dickey trips, Barron was promoted to command of his own crew and aircraft. Those introductory operations quickly inculcated the quiet New Zealander with an appreciation of the hazards to be faced in bombing ops. Two such sorties were in daylight, attacking Béthune and Hazebrouck, against moderately heavy flak and Luftwaffe fighter defences; while one of his night forays against the Ruhr Valley, as second pilot to the squadron commander, entailed bombing from some 800 feet due to bad visibility conditions over the briefed target. Inevitably, such a low altitude meant the Stirling having to run the gauntlet of murderous flak defences for almost twenty minutes approaching and leaving the target, and reaching base again well perforated. On 1 September 1941 Fraser Barron was promoted to Flight Sergeant, and nine days later was one of six Stirling skippers from 15 Squadron who made the unit's first attack against an Italian objective, in this case the Royal Arsenal at Turin.

Returning to Italy shortly after, to bomb Genoa, Barron's Stirling was hit by flak crossing the French coast near Dunkirk on the outward leg. Unbeknown to the crew, some flak splinters had sliced through part of the bomb-release electrical circuit, thereby isolating some 5,000 lb of bomb load in the fuselage bay from normal release. It was only the beginning of Barron's problems on that particular sortie. Reaching the objective, he made his run-in, then realised that only the under-wings' load had been dropped. All efforts to dislodge the bombs in the main bay were fruitless, so Barron prepared for the long haul home with the added burden. Matters grew worse on the return trip as deteriorating weather forced him to detour 100 miles off track, using up precious fuel, until when passing over the Channel Islands, Barron was informed that there was only enough fuel left for ten minutes' flying time.

Barron asked his crew whether they preferred to ditch quickly, or to press on and hope to make landfall; they chose the latter. As the first available airfield came into view Barron put the Stirling's nose down for an immediate landing, touched down smoothly on a concrete runway, then had three engines die on him halfway along his landing run, starved of petrol. The sortie had taken nine hours and ten minutes – 'not very comfortable', as Barron remarked modestly afterwards.

Further sorties followed – Frankfurt, Munster, Berlin, Karlsruhe, Bielefeld, Duisberg, Kiel, Nuremburg, Bremen, Cologne, Essen, Lubeck, Hamburg, Rostock, and the Ruhr – each against steadily increasing and more accurate German defences. After completing his 29th operational sortie – the third in 48 hours attacking Essen – Fraser Barron was awarded a DFM (gazetted 26 May 1942); but his 30th trip was almost his last ever.

Ostensibly a relatively 'soft' sortie – mine-laying – Barron's aircraft was hit by light flak on his first dummy run prior to releasing his mine load. A shell exploded inside the forward fuselage, cutting trim wires and therefore leaving Barron to fight for control of the heavy bomber. Aided by Flight Sergeant J. Cowlrick, however, he managed to return to base safely, but counted almost 100 holes in the scarred Stirling later. Undeterred, Barron flew a further twelve sorties, but was then notified that he had completed his first tour of operations, and was to be rested. Meantime, on 23 March 1942, Barron was commissioned as a Pilot Officer.

In June 1942 Barron was posted to No. 1651 Conversion Unit at Waterbeach, Cambridgeshire as an instructor, though while there being rested he flew four more operations – to Bremen, Hamburg, and Düsseldorf (twice). Then, on 20 September 1942, he returned to the

operational scene with a posting to No. 7 Squadron at Oakington, flying
Stirlings again, though this time with the recently inaugurated Path
Finder Force (PFF) as one of the spearhead marking formations
'preparing' each target for main force bomber streams. Several of his
initial sorties with the PFF were flown to Italy, visiting Milan, Genoa
and Turin. On his third successive trip to the latter, Barron again ran
into a variety of problems outside his control. In his own words:

'It was a filthy night with weather so bad that many aircraft iced up
and had to abandon the trip and return to base. We decided to fly below
the weather as long as possible, then climb quickly over the Alps and
rely wholly on Caldwell's* navigation. Everything worked well and we
waited until he said, "All right – come down". Down we went, holding
our breath and praying we weren't going to hit a mountain, then
suddenly we saw that we were just twenty miles north of Turin – it was
exceptional navigation. We were surprised by the stiff opposition we
encountered and, hearing flak exploding uncomfortably near us, we
flew right across the town, then circled and returned to drop our flares
and bombs. We were caught and held by searchlights for five minutes,
but managed to escape them and get back without incident. At base
we discovered the reason for that individual attention – we had been
the only aircraft over the target...'.

In October 1942 Barron was promoted to Flight Lieutenant, and in
December awarded the Path Finder Badge – the gilt eagle sewn below
his medal ribbon, on the flap of his tunic pocket – denoting his con-
firmation as a qualified member of the PFF. In the same month, on
21 December, he set out to bomb Munich:

'We were first to bomb, but on the return flight were surprised by
a nightfighter which raked us from end to end before we saw it. For a
moment or two I watched cannon-tracer going into the port wing, then
took violent evasive action. The gunners got in short bursts until their
guns failed due to mechanisms being damaged. However, we managed
to out-manouevre him and got away.

'Taking stock, we found that the changeover petrol cocks for tanks
on the port side had been severed. The tanks we were then running on
had very little petrol and we couldn't supplement them. Another
complication was a fire in the rear of the aircraft. The fire was put out
by the wireless operator, then our flight engineer, Flight Lieutenant
Robinson, a Scot with a DFM on his 77th op, managed to connect up
the tanks and get the petrol through . . . we got home all right but when
we reached England there was low cloud and suddenly we found our-

---

* Flight Sergeant P. R. Caldwell, later, Squadron Leader, DSO, DFM.

selves flying over Luton with a big chimney sticking up *above* us. We shot up again, then when about to land found that one main wheel would not come down. Well, Robinson fixed that too, we braced our-selves for a crash, but the wheel held.' Robinson was awarded a DFC for that night's work especially.

Barron's 57th operational sortie was a raid on Cologne as one of the first three aircraft over the target. One companion was almost immediately brought down, while the other was forced to abort with mechanical defects. Running up to his target Barron was coned at 18,000 feet by an estimated 50 searchlights, and within seconds was the focal point of a fury of flak. One propeller was damaged, while his tail turret was smashed. Despite Barron's every attempt to escape the searchlights' glare, he remained coned for some sixteen minutes before finally releasing his load and diving away into the protective blackness away from the target. The return leg, with defunct compasses, led him over Ostend and yet another barrage of flak too close for comfort, but he returned to base without further damage. Shortly after, on 9 February 1943, he was awarded a DSO for '. . . exceptional gallantry and devotion to duty, setting an example of the highest order.'

His 61st sortie was to Hamburg. Flying above a heavy storm en route, he reached the port, began his run-in, only to have one engine cut out abruptly. Completing his bomb run, he turned for home, know-ing he would not have sufficient power to climb over the bad weather ahead. Soon he entered the heart of a storm and icing became bad enough to force the Stirling down to 2,000 feet and reduce its speed to only a fraction above stalling. Then, passing over Rotterdam, he ran through a rainstorm which melted the accumulated icing, allowing him to gradually gain height to 4,000 feet, after which Barron managed to regain base. His next sortie came on 14 February to Cologne, and was completed successfully despite engine problems. With this he had completed 62 operations and the end of his second operational tour. On 7 March he received further promotion to Squadron Leader, then a week later went to No. 11 OTU, Westcott as a senior instructor.

Barron remained on instructional duties for the next nine months, but then volunteered to return to operations. Accordingly, he was posted back to No. 7 Squadron on 27 December 1943 as a flight commander. By then his old unit had converted from flying Stirlings to Avro Lancasters, though it remained based at Oakington. Barron soon started operating, bombing Berlin on three trips, apart from Magde-burg, Schweinfurt, Augsburg and others, but on the night of 19/20 February 1944 he went to Leipzig – a raid which cost the RAF 78 bombers lost, mostly to Luftwaffe nightfighters. Of that sortie, Barron said later :

'It was one of the toughest I've been on. German fighters appeared to be waiting for us everywhere, and they laid an aerial flare path for a distance of 100 miles to the target. It was just like daylight. We saw kite after kite in combat, and watched several go down in flames. So we were highly relieved when we reached the target, bombed, and got out of it without any trouble.'

The early months of 1944 were to witness the loss of many veteran PFF crews, particularly those of Master Bombers and/or their deputies. No. 7 Squadron, for example, lost its commander, Group Captain K. R. Rampling, DSO, DFC, on 24 March, then his successor, Wing Commander W. G. Lockhart, DSO, DFC, a month later, on 27 April. Fraser Barron, who had been promoted to Wing Commander on 12 February, was appointed CO of 7 Squadron on the day after Lockhart 'failed to return'. Most of his operations by then were in the role of Master Bomber, carrying a load of flares and target indicators (TIs) for initial target-marking, then remaining in the target zone to direct or amend the follow-up marker aircraft results and order in the main force bombers. Such a role meant deliberately staying in the danger zone, ignoring flak and searchlights to concentrate on directing as accurate an attack as humanly possible.

It was in precisely this role as Master Bomber that Barron set out on his 79th sortie on the night of 19/20 May 1944. The objective was the rail marshalling yards complex at Le Mans in France, and Barron's deputy was Squadron Leader J. M. Dennis. Having dropped the first markers, Barron was heard over the R/T giving directions to the others – then came an abrupt silence. Next day he had still failed to be accounted for, and was therefore officially recorded as 'missing'. Though claimed to have been a victim of flak or possibly a nightfighter in some subsequent histories, there is strong evidence that Barron's Lancaster had been the victim of a mid-air collision.

The Germans buried James Fraser Barron, DSO, DFC, DFM in Le Mans Cemetery. He was just 23 years old. In the following month the *London Gazette* announced the award of a Bar to Barron's DSO, its citation ending with the words, 'He is an outstanding captain, whose example of skill, bravery and determination has impressed all' – perhaps a fitting epitaph for the young Kiwi they described as 'the perfect gentleman' in RAF bomber messes.

CHAPTER SEVEN

Mick Martin

When speaking of his period of service in command of No. 617 ('Dambuster') Squadron during 1943–44, Group Captain Leonard Cheshire, VC, DSO, DFC, has been quoted as saying:

> The backbone of the squadron were Martin, Munro, McCarthy and Shannon, and of these by far the greatest was Martin. As an operational pilot I consider him greater than Gibson, and indeed the greatest that the Air Force ever produced. I have seen him do things that I, for one, would never have looked at . . . I learned all I knew of this low-flying game from Mick.*

Born on 27 February 1918 at Edgecliff, New South Wales, and later resident in Sydney, Martin joined the RAF in England on 28 August 1940 for pilot training, received his wings and a commission in June 1941, and joined his first operational unit, No. 455 Squadron RAAF in October 1941. Though originally formed in New South Wales on 23 May 1941, 455 Squadron's advance party of personnel – two officers and some 200 airmen – did not set sail for England until two months later, but meanwhile the squadron was officially formed under the aegis of No. 5 Group, RAF Bomber Command at Swinderby in June 1941, absorbing the RAAF contingent as these arrived in the UK weeks later. The Australian authorities had intended the unit to become a Wellington bomber squadron, but in the event the squadron was slowly equipped with Hampdens.

On the night of 25 August 1941 two of 455's crews took part in a raid over Germany, one of these in a Hampden 'borrowed' from No. 50 Squadron, also based then at Swinderby, but four nights later, led by Squadron Leader Dereck French, DFC, in Hampden AE296 'F', both squadrons raided Frankfurt – 455 Squadron's first *official* operations. By early 1942 the squadron was up to full strength in

* *The Dam Busters* by P. Brickhill; Evans Bros., 1951.

aircraft and crews, operating from Swinderby and its satellite airfield at Wigsley.

Martin was among the first skippers to undertake operational sorties, and on 21 February 1942 he piloted an all-Australian crew to Germany – the first all-Australian bombing sortie of the war in Europe – his crew being Jack Leggo, 'Tammy' Simpson and Toby Foxlee, all of whom were to remain with Martin for the following two years. Tallish, slim, with a fashionable wide-span moustache often affected by RAF air crews of the period, Martin was described by one contemporary as having a 'wild streak, no nerves, but well above the average in the precision of his flying abilities'.

His predilection for low-level flying in particular was demonstrated only too well on one occasion. The squadron commander, Wing Commander Grant Lindeman, was in the airfield's control tower with the visiting Air Officer Commanding, and was explaining that 455 Squadron *never* indulged in the dangerous and unauthorised practice of 'beating-up' airfields – only to have his words drowned by the fearsome noise of one of 455's Hampdens nearly taking the roof off above his head! The culprit – Martin – subsequently had a gigantic 'strip' torn off him by his highly embarrassed squadron commander.

In April 1942 the squadron flew its last bombing sorties on the night of the 15/16th and ten days later was officially transferred to Coastal Command for a future torpedo-bomber role. Martin, who had completed thirteen sorties over Germany by then, left the squadron on posting to the 'sister' unit at Swinderby, 50 Squadron, taking his regular Aussie crew with him, and continued his tour of ops. Still flying Hampdens, Manchesters and Lancasters, Martin completed a further 23 sorties with 50 Squadron before being 'rested' in October 1942 with a posting on instructional duties to No. 1654 Conversion Unit, and being awarded a DFC.

By then his growing reputation as a pilot who was seldom (if ever) deterred by any form of enemy opposition from completing every allotted task, apart from an instinctive skill in his 'trade', had spread around much of bomber circles, and led to his personal selection by Wing Commander Guy Gibson, DSO, DFC to become a 'founder-member' of the newly-forming No. 617 Squadron, based at Scampton, in early 1943. Accordingly, Martin arrived on 617 Squadron on 31 March, to be joined by his old crew of Leggo, Foxlee and Simpson, and immediately became involved in the intense training programme of the squadron as it prepared for its first operational task – Operation

Chastise – the projected breaching of several key dams in the Ruhr area of Germany. To Martin's personal delight, this working-up stage involved the unit's Lancaster crews in perfecting almost ground-level low-flying techniques – his 'speciality' – though until the last days of the trials he, like almost all other 617 Squadron personnel, had no precise idea of the eventual targets.

As the new squadron's acknowledged 'gen-man' on low flying by night or day, Martin gave the other crews several lectures on the art. He spoke from hard experience gained during his Hampden operations. On one such trip to Kassel he had hit a balloon cable at low altitude, severed it, but flew on with the steel cable still dangling from a wing. On the return leg his Hampden was attacked by a nightfighter, so he dropped down to some fifty feet height. Brushing the tips of some trees, one end of the dangling balloon cable wrapped itself in a branch cluster and was pulled clear – though only as the Hampden was pulled momentarily even lower! 617 Squadron's low-level training was not without incident, however, including one special trial on which Martin flew an actual bomb-dropping run across the waters at Reculver. He released his 'bomb', only to have the consequent spout of water hit one of his Lancaster's elevators, damaging its under surface. The bomber dipped its nose but Martin's expertise saved him and his crew from a watery grave.

His reaction afterwards was typical of the man – a cool appraisal of what had happened. Convinced, though not despondent, that he would die on operations 'sometime', Martin had long ago reconciled himself to living each day to the full while he could – a fatalism not uncommon among many other air crews who had survived an operational tour, then returned for a second spell of bombing.

Finally, on 16 May 1943, Operation Chastise (the Dams' raid) was 'on'. Nineteen Lancasters and their selected crews were prepared and briefed during the day, and by 8.30 pm the crews were waiting by their loaded aircraft awaiting the order to climb aboard and go. They were to fly the sortie in three waves. Guy Gibson was to lead one group of nine Lancasters, including Martin's 'P-Popsie' (ED909), to commence the actual attack pattern; followed by two more groups of five Lancasters apiece to complete the plan. Then, at 9.40 pm, Gibson, flanked by Martin and Flight Lieutenant J. V. Hopgood, DFC, began a 'Vic' take-off run from Scampton's grass airfield.

Leaving the English coast, Gibson, Martin, and the following aircraft eased down to fifty feet above the surface of the North Sea as they nosed towards the Dutch coast. From the coast to the Möhne

Dam they ran through a series of flak guns, but spent much of the trip dodging power cables, trees, and low hills as they hugged the ground contours. Arriving over the Möhne, Gibson made the first attack without breaching the dam structure, then called in Hopgood to commence his attack. Hopgood, already wounded by flak during his approach leg to the target, duly swung Lancaster 'M-Mother' across the dam waters, lined up for the drop of his 9,100 lb 'mine', released it, and was immediately hit by more flak which set fire to the Lancaster's port inner engine. As Hopgood struggled to keep airborne and was crossing the dam wall, his 'mine' exploded below on a power house. Then Lancaster 'M-Mother' erupted in flames, staggered on briefly, and dived into the ground. Now it was Martin's turn.

Gibson called Martin to begin his attack, adding that he would fly in ahead and off to one side to attract the flak away from 'P-Popsie' if possible. Roaring in at precisely sixty feet above the waters of the reservoir, Martin held his Lancaster rock-steady as the German flak-gunners concentrated on the incoming pair of bombers. Martin's aircraft received several hits on the run-in, including a direct hit in his starboard wing's centre fuel tank (luckily, empty by then) and damage to ailerons, but released his 'mine' accurately and turned out over the dam wall. The dam remained intact. It needed two more bomb-runs, by Squadron Leader H. M. 'Dinghy' Young, DFC and Flight Lieutenant D. J. Maltby, DFC, before the Möhne Dam was finally breached; each of whom's run-in was accompanied by Gibson and Martin, attempting to smother and confuse the flak opposition. As soon as Gibson saw that the target had been smashed, he ordered Martin and the other 'empty' Lancasters to go home, while he gathered his remaining aircraft together for the next targets, the Eder and Sorpe dams.

The outcome of Chastise was equally success and sacrifice. The Möhne, Eder and Sorpe dams were breached, apart from a partial breaking of the Ennepe. The resulting loss of water disrupted huge areas of the surrounding countryside, killed more than 1,000 German civilians, and seriously affected power supplies of every type to dependent industrial complexes in the area. The cost to 617 Squadron was the loss of eight of the nineteen Lancasters which had initially set out – in human terms 56 air crew members missing, of whom just three survived as prisoners of the Germans, and the remaining 53 were all killed. The 'rewards' to the survivors of this unique operation were generous, including a Victoria Cross for the leader, Guy Gibson, and a

DSO for Mick Martin, plus seven days immediate leave for the air crews.

During the following weeks 617 Squadron was brought gradually up to full strength again, with new crews to replace the casualties, and the Lancasters modified and replenished for more 'normal' bombing roles. For the future the squadron was to become a 'specialist' unit, operating against specific key targets requiring uncommon tactics (and, later, weapons). It resumed operations on 15 July with an attack on power stations in northern Italy, a long haul which meant the aircraft eventually landing at Blida in North Africa; then 'shuttling' back to the UK later, bombing another target en route. Two weeks later came another 'shuttle' trip, this time to 'bomb' Milan with propaganda leaflets.

At the end of August 617 Squadron moved en bloc to a fresh base, Coningsby, where the crews began intense training in low-level tactics again. Then, on 14 September, eight crews set out to attack the key Dortmund–Ems Canal in Germany, each carrying a 12,000 lb HC (High Capacity) bomb in their bomb bays – the first *intended* use of this new weapon. In the event, weather conditions resulted in the force being recalled, but one Lancaster was lost when Flight Lieutenant David Maltby, DSO, DFC crashed in the sea.

Next morning eight more crews were detailed for the same operation, including Martin who had returned from leave and immediately volunteered to take the vacancy left by Maltby's death. The eight were led by 617's latest commander, Wing Commander George Holden, DSO, DFC, into the night of 15/16 September, flying at fifty feet altitude in a full-moon sky. Before reaching the target, over Nordhoorn, a flak gun hit Holden's Lancaster, rupturing a wing fuel tank. Streaming a cone of flames the stricken bomber exploded into the ground, killing Holden and three men of Guy Gibson's original 'Dam-busting' crew.

Martin, in Lancaster EE150, assumed command of the raiders and finally reached the target area, to find it covered in dense mist and fog. For the next hour or more the bombers circuited the target zone, attempting to get a clear sight of their objective, flying no higher than 150 feet and continuously under fire from the heavy flak defences along the canal. In the event, only Dave Shannon and Martin actually managed to drop their monstrous blast bombs anywhere near the canal, and neither was able to breach the waterway; Martin made thirteen attempts before releasing his bomb. Of the others, one skipper was forced to jettison his bomb due to flak damage to his Lancaster and abort the sortie – the other five were all shot down. Five lost out of eight represented a casualty *rate* or percentage even higher than that suffered by 617 on its first epic operation.

On his return from this disastrous sortie, Martin was promoted to Squadron Leader and given temporary command of 617 on direct authority of Ralph Cochrane, the AOC of No. 5 Group. For Martin, unversed in the finer points of administrative niceties and their ramifications, such a jump to the dizzy heights brought him many minor problems of routine squadron matters, but it did not curtail his operational flying. His period of temporary command only lasted a few weeks, until the official appointment to the post in late September of Wing Commander Leonard Cheshire, DSO, DFC (later, VC), though the new CO was unable to exercise full command until a month or so later. Then, sufficiently familiar both with the Lancaster aircraft and the operational expectations of his squadron, Cheshire began to literally lead his crews into battle. At first, naturally, Cheshire leaned heavily upon the esoteric experience of Martin and the few other surviving 617 'originals', but soon brought his own incisive views to bear on the unit's patterns and modes of operations.

With Cheshire leading, backed by Martin, Shannon, McCarthy and others, 617 began bombing selected targets in Italy and Germany, but not always with marked success. One objective particularly – the Antheor Viaduct on the main German railway supply line between Marseilles and Genoa – proved to be a hoodoo for 617's crews. Two previous attempts to knock this down by 617, apart from a third try by the USAAF, had achieved nothing, but on the night of 12/13 February 1944 Cheshire led eleven Lancasters to the viaduct, each bomber carrying a 12,000 lb bomb, except Cheshire and the raid deputy, Mick Martin; the latter pair intending to be the initial markers.

The target lay at the foot of steep hills and a ravine leading down to the sea, leaving the bombers with few alternatives for their approach runs; a situation exacerbated by a heavy defensive force of searchlights and flak guns ringing the area. Moreover, it lay at virtually the extreme range for a loaded Lancaster, leaving little margin for 'reserve' fuel. On reaching the target, Cheshire and Martin found they needed to fly no higher than 3,000 feet if they were to keep the viaduct in vision, but as each in turn made their first attempts to mark the aiming point, each was forced away by a fearsome barrage of predicted flak and blinding searchlight beams. Each man tried again, with the same outcome.

Both men had so far approached from the sea, but Martin now edged inland and asked Cheshire to draw off the flak while making a third seaward approach, while Martin tried a run-in from the opposite direction. Skipping over the hills, Martin dropped down into the ravine with the viaduct dead ahead, outlined in his view clearly against its Mediterranean backcloth. Overhead, Cheshire flew a reciprocal course, absorbing a fair proportion of the flak barrage. Then, as Martin was diving and on the point of releasing his markers, a burst of 20 mm cannon shells exploded through his aircraft's nose section, killing Bob Hay, Martin's bomb aimer for so many past sorties, while other hits slammed into two engines, cut hydraulic pipe lines, and wounded the flight engineer in his legs.

Scraping over the viaduct at less than fifty feet, with every gun in range hammering at it, Martin's 'P-Popsie' fled out to sea. Once clear of the flak, Mick took stock of the damage. Apart from the holed nose and crew casualties, two engines were stuck in a throttle-back position, the bomb doors could not be closed, air pressure for brake controls had gone, and he still had a 4,000 lb 'Cookie' and several 1,000 lb high explosive bombs on their belly racks, unable to be dropped electrically due to a smashed circuitry.

Realising that there was an urgent need to get medical help for his injured flight engineer, Ivan Whittaker, Martin set course for Sardinia, and an American airfield there, Elmas Field. It would mean some 200 miles or more, keeping a battered Lancaster airborne somehow despite the widespread damage, but his first task was to get rid of the bomb load, not only to 'lighten ship' but to increase his slender chances of some form of safe landing on arrival at Elmas. Kenny Stott the navigator gradually got rid of the 'Cookie' and all but two of the thousand-pounders by manually tripping their release mechanism hooks, and all aboard sighed with relief – now their only problem was reaching Elmas, then landing.

When the air strip finally came into view Martin was disturbed to see that the overshoot area – which in his aircraft's sorry state, he'd probably need – was non-existent; the runway ended at a cliff's edge! With no brake pressure, and possible unknown damage to his Lancaster's undercarriage, Martin set her down smoothly at the end of the runway, immediately began fish-tailing the rudders to slow progress, then as the cliff edge loomed near, applied full rudder to swivel the aircraft around finally to a stop. The cliff drop was only 50 yards further on.

Whittaker, the injured man, received on-the-spot medical aid, thereby saving one leg from possible amputation, and was then whisked off to hospital; Bob Hay's body was interred locally; then after repairs locally and at Blida, Martin flew back to England.

On arrival in the unit's base, Mick Martin was told he was being ordered off operations by Cochrane himself – there was no argument would persuade the AOC to change this decision. Martin by then had been awarded Bars to his DSO and DFC for his trojan work with 617 Squadron, and was quietly shuffled off to a desk job at a Group head-quarters. He had by then completed some 49 sorties in all, but the prospect of sifting paper for the remainder of the war was just not Martin's 'style', and he quickly began wangling himself back to the operational scene.

The result was a posting to No. 515 Squadron in 1944 to fly Mosquito VIs from Little Snoring near Norwich on night intruder and escort duties over Europe and, after D-Day (6 June 1944), day Ranger patrols over France and the Low Countries. By late 1944 Mick Martin had brought his sorties' total up to 83 and was awarded a second Bar to his DFC before finally coming off operations.

After the war Martin remained in the RAF, gaining further steady promotion and honours, and eventually retiring from the Service on 31 October 1974 as Air Marshal Sir Harold Martin, KCB, DSO, DFC, AFC. Such an impressive status may well tend to overshadow earlier achieve-ments in the mind of the layman, but contemporaries of Mick Martin are unlikely to think of him in any other terms than the description in the official history of the European bomber offensive : *

Though not the most famous, (he) was certainly one of the greatest bomber pilots who ever set course from British bases. His genius for flying was unsurpassed and his relentless determination in the face of any hazard was unquenchable.

* *The Strategic Air Offensive against Germany, 1939–45* by Sir C. Webster/ N. Frankland, Vol 2; HMSO, 1961.

CHAPTER EIGHT

Dennis Witt

When war with Germany was declared on 3 September 1939 the great majority of RAF personnel, particularly air crews, were men who had already signed on, serving some form of regular service engagement. They came from many differing backgrounds, including no few from the various member-countries of the British Empire, each merging easily into a uniform 'whole' RAF. Yet the real backbone of the 1939 RAF had been nurtured from within the Service's own auspices: products of Cranwell, Halton, Flowerdown, Eastchurch, Cosford and similar establishments initiated on the foundation of Hugh Trenchard's visionary 1919 schemes for the post–1918 Royal Air Force.

Of these breeding grounds, Cranwell and Halton were possibly the most significant. While the RAF College at Cranwell had, by September 1939, passed more than 1,000 young officers into service, the station had also been the training school for aircraft apprentices of the electrical and wireless ground trades; in parallel with Halton's 'Trenchard Brats' of the other top skilled trades. These boys, destined to serve as the technical spine of the regular RAF, also provided a steady flow of air crews. Once having attained the status* of Leading Aircraftman (LAC) in their trade, ex-apprentices became eligible for possible aircrew training should they so desire, and for many ex-apprentices this was their ultimate ambition – to fly.

One ex-Cranwell 'Brat' who achieved that ambition was Dennis Theodore Witt who commenced the war as a Sergeant Pilot and five years later had become Wing Commander, DSO, DFC, DFM, veteran of 100 operational sorties over Europe in bombers.

A native of Swanage, Dorset, Witt was born on 27 September 1915 and joined the RAF as an Aircraft Apprentice (23rd Entry) in January 1931 to be trained as an electrician at Cranwell. During his three years' apprenticeship his athletic prowess was exemplified

---

* Unlike today, LAC at that period was not a rank, but the ultimate trade proficiency status prior to acquiring NCO rank *et al.*

when he represented the RAF at cross-country running, and on leaving Cranwell as an Aircraftman 1st Class (AC1) he was posted to Henlow. He soon attained his LAC 'props' via various trade tests and wasted no time in applying for pilot training, but a posting to No. 7 Squadron (Handley Page Heyfords) at Worthy Down intervened; his application apparently strayed in the official channels, and he received no response.

Determined to achieve his ambition, Witt re-applied and this time was accepted; he moved to the Bristol Flying School, Filton, in September 1936 for elementary instruction initially, then graduating to No. 9 FTS, Thornaby and Hullavington. One of his fellow-pupils and close friends throughout this training period was Geoffrey 'Sammy' Allard, an ex-Halton Apprentice, who later rose to fame as Flight Lieutenant, DFC, DFM and one of the RAF's leading fighter pilots of 1940–41 before his death. Finally, he was awarded his wings and promotion to Sergeant in October 1937, and proceeded to his first unit as a pilot, No. 10 Squadron, based then at Dishforth, Yorkshire.

No. 10 Squadron, formerly equipped with Heyford biplane 'cloth bombers' had been chosen to introduce the new, all-metal monoplane Armstrong Whitworth Whitley bomber into operational use, receiving its first example in March 1937 and, by June, had its full complement of twelve Whitleys. Witt quickly mastered the art of piloting the lumbering Whitley and remained with 10 Squadron for the last two years of the peace, then flew his first wartime sortie on 5 September 1939, a rather harmless leaflet raid. In that same month he was promoted to Flight Sergeant. Still with 10 Squadron, Witt took part in various operations over Germany and occupied France during 1939–40 and by September 1940 completed his first tour of 38 sorties, having been awarded a DFM in the previous April.

Shortly after leaving No. 10 Squadron he was commissioned as Pilot Officer, then posted to his old unit, No. 7 Squadron for a further spell of operations. By coincidence he was again joining a unit about to introduce a new bomber to service, in this case the giant Short Stirling 'heavy'. By 30 November 1940, No. 7 Squadron, based at Oakington and commanded by Wing Commander Paul Harris, had nearly its full establishment of air crews, but only five Stirlings. These five were still, ostensibly, training aircraft, intended to familiarise air and ground crews with the new type, and a myriad of technical problems already plaguing the Stirling prevented its use on true operations until 10 February 1941, when three of the squadron's crews managed to participate in a bombing raid on Rotterdam and returned safely, albeit with two of the three having bomb hang-ups.

For the next two months Stirling sorties followed a spasmodic pattern, often with only solitary or pairs of crews undertaking sorties. On 28 April, piloting N6010, Witt bombed Emden at mid-day, dropping eighteen 500 lb GP bombs in the city centre, then dropping to 2,000 feet and recrossing the target to allow his gunners to conduct a 'street-strafe' and splash bullets in the docks area.

By June 1941, No. 7 Squadron had managed to despatch an overall total of 100 operational sorties in some five months, but had lost three Stirlings in action and four others written-off in pure accidents. By then Stirlings were being employed mainly on daylight raids, thereby being dangerously exposed to attack by Luftwaffe fighters. On 4 July, for example, Witt was one of three Stirling skippers who set out to bomb Borkum seaplane base. They were jumped by a horde of Messerschmitt Bf 109s which quickly shot down one Stirling, then turned their attentions to Witt and his companion. Four times the Bf 109s raked Witt's aircraft, wounding his air gunner, Flying Officer J. L. A. Mills, who managed to drive his tormentors away. Leaving his turret then to have treatment for his wounds, Mills quickly returned to his guns as a fifth attack bore in and shot one Bf 109 down. Running a gauntlet of flak and fighters by day had by then become a familiar adjunct to Stirling operations, due to the contemporary use of the bombers in 'Circus' raids; blatant bait for drawing up German fighter opposition in order that the often heavy RAF fighter 'escorts' could conduct battles of attrition with their Luftwaffe counterparts.

In early July 1941 Witt raided Texel, only to be attacked by a swarm of Messerschmitts. Using the Stirling's remarkable manoeuvrability, he managed to give his tail gunner a no-deflection target, which the gunner promptly acknowledged by destroying one Messerschmitt in flames. Ten days later, while leading a Vic of three Stirlings over Béthune, Witt ran into a fiercely accurate flak barrage which shot down one bomber. Undeterred, Witt completed his bombing run, despite further flak opposition, and returned by jinking his way through several determined attacks by roving German fighters. These and previous hazardous sorties resulted in Witt being awarded a DFC in August 1941.

After completing his second operational tour of 27 sorties, Witt left the operational scene in September 1942 on posting to Canada for pilot navigational training duties, where he remained until August 1943, then returned to England to take up an appointment as a staff officer at the headquarters of No. 8 (PFF) Group. There followed a course at the RAF Staff College, Bulstrode Park, but Witt then managed to wangle himself back on operations, being posted as a flight commander to No. 635 Squadron, at Downham Market, Norfolk. Equipped with Avro Lancasters, 635 Squadron had been formed on 20 March 1944 from detached flights of Nos. 35 and 97 Squadrons, as the latest Path Finder unit to join No. 8 (PFF) Group.

Qualifying soon after as a Master Bomber, Witt flew a further 35 sorties with the Path Finders, thereby completing an operational career of 100 sorties; his ultimate 'century op' in November 1944 being a blind sky marking and bombing of Duisberg. On 16 February 1945 the *London Gazette* announced the award to Dennis Witt of a Distinguished Service Order (DSO), its citation ending with the words. 'He has displayed the highest standard of skill and bravery, setting an example of a high order.'

Witt saw the remaining months of the war out as an instructor at the Empire Central Flying School, and with the arrival of peacetime continued in regular service. With various appointments in the UK and overseas, including command of Nos. 15 and 109 Squadrons in England and 88 Squadron in Germany, he was promoted to Group Captain in 1959 and became Deputy Director of Operational Requirements 1 at the Air Ministry. Tragically, he died less than four years later.

CHAPTER NINE

Jo Lancaster

Ask any wartime bomber air crew member who initially joined the RAF in 1939–40 what he had hoped to become and the odds are that a large majority of those embryo fliers would reply 'Fighter pilot'. The first year of the war had brought the exploits of fighter pilots into the glare of media limelight, heavily playing up the pseudo-glamour attached to such individuals from the days of the 1914–18 aerial conflict. This popular legend of the dashing, steely-eyed 'knight of the air' became particularly emphasised in 1940 as RAF Fighter Command fought a desperate battle of attrition with the German Luftwaffe over (mainly) south-east England during the Battle of Britain. The equally trojan work of the 1939–40 crews of Bomber Command rated few headlines in the contemporary news outlets, and in any case – to the lay mind – bombers evoked no image of glamour or glory. Little wonder that newly-joined airmen of eighteen or nineteen primarily opted for training as fighter pilots, each imagining himself as a future ace. J. O. – 'Jo' – Lancaster was no different in his views when he was first called to 'the colours' for air crew training with the RAF; he too distinctly fancied himself as a glamorous fighter boy.

Lancaster's early post-school years had always been tied in with aviation, having been apprenticed to Armstrong Whitworth Aircraft Ltd at Whitley airfield, near Coventry. While still a humble apprentice he was given leave to join the RAF Volunteer Reserve in June 1937, undertaking his elementary pilot training at Sywell. His spare time from then on was mainly devoted to flying, though an untoward incident in 1938 led to his 'discharge' from the RAFVR. For almost eighteen months Jo Lancaster tried to rejoin the RAF, to no avail until late 1939 when – to his surprise – he received instructions from the Air Ministry to report to RAF Cardington for enlistment as a 'U/t' (Under Training) pilot. In July 1940 he commenced the elementary circuits and bumps training in Tiger Moths at Desford, near Leicester, then progressed to No. 5 FTS, Sealand and Ternhill to fly Miles Masters, taking with him a recommendation from his former instructor for selection as a future fighter pilot. At No. 5 FTS Lancaster's particular flight was also given night flying instruction, a circumstance which resulted ironically in him being posted on to No. 20 OTU, Lossiemouth – for final training as a bomber pilot! Having resigned himself to the 'fickle finger of fate' and a future of 'driving airframes with bombs', Jo – logically – thought he would best be trained on Whitley bombers at the nearby Kinloss OTU; after all, he *had* done an engineering apprenticeship helping to build Whitleys. His application for such a transfer was firmly refused – logic had little part in the thinking of contemporary RAF administration policy.

At Lossiemouth Jo crewed up with a mixed batch of internationals – a Welshman, a Scotsman, a New Zealander, and two Canadians – and soon completed their operational 'work-up' on Wellington bombers before being posted as a crew in May 1941 to No. 40 Squadron, a Wellington unit based at Alconbury. Here Lancaster flew his first eight sorties 'in anger' as second dicky to an experienced skipper before finally being allotted his 'own' Wellington. At that period of the bomber offensive operational routine was – relatively speaking – leisurely, almost casual, compared to the intensity of later war years. By mid-morning the crews usually knew if 'ops' were on or off, and if on the detailed crews would carry out a night flying test (NFT), which in Lancaster's case invariably consisted of a deck-level beat-up one side of the Bedford Canals and back alor the other side, terrorising Land Army girls and other labourers in the surrounding farmlands en route. Social calls on friends at neighbouring airfields – by air – were common, while at briefings no specified or mandatory routes to or from targets were imposed, or specified take-off times or times over target. Each crew had its 'own' Wellington, and the peacetime traditional individual ground crew – two engine fitters for the engines and two airframe fitters – thereby welding both air and ground crews on each aircraft into tight-knit teams with mutual loyalties, pride and confidence in each other's efforts. Even actual sorties were individual, each aircraft and its crew being virtually on their own once they left base – the days of bomber streams were things of the future.

If the background to operations seemed almost casual at that period, the hazards and dangers of operations over enemy-occupied lands were nevertheless acute. On 24 July 1941, piloting Wellington T2701, 'S-Sugar', Jo Lancaster was one of six skippers from 40 Squadron tasked with a daylight attack on German shipping in the harbour of Brest. In a hot, cloudless sky, Lancaster and his fellow Wimpy captains made their way to the target via the Scilly Isles, then made their bombing runs in to the target at 10,000 feet through air thick with black flak smoke and running a gauntlet of wheeling Messerschmitt Bf 109 fighters. Having bombed Jo swung out to turn for home and saw another Wellington close by being attacked by a Messerschmitt from its rear. As the German climbed away from its first pass, Lancaster's rear gunner, Keith Coleman (the New Zealander) raked the fighter from end to end and saw its pilot bale out. The return trip for Lancaster was, to say the least, 'hairy'. His aircraft was liberally perforated with flak hits, including a holed windscreen and a ruptured hydraulic system, and his fuel state did not inspire too much confidence in reaching England again. Accordingly, Jo set course for St Eval, Cornwall where he landed safely, one of many returning bombers bearing battle scars, some carrying dead or wounded crews.

Most of Jo's sorties during his tour with 40 Squadron, however were night sorties over Germany, bombing targets such as Stettin, Hanover, Cologne, Essen, the Ruhr, and the 'Big City' – Berlin. Most such trips involved long hours for Jo in his pilot's bucket seat – his longest such flight being to Stettin on 29 September in Wimpy Z8859, 'S'. With overload tanks fitted on this occasion he was airborne for just over nine hours. Though his aircraft was fitted with an early version of auto-pilot, this (like the cabin heating system) seldom worked for long, leaving the pilot to 'pole' his machine manually for long weary hours. Fortunately, on the Stettin trip Lancaster found little opposition over the target, allowing his navigator the luxury of four 'practice' bombing runs before finally releasing the bomb load precisely on target.

If the occasional sortie proved relatively uneventful, the many other hazards of operational flying kept the risk factor high. On 25 August 1941, for example, Jo had only just taken off from Alconbury in T2701 with a full bomb and fuel load when, at a mere 750 feet altitude, he saw that all oil pressure on the port motor had gone. Oil was streaming back over the wing from the engine and seconds later the engine seized up solid. Using every available muscle – and a brief prayer – Jo managed to scrape in to nearby Wyton airfield, unannounced but unscathed; a main oil pipe had broken. On another occasion, as he waited his turn to taxy out for take-off, a nearby Wellington skipper on his first trip as captain put his aircraft's wingtip through Lancaster's front gun turret as he swung onto the perimeter track. Lancaster and his crew were uninjured, but had to scrub the sortie – the sprog skipper, however, failed to return that night.

Other incidents during this first tour included becoming iced-up in the centre of a severe electrical storm, being struck by lightning, having both engines cut out, and being strafed by flak – all at the same time. A return trip from Berlin saw him as the intended victim of a Messerschmitt Bf 110 nightfighter which made several determined attacks before Lancaster's gunners managed to sink an accurate burst into its belly and sent it down vertically into cloud below.

By October 1941 Jo Lancaster had completed 31 sorties with No. 40 Squadron and was therefore rested from ops with a posting to No. 22 OTU, Wellesbourne Mountford, and promoted to Pilot Officer. Here he became an instructor on Wellingtons, but took part in two of the '1,000-bomber' raids laid on by the Bomber Command chief, Butch Harris in early 1942. The first of these, to Cologne on 30 May, he flew in a dual-instruction equipped 'tired' Wellington with a scratch crew, returning without undue problems; then flew the same aircraft, X9932, to Essen on the second Operation Millenium two nights later. These were the only bright spots for Jo in the monotony of his instructional duties. Several applications for a return to operations had been rejected by officialdom, though he moved from 22 OTU to 28 OTU, Wymeswold when this came into being. His persistence finally paid off when, in October 1942, he was posted back on operations by joining No. 12 Squadron at Wickenby, a satellite field to Binbrook. His arrival on 'Shiny Twelve' almost coincided with the squadron's re-equipment from Wellingtons to Avro Lancasters, but his first three sorties with No. 12 Squadron were flown at the helm of Wellingtons; the first was a 'Gardening' (Mining) trip to Hungersund Fiord under a full moon, lasting eight hours. In November 1942 the squadron's first Lancaster arrived and conversion training for the crews began immediately, lasting until the close of the year as Lancaster strength was steadily increased. During those weeks Jo Lancaster and his crew spent many hours learning about the various new radio and radar 'black boxes' they would be using on operations, and flew numerous lengthy cross-country training exercises – up to nine hours' duration on occasion – familiarising themselves with Jo's namesake 'kite'. Actual operations with the Lancaster on 12 Squadron commenced on 3 January 1943 when ten aircraft 'sowed' mines in the La Rochelle area. Shortly after ten aircraft set out for Berlin, and only six returned – a sharp reminder to the crews of the ever-stiffening German defences awaiting them every night.

By April 1943 the squadron could usually only muster ten Lancasters and crews for operations, but this figure rose to 21 in May and 24 in June, despite casualties amounting to 33 aircraft and crews which failed to return from operations during the first six months of 1943 – the rough equivalent of 130 per cent of the squadron paper establishment. For Jo Lancaster and his crew, usually flying in Lancaster W4366, PH-R 'Robert', it was a period of intense strain as they witnessed the mounting casualty toll of friends and acquaintances; a far cry from the easy-going, near-casual atmosphere of Jo's initial sorties of his first operational tour. In less than four months Jo had brought his overall sorties' total to 54, thereby completing his second tour, and receiving a DFC in recognition of his doughty efforts. He was offered a rest posting as an instructor on Wellingtons at Harwell – a thought which appalled him and which he abruptly declined. Instead he was sent to No. 1481 Flight at Binbrook, in command of the Wellington Flight of No. 1 Group's gunnery training set-up. It amounted to a euphemism for more instructing duties, and Jo began agitating for a more active flying appointment. Again his determination bore fruit and in October 1943 he joined the staff of the Aeroplane and Armament Experimental Establishment (A & AEE) at Boscombe Down in Wiltshire, going specifically to B Flight of the Armament Testing Squadron. As such he now became engaged in highly secret experimental testing and proving of a bewildering variety of airborne armament, in an equally mixed bag of aircraft types; an aspect which particularly appealed to Jo's prime enthusiasm – flying. Among the many trials undertaken by Jo Lancaster was the initial test-drop of Barnes Wallis's brainchild, the 12,000 lb DP/HE bomb, more usually titled 'Tallboy', which Jo released from a Lancaster at 18,000 feet over a test target precisely.

Jo remained with the A & AEE for two years, accumulating many flying hours in various types of light, medium and heavy aircraft; then in February 1945, having completed the appropriate Empire Test Pilots Course, he was posted to the Test Pilots School. A year later Jo was seconded as a test pilot to Boulton & Paul Aircraft at Wolverhampton, but soon transferred to a similar post with Saunders-Roe of the Isle of Wight. Here he was able to broaden his experience by learning to handle maritime aircraft, then undertake part of the flying test programme of the SRA.1 – a jet-propelled fighter flying boat design of huge potential. Three years of flying for Saunders-Roe came to an end in January 1949 when Jo decided to rejoin the firm he'd been apprenticed to some ten years previously,

Armstrong Whitworth, based at Baginton. Here he handled the firm's production aircraft – mainly Avro Lincolns and Gloster Meteor nightfighter adaptations – but his continuing delight in flying new types of aircraft was particularly satisfied when he undertook some of the flying trials of the unorthodox, tail-less 'flying wing' design, the AW52.

In the event, this aircraft almost cut Jo's career (and life) to a sudden stop. On 30 May 1949, Jo took off in AW52, TS363 for yet another routine flight in the design's test programme when an asymmetric flutter developed in one wingtip, spreading rapidly across the whole aircraft and shaking the airframe to a pitch threatening to disintegrate it. In the tiny cockpit Jo was literally bounced up, down, and sideways in increasing severity until he could no longer focus his vision. Finally, at 5,000 feet, with the air speed indicator building above 300 mph, Jo used his ejection seat to abandon the uncontrollable aircraft – the first man to utilise the Martin-Baker ejection seat 'live' in a real emergency to save his life. Though his parachute opened at some 2,000 feet, Jo landed heavily, chipping a shoulder and slightly fracturing his spine, apart from myriad bruises from the battering around the interior of the cockpit.

Three months later Jo Lancaster was back on the flying line and in subsequent years was to survive even more potentially disastrous situations, including having the perspex hood of a 500 mph jet aircraft disintegrate around his head, losing an undercarriage leg on a Meteor during a practice forced landing, and having both starboard engines of a Liberator suddenly feather and stop on take-off. To Jo Lancaster these were simply part of a pilot's life – but nothing ever diminished his lifelong love of flying.

CHAPTER TEN

John Wooldridge

Speaking of the air crews of No. 106 Squadron, to which he had been appointed commander in March 1942, Wing Commander Guy Gibson, DSO, DFC (later VC), said:

> Their keenness and skill was largely due to an excellent flight commander who had just come to take the place of a vacancy. Wooldridge was his surname, but he was rarely called that. He had been known as 'Dim' ever since he learned to fly. He was a sort of 'Algy' of the air, with a large moustache and a drawling voice. He had amazing habits, and at the time he joined, he was engaged in the doubtful art of composing a concerto for piano and orchestra. I think it was a ruse on his part to keep him away from the boys. He had stomach trouble. He couldn't drink a lot, and his excuse always was that he must sit down quietly in his sitting room, and write his concerto rather than go out and drink beer. Poetry was his line as well, but he was an excellent type and, apart from all this, had done 67 trips over the Third Reich.*

Academic, classical musician-composer, poet, with the carefully-posed 'coolness' of the caricature English 'gentleman', John Wooldridge's wartime career saw him rise from Sergeant to Wing Commander, DSO, DFC, DFM while flying a total of 97 sorties over Germany, to which impressive record he added postwar the talents of musical conductor and director, playwright and author.

John de Lacy Wooldridge could have been said to have been destined for a life career in aviation. His father, Gilbert, had qualified as a pilot in July 1915 and seen service with the Royal Flying Corps during 1915–18 in France and Mesopotamia (Iraq), later becoming 'adviser' to the embryo air forces of Italy and Japan. Thus John and a brother, Peter, grew up with their father's example dominating their

---

* *Enemy Coast Ahead* by Wg Cdr G. P. Gibson, VC, DSO, DFC: Michael Joseph, 1946.

outlook of their futures.* John's early promise of academic abilities led him to becoming a teacher in Suffolk, and eventually a pupil of Sibelius, but in 1936 he learned to fly at Marshall's Flying School, Cambridge as a member of the RAF Volunteer Reserve. In April 1939, as war with Hitler's Germany drew nearer, John was called up for full-time flying duties with the RAF, and after a brief spell of advanced training joined his first squadron, No. 44, based at Waddington, Lincolnshire to pilot Handley Page Hampden bombers. A brief spell with 76 Squadron at Finningley, then a Group Pool training unit, was next followed by a posting to No. 61 Squadron at Hemswell, to commence an operational tour on Hampdens.

For some nine months Wooldridge took part in the varied operations undertaken by 61 Squadron: mine-laying, 'armed recces', bombing invasion barges, ports, docks and airfields, attacking vital targets like Kiel and Dortmund. During one such trip bombing Calais a flak shell exploded in the nose section of his Hampden, wounding Wooldridge in several places and damaging the bomb-release circuitry. Ruptured hydraulics left him with minimal control of the Hampden but by cool skill and no little determination, Woodridge guided the bomber home. On reaching base he brought the Hampden in for a skilful forced landing but on touchdown the aircraft fell apart; yet despite a full bomb load still aboard, which mysteriously failed to detonate, and the disintegration of the Hampden, none of Wooldridge's crew received further injuries. By the autumn of 1940 Wooldridge had been awarded a DFM, then a commission, and completed 41 sorties, after which he was sent to No. 16 OTU, Upper Heyford for a 'rest 'as an instructor. Here the monotony of the daily routine of initiating fresh crews to the idiosyncrasies of Hampdens and operational procedures was part-relieved for Wooldridge when he was 'detached' for a month to the Ealing Film Studios as 'air adviser' for the film *The Big Blockade*.

In August 1941 he returned to his old unit, 61 Squadron, for a second spell of operations. The squadron by then had become based at North Luffenham, and was now equipped with tired Hampdens which were about to be exchanged for Avro Manchesters. The unit had received its first examples of Manchesters in June 1941, but did not complete full re-equipment until October, having no more than six Manchesters on strength until the latter date. Though basically a fine design, the Manchester's operational career was to be dogged throughout by a myriad of technical defects, mainly due to its unorthodox – and highly

* Peter also joined the RAF, as a fighter pilot, and failed to return from a Typhoon sortie off the Dutch coast in 1943.

unreliable – Vulture engines. Nevertheless, Wooldridge completed fourteen sorties with 61 Squadron, then moved to another Manchester unit, 207 Squadron at Bottesford, where he converted to Lancasters during the winter of 1941–42. After only four sorties with 207 Squadron, however, he was transferred to No. 106 Squadron at Coningsby to fill a vacant flight commander's post – and received direct promotion from Pilot Officer to Acting Squadron Leader on the spot! As with his previous units, Wooldridge joined a unit equipped with the notorious Manchester bomber but in the process of converting to Lancasters. The commander of 106 Squadron was Wing Commander Guy Gibson, DFC, later to gain a VC for his leadership of the famed 'Dam-busting' sortie of 16 May 1943, whom Wooldridge had previously met and befriended when both men had been on instructional duties.

As commander of 106's B Flight, Wooldridge proved not only popular but, far more important, respected by his crews; leading them personally on fourteen sorties, including the first three '1,000-bomber' raids by May/June 1942. These completed his second tour, during which he had added a DFC and Bar to his decorations and had now logged a tally of 73 operational trips overall. Handing over his flight commander post to John Searby, Wooldridge was promoted to Wing Commander and posted to the tri-Service Petroleum Warfare Department in London. Here he applied his academic knowledge to various scientific projects relevant to Bomber Command's growing offensive. In particular, he helped develop Fido, the fog-dispersal petrol-pipe burner system alongside selected bomber airfield runways which, from November 1943 until the end of the European war enabled almost 2,500 returning bombers to land safely in atrocious fog conditions. Other projects to come within his aegis included various flame-throwing devices, Pluto (Pipe Line Under the Ocean), and his own 'invention' of a 4,000 lb flame-throwing 'aeroflame' bomb.

After many months of shining a desk seat, however, the urge to return to operations led him to approaching the C-in-C, Bomber Command, Arthur Harris, in early 1943 with a request for a more active post. His wish was quickly granted, and on 17 March 1943 he arrived at Marham, Norfolk to command No. 105 Squadron; thereby filling the vacancy caused by the loss of the previous unit commander Wing Commander G. P. Longfield.

No. 105 Squadron had pioneered the operational use of the unarmed DH Mosquito bomber, and by the time of Wooldridge's arrival had become renowned, alongside its 'sister' Mosquito unit, No. 139 Squadron, for daring, low-level, high precision day raids on specific enemy installations around northern Europe. Between March and July 1943, Wooldridge flew 24 such daylight trips, each fraught with hazards of accurate flak, Luftwaffe fighters, and no less from such 'natural' obstacles as bird-strikes – which at speeds of 200 mph or more could be lethal – chimney stacks, trees, telephone wires *et al.* One such trip was an ultra-low level attack on Tours, which Wooldridge described amply later in a letter to the Mosquito's designers, De Havilland :

> While approaching the target at approximately 100 feet, with bomb doors open, my aircraft was hit by three Bofors (*40 mm*) shells. Apart from the distinct thuds as the shells exploded, and a rather unpleasant smell of petrol, the behaviour of the aircraft after impact appeared to be normal and the bombs were dropped successfully. Actual damage was; the first shell entered the lower surface of the port mainplane, approximately four feet from the wing tip, and burst inside removing three square feet of the upper wing surface . . . the second shell hit the port engine nacelle fairly far back, wrecking the undercarriage retraction gear, severing the main oil pipe line, damaging the airscrew pitch control, and putting the instruments of the blind flying panel out of action. The third shell entered the fuse-lage just in front of the tailplane and severed the tailwheel hydraulic line and the pressure head line, rendering the ASI (*Air Speed Indicator*) useless.

On the return journey the ruptured port engine failed but its propeller could not be feathered. Wooldridge maintained a ground speed of almost 200 mph and on reaching base in pitch darkness, with virtually no hydraulics or electrics left to him, no flaps, no indication of actual air speed, belly-landed safely.

A few days later, en route to France across the Channel, he almost collided with a roving Focke Wulf Fw 190, and (in his words) '. . . an extremely hectic few minutes ensued'. Nor was this the only occasion when he and his crews encountered Luftwaffe fighters. Being unarmed, except for a bomb load on the outward leg of any sortie, the Mosquito had only one prime means of defence – sheer speed, combined with superlative manoeuvrability; facets of the 'Mozzie's' character which time and again brought its crews home alive and unharmed. By June 1943 No. 105 Squadron, with No. 139, had completed virtually a year's operations by day, and a fresh policy for employment of the Mosquito as a night bomber was about to be implemented, prior to the two units being used for pathfinder roles. Wooldridge remained in

1. Marshal of the RAF Sir Arthur Harris, Bt, GCB, OBE, AFC, LLD, AOC-in-C, Bomber Command from 22 February 1942 to 14 September 1945 - 'Butch'.

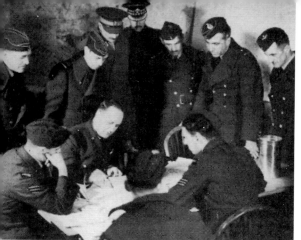

2. Early days. HM King George VI (third from left standing) attends a bomber crew debriefing, early 1941. Second from left standing is Air Vice Marshal John Baldwin, and second from right standing is Air Marshal Sir Richard Peirse, AOC-in-C, Bomber Command at that time.

3. Veteran Lancaster B1 R5868, PO-S 'Sugar' of 467 Squadron RAAF at Waddington, June 1944, with 107 of its eventual 135 ops recorded on the nose. Group Captain Bonham-Carter (left) and Wing Commander W. Brill, DSO, DFC (OC 467 Squadron) (right) with HRH The Duke of Gloucester (centre). This Lancaster now resides in the RAF Museum at Hendon.

5. Major H.C. Knilans, DSO, DFC, in USAF uniform.

4. Top Dog. Mosquito LR503, GB-F, of 105 Squadron which ended the war with a tally of 213 sorties completed.

6. Knilans (third from left) and his 617 Squadron Lancaster crew, 1944.

7. Wing Commander A.P. Cranswick, DSO, DFC.

8. Wing Commander F.J. 'Popeye' Lucas, DFC.

9. Air Commodore Sir Hughie Edwards, VC.

10. Wing Commander J.F. Barron, DSO, DFC, DFM (centre).

11. Group Captain Dennis T. Witt, DSO, DFC, DFM.

12. 'Jo' Lancaster at Wickenby, April 1943, when serving with 12 Squadro

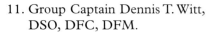

13. Wing Commander John de L. Wooldridge, DSO, DFC, DFM, when OC 105 Squadron, August 1943.

14. Flight Lieutenant Syd Clayton, DSO, DFC, DFM, and Wing Commander Roy Ralston, his usual pilot on 105 Squadron.

15. Group Captain T.G. 'Hamish' Mahaddie, DSO, DFC, AFC.

16. Air Vice Marshal D.C.T. Bennett (left), Marshal of the Royal Air Force Lord Trenchard, and Lord Cherwell in Wyton's Officer's Mess.

17. Air Vice Marshal Basil Embry.

18. Flight Lieutenant Jo Capka.

19. Wing Commander Hope, Group Captain P.C. Pickard, DSO, DFC, with his dog 'Ming' and Flight Lieutenant Johnson.

20. Pickard's usual navigator, Flight Lieutenant J. 'Bill' Broadley, DSO, DFC, DFM, seated in a Mosquito.

21. Pilot Officer R.H. 'Ron' Middleton, VC, RAAF.

22. Wing Commander G.P. Gibson, VC, DSO, DFC.

23. Cheshire as Station Commander at RAF Marston Moor.

24. Cheshire being congratulated on his VC award by Flight Lieutenant C.K. Astbury, RAAF, 617 Squadron.

25. Cheshire with Warrant Officer Norman Jackson, VC at Buckingham Palace, 1945.

26. Wing Commander J. 'Moose' Fulton, DSO, DFC, AFC.

27. Squadron Leader Jamie Pitcairn-Hill, DSO, DFC.

28. Squadron Leader T.W. 'Tommy' Blair, DSO, DFC.

29. Group Captain
H.E. 'Hal' Bufton, DSO,
OBE, DFC, AFC.

30. Squadron Leader 'Danny' Everett, DSO, DFC
(centre) as a Sergeant, with members of his first
operational crew.

31. Pathfinders. From left: Group Captain John Searby, Wing Commander S.P. 'Pat'
Daniels, Group Captain R.W.P. Collings, Group Captain T.G. 'Hamish' Mahaddie,
Air Vice Marshal Don Bennett.

32. Squadron Leader W.W. 'Bill' Blessing, DSO, DFC (centre) at a medal investiture, with Group Captain P.C. Pickard, DSO, DFC (left) and Group Captain G.L. Cheshire, VC, DSO, DFC.

33. Wing Commander Ray Hilton, DSO, DFC, who was killed in action on 23 November 1943 over Berlin.

34. Squadron Leader Julian Sale, DSO, DFC (standing third from left), with his 35. Squadron air and ground crews. Standing, left to right; Lamb, Carter, Sale, Bodnar, Cross, Rogers.

35. Group Captain Johnny Fauquier, DSO, DFC (centre), the tough CO of 405 Squadron RCAF, then 617 Squadron RAF, with AVM Don Bennett, the PFF's AOC-in-C (left).

36. Wing Commander Alan J.L. Craig, DSO, DFC.

37. Wing Commander W.D.G. Watkins, DFC, DFM (left), OC 15 Squadron, with Wing Commander I.C.K. Swales, DSO, DFC, DFM. Watkins, a navigator, became OC 15 Squadron in April 1944, but was shot down in Lancaster PB137, LS-U, over Heinsberg on 16 November 1944 and became a prisoner-of-war.

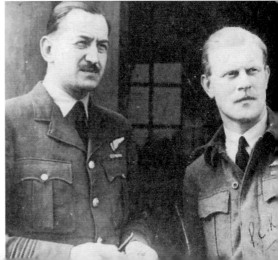

38. Wing Commander J.B. 'Willie' Tait, DSO and 3 Bars, DFC, who eventually commanded 617 Squadron, with Air Vice Marshal Sir Ralph Cochrane, AOC-in-C, No. 5 Group, Bomber Command.

39. Group Captain G.H. Womersley, DSO, DFC.

40. Group Captain George F. Grant, DSO, DFC.

41. Air and ground crews of Lancaster PA187 'O-Orange', 467 Squadron RAAF, April 1945. Pilot Flying Officer 'Kitch' Boxsell is centre, with peaked cap.

42. Wing Commander Maurice Smith, DFC (far left) and, far right, Wing Commander John Woodroffe, DSO, DFC. Smith was Master Bomber for the first attack on Dresden on 13 February 1945, while Woodroffe has been described as the 'doyen' of Master Bombers.

43. Hughie Edwards VC (left) and his navigator about to board his 105 Squadron Mosquito

44. Dambusters. Left to right; Flight Lieutenant J.F. (now Sir Jack) Leggo, DFC; Flight Sergeant T.D. Simpson, DFM; Flight Lieutenant R.C. Hay, DFC; Pilot Officer B.T. Foxlee, DFM and Flight Lieutenant H.B. 'Mick' Martin, DSO, DFC, in London shortly after the famous dambusting sortie by 617 Squadron in 1943.

45. Mosquito XIX, WM-Z, of 68 Squadron and Czech crew, 1944.

46. Gibson VC (front row, 4th from left) and his 106 Squadron crews on the morning after the first 1000-bomber raid against Cologne.

47. Gibson, HM King George VI, Group Captain John Whitworth, DSO, DFC, at Scampton on 27 May 1943.

command of No. 105 until the last day of June, supervising the conversion training of his crews for their future tasks, then on July 1 relinquished his command to a veteran PFF pilot, Group Captain H. J. Cundall, DFC, AFC. Shortly after Wooldridge was awarded a DSO, and then returned to his former appointment with the Petroleum Warfare Department.

Sent on a short tour of the USA and Canada to help co-ordinate the final arrangements for the Pluto project, Wooldridge took several opportunities to demonstrate the superb flying qualities of the Mosquito aircraft, culminating in a new trans-Atlantic record flight in May 1944 when he flew from Labrador to Prestwick direct in five hours and 40 minutes (total time runway to runway being six hours 46 minutes) – the first time either Wooldridge or his navigator, Flying Officer C. J. Brown, RAAF, had ever crossed the Atlantic by air. On his return, Wooldridge was appointed Chief Flying Instructor at a Nottinghamshire OTU where he remained until the cessation of hostilities in Europe. Leaving the RAF shortly after, he turned to his first love, music, as his future career. In 1948 he married the actress Margaretta Scott, and in the following years became heavily involved in composing and directing music for films, radio and television, apart from appearing as guest conductor of many leading international orchestras.

Equally talented as a writer, Wooldridge had compiled and edited a book, *Low Attack*, in 1943*, an authentic account of the operational activities of Nos. 105 and 139 Squadrons, 1939–43, now regarded as a minor classic in RAF history literature; while in 1952 he wrote the script for an equally authentic film, *Appointment in London*, depicting life on a Bomber Command heavy bomber squadron. In addition, in the 1950s, he wrote several plays successfully presented in London's theatre-land, but in 1958 his potentially brilliant future was cruelly cut when he died as the result of a car accident.

---

* *Low Attack* : Sampson Low, London, 1944.

CHAPTER ELEVEN

Roy Ralston

The aircraft apprentice scheme inaugurated in 1920 by Hugh Trenchard at Cranwell and Halton was to produce not only a highly skilled technical spine for the regular Royal Air Force during following years, but – when war erupted in Europe in September 1939 – provided a large number of 'ex-Trenchard Brats' (as such ex-apprentices came to be universally dubbed) who carved out distinguished careers as operational air crews of all types. Wing Commander Joseph Roy George Ralston, DSO (BAR), AFC, DFM was one such 'ex-Brat' who, like so many of his contemporaries initially trained as a technical tradesman at RAF Halton, spent several years as an 'erk' before eventually achieving his ambition to fly, and then proved to be an outstanding pilot and leader.

Born in Manchester on 12 January 1915, Ralston enlisted in the RAF as a Halton Aircraft Apprentice of the 20th Entry on 9 September 1930 and was trained as a metal rigger, graduating three years later and being posted as an AC1 (Aircraftman 1st Class) to Hornchurch, to service No. 54 Squadron's Bristol Bulldog fighters. Four years later he was accepted for pilot training at Hamble and, later, Brize Norton, and gained his wings as a Sergeant pilot on 15 December 1937. In May 1938 he joined No. 108 Squadron at Bassingbourn, flying Hawker Hinds and, later, Bristol Blenheims, but on 8 April 1940 his squadron was 'married' to No. 104 Squadron to form No. 13 OTU at Bicester, and he became an instructor on Blenheims. Just four months later, however, came his opportunity to join the sharp end of operations when, on 18 August 1940, he was posted to No. 107 Squadron at Wattisham, a Blenheim IV bomber unit under the aegis of No. 2 Group.

Only five days later Roy Ralston flew his first operational sortie. His crew were Sergeant 'Jackie' Brown (Wop/AG) and Sergeant Syd Clayton, a trio who were destined to fly 42 sorties together before Brown was killed during a low-level attack on a German convoy off the Norwegian coast. Thereafter Ralston and his navigator, Clayton, remained together for some three years, completing seventy-eight sorties as a 'team'. Their first year of operations brought a succession of 'hairy' sorties, mainly ultra-low level attacks against well-defended targets and enemy shipping around the North Sea zones. Promoted to Flight Sergeant, then Warrant Officer, Ralston remained with 107 Squadron when it moved base to Great Massingham on 12 May 1941, and on 21 May was one of a squadron formation which set out to bomb Heligoland.

Flak was intensely accurate as they approached their objective, and as the Blenheims swept over the cliffs of the island one of the leading Blenheims, piloted by Ken Wolstenholme*, suffered direct hits, killing its navigator Sergeant Wilson. Wolstenholme spotted two other Blenheims pulling away after making their bomb-drops and flew to join them for protection. One of this pair almost at once nose-dived and ditched, but the second, piloted by Ralston, immediately climbed to 1,500 feet and sent off a plain language signal to base giving the ditched Blenheim's location. In the event the ditched crew escaped safely, but Ralston's selfless action, which might well have pinpointed him for any marauding German fighters, resulted in the award of a DFM to Ralston.

Roy's lengthy operational stay with 107 Squadron came to a close in December 1941 when he was commissioned as a Pilot Officer and posted to instructional duties at No. 17 OTU, Upwood. His rest from operations lasted only until 22 May 1942, when he joined No. 105 Squadron at Horsham St Faiths (now, Norwich Airport). 105 Squadron was the first squadron (though not the first *unit*) to be equipped with De Havilland Mosquito bombers, an aircraft destined to prove itself as one of the most versatile and ubiquitous aircraft ever to see RAF service.

On arrival in Norfolk, Ralston was rejoined by his former navigator, Syd Clayton, and the duo immediately teamed up. Quickly adapting to their 'Wooden Wonder' Mosquito, they were one of six crews, led by Squadron Leader P. J. Channer, DFC, which set out on 11 July 1942 to participate in a raid on U-boat slipways at Flensburg – actually a diversionary sortie for a main Lancaster force attack against Danzig on that date. Flying at some thirty feet altitude for most of the trip, through a succession of blinding rainstorms, one Mosquito aborted with engine problems, while a second was shot down as the bombers emerged into clearer skies near their target. Despite fierce flak opposition the remaining four Mosquitos hit their target and returned to base.

* Later, Flight Lieutenant, DFC (Bar) and a well-known BBC sports commentator.

In September 1942 the squadron moved base to Marham, but were soon joined by a second Mosquito unit, 139 Squadron, and the two squadrons combined to pursue their 'speciality' – low level precision raids against enemy objectives. On 15 October, for example, one Mosquito from 139 Squadron flew as part of a formation led by Roy Ralston (by then a Flight Lieutenant). The target was the Stork Diesel works at Hengelo in Holland. Ralston released his bombs precisely on target, but the 139 Squadron aircraft was slightly slow in following and its crew were lucky to escape almost unscathed from the explosion of Ralston's bombs. Five days later Ralston was awarded a DSO for his 'outstanding leadership and determination', and on 7 November was promoted to Squadron Leader and commander of 105 Squadron's B Flight. He promptly celebrated these honours by leading a specially requested raid that same day of six Mosquitos against two German blockade-runner ships carrying (reportedly) a precious cargo of raw rubber in the Gironde Estuary. Airborne by 1345 hrs, they flew at literally wave-top height towards the French coast.

Just before their ETA (Estimated Time of Arrival) Ralston spotted some ships which he took to be the targets. With bomb doors open, he commenced his bombing run before realising he was mistaken in his identification. He immediately swung away but was unaware that because of an electrical fault his bombs had been released. Finding his briefed targets, Ralston again made a bombing run, sweeping in from wave-level and achieving complete surprise. Hits were seen on one ship before the tardy flak gunners finally opened fire on the retreating Mosquitos, one of which was unlucky enough to be brought down, though its crew survived as prisoners of war.

On 9 December 1942 the Ralston-Clayton partnership hit the headlines with an almost unique operation. Detailed as one of three crews to undertake 'rail intruder' sorties over France, Ralston's specific objective was the Paris-Soissons railway line and, in particular, a large rail tunnel thereon. Reaching the target, Ralston dropped two 500 lb bombs accurately onto the tunnel entrance just after a train had entered, then quickly 'sealed' the train and its occupants inside by bombing the tunnel exit. Flying Mosquito DZ353, 'E-Easy', Ralston led six Mosquitos in a low-level assault on rail installations at Hengelo on 20 January 1943, two aircraft bombing from no more than 1,000 feet and thereby epitomising the form of attacks which had become 105 and 139 Squadrons' 'trademark' by then. In essence, such diver' sections on most sorties, involving separate, but co-ordinated formations, with each squadron taking its share of both styles of assault.

On 9 March 1943, Ralston led a mixed formation of fifteen Mosquitos from 105 and 139 Squadrons against the engine shed complex of the Renault works at Le Mans. Ralston spearheaded five 105 aircraft in the low-level role, while the remaining ten, from 139 Squadron, were led by Squadron Leader Bagguley at higher altitude. All aircraft hit their target as dusk began closing in, but Bagguley in Mosquito DZ469 was shot down – the only loss, despite severe flak damage to several other raiders.

Then, on 1 April 1943, came the last sortie by the Ralston-Clayton duo. It was to be Syd Clayton's 100th operation as a navigator, and Roy Ralston's 83rd sortie. Again, Ralston was the formation leader, and the objective for this raid was a rail complex in the Trier and Ehrang area. Despite appalling weather conditions, the Mosquitos hit their targets with great success. On their return, Clayton received an immediate award of a DSO to add to his DFC and DFM, and then left the ops' scene to undergo pilot training; while Roy Ralston received a Bar to his DSO, an extract from its citation read, '. . . undeterred by the fiercest opposition, he has invariably pressed home his attacks with the greatest vigour. His unswerving devotion to duty and heroic endeavours have set a standard beyond praise.' Promotion to Wing Commander soon after meant a temporary respite from operations for Ralston when he was appointed OC No. 1655 Mosquito Training Unit (MTU) at Marham, which unit later moved to Warboys as part of No. 8 (Pathfinders) Group.

This post lasted until August 1944 when he joined the staff of No. 8 Group's headquarters at Castle Hill House, Huntingdon as Group Training Inspector for the elite PFF. Interesting and varied as his latest duties were, Ralston still itched to return to the operational scene, and his wish was eventually granted on 1 March 1945 when he was appointed as the latest commander of No. 139 Squadron, operating in Mosquitos from Upwood. Despite the inevitable administrative and other routine duties involved in his appointment, Ralston still managed to fly occasional sorties leading his squadron, flying eight such trips to bring his operational tally up to 91 before Germany surrendered in May 1945.

As a 'career' man originally, Ralston naturally hoped to remain in the RAF and, indeed, was granted a permanent commission in 1946, only to fail the requisite medical examination and be officially invalided out of the service. Unable to take up any civilian career in flying, Roy Ralston next displayed the self-dependence and individuality fostered in so many men whose early training had been inculcated as an aircraft apprentice at Halton, and set up his own sign and nameplate manufacturing business near his birthplace, Manchester.

CHAPTER TWELVE

Syd Clayton

To rise from Sergeant to Squadron Leader during the course of 100 operational sorties as a navigator, and be awarded a DSO, DFC, and DFM along the way, was a relatively rare achievement even by RAF wartime standards. To then undertake pilot training, return to operations, and undertake a further 46 operational trips was virtually unique. Yet Syd Clayton achieved all these things – and, moreover, despite many decidedly 'dicey' trips, was never once wounded or even injured.

Born in Lancashire in March 1916, Clayton's first operational unit was No. 107 Squadron in 1940, flying Blenheim IV bombers on daylight sorties. In August that year he teamed up with Roy Ralston as his regular pilot, and flew a total of 72 sorties in Blenheims, resulting in the award of a DFM in June 1941 and promotion to commissioned rank as a Pilot Officer. He was then rested from operations with a posting to instructional duties at No. 17 OTU, Upwood, but in early 1942 the legendary grapevine whispered that No. 105 Squadron, a former Blenheim unit, was due to be reformed with the new De Havilland Mosquito bomber; a design already regarded by many bomber crews as a coveted prize in terms of operational postings. On hearing this whisper, Clayton 'did the necessary spadework' (as he termed it) and on 1 June 1942 he arrived on 105 Squadron, based then at Horsham St Faiths, near Norwich, and commanded by Wing Commander Peter Simmons. A shortage of Mosquito aircraft at that time meant that the unit's crews had to work up on a motley mixture of Blenheims, Oxfords and Masters, but Syd's first Mosquito operation came on 11 July, in DK300, 'delivering' four 500 lb bombs on the submarine base at Flensburg. It was a low-level raid and Clayton's aircraft met medium flak which damaged its fin and rudder, severed the pitot-head pipe, and ruptured its hydraulic system. Arriving safely back over base, the Mosquito was led in to land by another aircraft, belly-landing at 160 mph – a somewhat abrupt introduction to 'Mozzie' operations, yet one which gave Syd full confidence in the structural strength and abilities of the design.

For the following three months Clayton participated in alternate high- and low-level sorties, attacking targets at Ijmuiden, Frankfurt, Essen, Wiesbaden, Kiel *et al* in the teeth of increasingly heavy and accurate flak opposition. A brief respite at Manby in September for a bombing leader's instructional course came next, but on his return to 105 Squadron Syd continued the near-daily routine of daylight assaults against German-occupied targets. On 21 October, in DZ343, Syd and his pilot were given a free-hand 'roving commission' trip. In his own words, 'The general idea was to bomb four separate targets in different areas, so that apart from bomb damage, production was lost due to air raid alerts. We made a general nuisance of ourselves for about three hours and then, while crossing the north Dutch coast, we were jumped by two Focke Wulf Fw 190s who had obviously been vectored onto us. Cloud was about six-tenths at 3-4,000 feet and on sighting the Ea (enemy aircraft) we entered cloud, turned north and dived for the deck.

'On breaking cloud cover we had gained some distance but the Fw 190s were being controlled and turned on to us. However, with our dive we managed to hold them off although they chased us for about fifteen minutes. The big snag was trying to keep a sight on their position and distance away. The Mozzie wasn't fitted with VHF but we had a Marconi 1154/1155 W/T, and the only way to keep check was to slip your head sideways between the top of the radio and the canopy. Being more or less at sea level, and going flat out, it was a *very* bumpy ride, with my head vibrating between radio and canopy. Luckily the 190s finally broke away and we could then make for base.'

From October 1942 to March 1943, Syd Clayton and his constant pilot Roy Ralston continued their depredations of the German communication systems, raiding rail sheds and stations at Lier, Montgen, Berman, Raimses, Liège and Rennes, interspersed with attacks on the Hengelo Diesel factory, Liège steel works, and the Le Mans Renault Aero works. A repeat sortie against Hengelo on 20 January 1943, in Mosquito DZ353, proved near-fatal. Hit by flak on the outward leg, their Mosquito seemed still flyable so they pressed on and bombed their target, but with no air speed indication available the return to base meant another hazardous belly-landing.

All these sorties had been in the low-level role, and on 1 April 1943 – the 25th anniversary of the original formation of the Royal Air Force – the Clayton/Ralston duo flew their ultimate sortie together, yet another low-level trip, this time to the Trier railway engine repair depot, in Mosquito DZ462. It was to be Clayton's 28th operation in Mosquitos, but much more significantly his 100th overall operational trip – and his last as a navigator.

Syd's own account of his 'hundredth' shortly after its completion read: 'For three weeks I'd waited for my century and at briefing on 1 April I learned that I'd got it – a trip to Trier. The weather boys forecast low cloud and rain extending right across our target area between 1500 and 1700 hrs, so we planned to drop in at 1600 hrs. Nevertheless, we had orders to abort the trip if no cloud cover became available. Take-off commenced at 1400 hrs and ten minutes later we were airborne, circled the 'drome to pick up formation, then set course at 1430. Down to Beachy Head, flying no more than 100 feet off the deck – an exhilarating sensation, but an altitude which meant keeping a wary eye open for flocks of birds which occasionally crossed our front. Weather was good – too good, with cloud base at about 3,000 feet and clear visibility. Course change at Beachy Head, but the clouds still stayed too high for us – it looked as if our orders would mean scrubbing the sortie. Roy (Ralston) decided to carry on a bit longer, to within ten miles of the French coast anyway, then just as I was getting ready to be disappointed the forecast bad weather front appeared on the horizon. Cloud came lower, visibility decreased, and we crossed the coast in pouring rain with vis down to 400 yards.

'It stayed that way for the next 250 miles, with visibility slowly getting worse, yet the other Mossies stayed in good formation. We crossed over several airfields en route, apart from apparently deserted French villages. Ten miles west of Luxembourg the weather cleared, with cloud rising to some 3,000 feet and visibility ahead suddenly lengthening up to about ten miles. Skirting south of Luxembourg, we crossed the German frontier, and settled onto the final leg into target. I next saw smoke rising from Trier ahead. Bomb doors were opened and within seconds we were nipping over the hills and down into the valley heading for target. I watched Roy's thumb on the bomb-release tit as the sheds steadily came towards us . . . he sat dead still . . . then suddenly his thumb jerked once, and he laughed. Then we were climbing away up the hillside north-east of the town. Looking back I saw tall columns of smoke rising from the target centre.

'We had already decided that we'd follow the bad weather front out over enemy territory, so reached cloud cover which sheltered us to within fifty miles of the coast before breaking out below a 4,000 feet cloud canopy with clear visibility. Roy decided to climb into cloud again and, looking back, I saw the rest of the Mossies come up with us, still in a good formation. Some flak reached for us from Merville, but it did no damage, and when we finally came down out of cloud later the enemy coast was well behind us. I looked down and saw the quilt of English fields – it was over. I'd done my 100th operational sortie.'

Clayton had already been accepted for conversion training to pilot, and therefore left 105 Squadron as a senior member of the legendary 'Navigators Union', with the ribbons of DSO, DFC, DFM on his tunic, to become one of the latest sprog pilots at Carlisle undergoing *ab initio* instruction in Tiger Moths. Further training at 28 EFTS, Wolverhampton and 17 SFTS Cranwell followed, and he then reported to No. 2 Group SU at Swanton Morley for final training, making his first solo flight as pilot of a Mosquito in LR535 on 31 May 1944. His first night cross-country exercise, in Mosquito HX963, caused Syd a few grey hairs when, having only just become airborne with undercarriage and flaps fully retracted, he saw the coolant and oil temperatures for his port engine soaring up the scale. Feathering quickly, he was forced to make a single-engine landing. Examination afterwards discovered that the cap on the coolant tank had not been correctly fastened.

With the award of his pilot's wings, Syd Clayton was posted to No. 464 Squadron RAAF of No. 140 Wing, 2nd Tactical Air Force at Thorney Island, to fly Mosquitos again. His first operational sortie was flown on the night of 26 August 1944, in NT144, an attack on rail and road transport, using flares to illuminate targets; a type of operation which continued when the squadron moved to Rosières, then Melsbroek on the Continent in direct support of the Allied armies advancing into Germany. An occasional daylight sortie came his way, including the pin-point bombing of a Gestapo headquarters at Aarhus on 31 October 1944, and Operation Clarion on 22 February 1945. Apart from '. . . the odd bit of flak or an encounter with night fighters, nothing terribly exciting happened in my ops as a pilot' (quote). Then, on 8 May 1945, Victory in Europe Day (VE Day) was declared officially.

Leaving the RAF 'shortly after peace broke out', Clayton returned to his native county, Lancashire and initially opened an hotel in Morecambe for some eight years, before taking over some newsagent shops. In 1971 he became a Civil Servant after selling his newsagency business, but died at his home in November 1976 in tragic circumstances.

CHAPTER THIRTEEN

Hamish Mahaddie

When, on 15 August 1942, the Path Finder Force came into being, it was, at best, a motley mixture of aircraft types for a force intended to become the target-locating and marking spearhead of the future heavy bomber offensive against Germany and its Axis partners. The same might be said of the original air crews allotted to the PFF. Each of the four founder-member squadrons had a fairly even composition of in-experienced and veteran crews, typical of virtually all bomber units then, and each crew member had been 'volunteered' for an extended operational tour of 60 (later amended to 45 minimum) sorties with the PFF. Thus, being already volunteers for aircrew duties, the PFF crews were in essence 'double 'volunteers, undertaking to complete at least fifty per cent more operational sorties in one tour than any other member of Bomber Command air crews. Since the prospects of any 'normal' bomber boy surviving his normal ops tour of 30 trips were theoretically no better than one in three, his survival factor in the PFF was even further reduced. One of the more experienced skippers of the PFF's original crews was Thomas Gilbert Mahaddie – 'Hamish' – who flew his 36th operational sortie on the night the PFF was born.

Born in Leith, Scotland in March 1911, Mahaddie had entered the RAF as a Halton Aircraft Apprentice on 9 January 1928, where for the next three years he was trained in the craft of metal rigger. Leaving his alma mater in December 1930, he was posted to the RAF College, Cranwell and within a year had achieved upgrading to Leading Air-craftman (LAC), thereby making him eligible to volunteer for pilot training – his ultimate ambition. Ignored by higher authority, however, he remained at Cranwell until October 1933 when he boarded a troop-ship bound for the Middle East, where he eventually arrived at his next posting, Hinaidi, Baghdad, on the strength of No. 70 Squadron. Once settled in, Mahaddie renewed his quest for air crew training, was accepted, then posted to Egypt to No. 4 FTS, Abu Sueir in August 1934 to commence pilot instruction. Undertaking his first solo flight in Avro 504N, J8679, Mahaddie eventually gained the coveted 'wings' on 13 June 1935, along with promotion to Sergeant, then returned to

Hinaidi to join A Flight of No. 55 Squadron, flying Westland Wapitis. He remained with 55 Squadron for the following two years, during which time he acquired an Arab blue roan '. . . with legs like a Tiller girl' which he promptly named Hamish. Accused by his fellow pilots of bearing a distinct resemblance to his steed, Mahaddie protested at this insult – to the pony! Nevertheless, thereafter Mahaddie was to be invariably nicknamed Hamish.

Returning to England in July 1937, Hamish's next posting was to No. 77 Squadron, based then at Honington and equipped with Audax biplanes and Wellesley monoplanes initially. In October 1938 the squadron began receiving Whitley bombers to replace its Wellesleys – Hamish having his first flight in the type on October 17 in K8949 – and it was at the helm of a Whitley that Mahaddie went to war a year later. Throughout the winter of 1939–40, operations varied widely – reconnaissance trips over the North Sea, leaflet raids over Germany, bombing attacks on coastal targets in the Low Countries, as on 19/20 March 1940 when 77 Squadron contributed seven Whitleys to a force of fifty aircraft despatched to bomb the German seaplane base at Hornum, Sylt; Hamish piloted Whitley N1355, carrying six 250 lb GP bombs that night. Attacks on Oslo and Stavanger followed in April, but in May 1940, with the German *blitzkrieg* assault rolling westwards into France, operations became hectic. An indication of this increase in the operational pace is the fact that between 9 May and 29 June Hamish and his crew flew a total of 23 sorties over France, Germany and Italy. Meanwhile, on 1 April Hamish received promotion to commissioned rank as a Pilot Officer.

In early July 1940, though at that stage of the war there was no officially defined limit to an operational tour, Hamish was rested by being posted as an instructor to No. 19 OTU at Kinloss, Morayshire, flying Whitleys still. He was destined to remain on instructional circuits and bumps for two years, during which period he rose steadily in rank to Squadron Leader, and for which duties he was later awarded an AFC – or 'Avoiding Flak Cross' as Hamish personally referred to his decoration.

He finally escaped from training duties in early August 1942, joining No. 7 Squadron at Oakington on 5 August, and just four nights later commencing his second tour of ops in Stirling N3764 to Osnabrück as second pilot to Pilot Officer Heywood. Two more sorties as 'second dickey' followed – to Mainz and Düsseldorf, then on 27 August, as captain of his own Stirling, BF339, and crew he 'nickelled' Lille. On 8 September, he set out to bomb Frankfurt with a 9,000 lb bomb load,

but on crossing the French coast inward had trouble develop in his
port inner engine, causing excessive fuel consumption. Pressing on, he
reached the target, but on return he brought BF339, flak-damaged, in
for a crash-landing at Manston. Two nights later he piloted Stirling
W7581 back to Germany, dropping 9,000 lb of high explosive bombs
on Düsseldorf on what he personally termed an 'uneventful trip'.

Hamish's 40th sortie was to Bremen on 13 September in W7581,
carrying a 9,000 lb bomb load, a successful trip though he was slightly
shaken when, after running through the fierce flak, his newly-joined
bomb aimer calmly decided to change the aiming point briefed to the
railway station. . . . In October Mahaddie began true PFF marking
on operations, dropping flares over Krefeld on 2 October and Osnabrück four nights later. Another flare-sortie to Cologne on 15 October
was followed eight nights later by a long haul in Stirling BF385 to
Genoa, Italy. He returned to Genoa on the night of 7 November with
a mixed load of incendiaries and high explosive 'stores'. It was a very
successful sortie, though as Hamish pulled away for the return trip his
second pilot, Flight Lieutenant Thompson coolly requested that he
return over Genoa one more time 'to get a better view of the attack'.
Forty-eight hours later Hamish was helping to mark Hamburg, despite
severe icing conditions and a ten-tenths cloud blanket over the whole
of north-west Germany. On 15 November he flew to Genoa yet again,
carrying out what he privately noted as 'the most perfect sortie to date'.
Two more trips in November – to Stettin and Turin – were followed by
his 50th sortie, to Frankfurt on 3 December. As a marker, his bomb
bay contained 24 x 250 lb incendiaries, but the hellish flak severed the
Stirling's bomb release circuit, and he only managed to drop three
stores; the remainder hung up. With typical honesty Hamish summed
the trip as 'a waste of time from start to finish'.

By then officialdom had suddenly begun to recognise Mahaddie's
operational efforts. On 1 December he was promoted to Wing Commander, and though already Mentioned in despatches twice during
1942, was further awarded an AFC on 1 January 1943, a DSO on
11 January, the Czechoslovakian Military Cross on 12 January,
followed by a DFC on 27 February. To receive four awards within a
period of eight weeks probably constitutes an RAF record, though
Hamish's only comment was to recall that remarkable period as 'the
most expensive in my career' – referring to the cost of the various parties
thrown in his honour in the mess. His natural modesty about his own
achievements, nevertheless, did not blind him to the doubts and fears
of the young air crews under his command. His personal methods of

bolstering the morale of his men varied in individual cases from a brusque yet kindly chat in private, to elaborate hoaxes to help relieve the ever-present tensions of operational flying. One example of the latter method was the occasion he heard that an elephant had escaped from a local zoo. Assembling a Mosquito crew in his office, he briefed them for '. . . a mission of utmost importance where success was essential'. Then, with a perfectly straight face, he told them to fly north along the old Great North Road (A.1) until they found an elephant! For once Hamish had underestimated his man, because the pilot's laconic but equally serious reply was, 'Yes, sir. What colour?' . . .

It was but one facet of a man whose various award citations contain such tributes as 'consistently attacked heavily defended targets with coolness and determination, often in adverse weather' and 'powers of leadership of a very high order, and his unflagging enthusiasm has had an inspiring effect on his comrades'. Hamish's reply to all problems or allotted duties was invariably 'It's nae bother, laddie' – a phrase which inevitably became his virtual 'trademark' with fellow crews – but few realised that, on return from any particularly sticky sortie, Hamish often left the de-briefing room and, instead of seeking his bed like most crews, made his way to the banks of the nearby River Cam, there to sit alone, peacefully watching the dawn and 'reviving his sanity' after the previous night's job of pure destruction.

On the night of 1/2 February 1943 he had needed every ounce of that sanity just to survive. Detailed as the 'Y' target-marker for a raid on Cologne – his 52nd sortie – he piloted Stirling R9273, MG–C to the target without undue trouble, but just as he had released his target indicators the scanty cloud cover ran out. He was almost immediately attacked by fierce flak which shattered the crew's inter-comm system and put the rear turret out of action. Simultaneously – it seemed – a roving Junkers Ju 88 nightfighter bore in to eighty yards range, pumping cannon shells all along the Stirling's fuselage.

The mid-upper air gunner, bomb aimer, and wireless operator were all wounded, the 'G' and 'Y' compasses smashed, all navigation aids rendered useless, and the aileron controls were shot away. Using every known trick in the book, Hamish managed to retain control and evaded any further attack from the Ju 88, then set the nose of the crippled Stirling homewards. With only the astro compass to aid navigation, his second pilot, Thompson managed to supply accurate bearings back to base; while Flight Sergeant Stewart first attended to the wounds of the three injured crew men, then repaired the severed controls. Next morning Hamish counted 174 cannon shell holes in 'C-for-Colander' – probably his closest brush with the Grim Reaper of his whole operational career.

Six nights later, however, Hamish had the same crew with him in Stirling R9257 – another 'C' – raiding Lorient, and they stayed with him until the end of his operational tour with the PFF in March. Tragically, their first sortie thereafter, with a fresh skipper, was to be their last – the aircraft was lost in action. This crew, with Hamish, had been due to attend an investiture at Buckingham Palace where, between them, they were to have received a total of eleven decorations. Only Hamish remained alive now for the royal occasion.

On 23 March 1943, with further promotion to Group Captain, Mahaddie was posted to No. 8 (PFF) Group Headquarters to become Group Training Inspector, a 'label' which in practice meant that Hamish now became the PFF's chief 'horse-thief' (his term). His prime task henceforth was recruiting the right men as volunteers for PFF operations; entailing constant visiting of all main Bomber Command stations giving lectures to the operational crews on PFF methods and overall purpose, then by fair – and occasionally foul – methods extracting the most suitable crews from their units to re-volunteer for ops with No. 8 Group. Within the following year Hamish became a familiar figure in every bomber mess, and in that period 'recruited' nearly 19,000 individual air crew men for the PFF.

Hamish's final appointment of the war came on 24 July 1944, when he succeeded Group Captain John Searby, DSO, DFC in command of RAF Warboys, a satellite airfield which was the home of the PFF Training Unit, equipped mainly with Lancasters. After the cessation of hostilities in Europe, Hamish remained in the RAF on regular service, with appointments to Germany and the Middle East, apart from flying duties in Lincolns. The New Year's Honours List for 1952 announced an award of a Bar to his AFC, while in 1954–55 he was again stationed in Germany; finally retiring from the RAF in March 1958. In 'Civvy Street' Hamish became an aviation consultant, and one of his jobs entailed gathering a virtual fleet of World War Two Spitfires, Hurricanes, Heinkels and Messerschmitts together for the epic film *Battle of Britain;* just one example of his many ventures into the worlds of cinema and television.

CHAPTER FOURTEEN

Don Bennett

'He was, and still is, the most efficient airman I have ever met. His courage, both moral and physical, is outstanding, and as a technician he is unrivalled.' In these words Marshal of the RAF Sir Arthur Harris described Donald Clifford Tyndall Bennett in his auto-biography.* He was referring to the man he had selected to command the freshly inaugurated Path Finder Force of RAF Bomber Command in early 1942, and who remained in command of that élite formation until the final surrender of Nazi Germany in May 1945. Butch Harris, ever noted for blunt honesty in his pronouncements and sparing in unnecessary praises, was not without ample foundation for his opinion of Bennett.

A navigation expert without peers, widely experienced as a pilot of aircraft ranging from fighters to flying boats and bombers, by the time of his appointment Bennett had also commanded two frontline operational bomber squadrons. Such deep practical experience and abilities, combined with relative youth for such a responsible command post, made Bennett virtually unique amongst contemporary group commanders. Moreover, much of that experience had been *recent* – something few other officers of Air Rank then could claim.

Australian-born in Fairthorpe, his family home in Toowoomba, Queensland on 14 September 1910, Bennett's early life had been the open-air, hard-working routine of a cattle farmer's son, and by the age of eleven he could not only ride any horse but drive a car. In contrast to his three elder brothers, he did not shine academically in his schooling. Intended for a career in medicine, young Bennett showed early signs of individuality by concentrating mainly on those subjects likely to be of most help in becoming a doctor, but tended to ignore all others. Leaving school he entered his father's business, but soon decided to make aviation his future career. As soon as he was the minimum age required by officialdom, he applied to join the RAAF and, after various setbacks and delays not of his own

* *Bomber Offensive* by Sir A. Harris : Collins, 1947.

making, in July 1930 he duly enlisted as a Cadet-Officer for pilot training. Trained at Point Cook, he had been told from the outset that he and his fellow cadets would eventually be attached to the RAF due to the economic strictures then in being for the RAAF during those depression years, and after one year Bennett sailed to England.

After a brief stay at Uxbridge and Sealand, he was posted to No. 29 Squadron at North Weald to fly Armstrong Whitworth Siskin fighters. After a year on these he applied for a course of instruction on flying boats and completed this, flying Supermarine Southamptons, at Calshot before being posted to No. 210 Squadron at Pembroke Dock, to fly Southamptons again, then Short Singapores. Here his commanding officer was Arthur Harris whose eminently down-to-earth views of how a peacetime RAF squadron *should* be operating meant that Bennett and the other pilots obtained plentiful practical knowledge of their job.

To his initial dismay, Bennett was next posted back to Calshot to become a lecturer on flying boat techniques and aerial navigation, but soon became a pure instructor of the various courses held on the station. He remained at Calshot until leaving the RAF in August 1935, but in the interim had broadened his knowledge of all aspects of flying considerably; obtaining his B Pilot's Licence, First Class Navigator's Licence, Wireless Operator's Licence, Ground Engineer's A, C, and X Licences and an Instructor's Certificate. Added to these – all with his eye on a future career in civil aviation – he spent many of his week-ends at Calshot flying De Havilland Dragon airliners for Jersey Airways Ltd, unpaid, but invaluable base-rock experience. When he finally shed his RAF uniform in August 1935, Bennett could show in his log books a total of 1350 flying hours on twenty-one different aircraft types; eight of these marine aircraft and the rest landplanes.

Just ten days after demobilisation Bennett married, then spent the rest of the year travelling to Switzerland – his bride's birthplace – and to his home in Australia. Then, in January 1936 he joined Imperial Airways back in England as a First Officer. For the next three and a half years he roamed the world, piloting flying boats and landplanes along the airline routes, interspersed with a host of individual flying exploits which brought him such awards as the Johnston Memorial Trophy and the Oswald Watt Medal for outstanding achievements in aviation. Such feats included the much-publicised Mercury-Maia composite flying boat flight across the North Atlantic in July 1938 – the first commercial half-ton payload to be flown by direct air route there.

In early 1939 he also participated in various flight refuelling experimental flights, and for the first ten months of the war was engaged in a number of VIP flights around Europe, including a clandestine trip to Bordeaux after France had capitulated to the Germans, to rescue Polish military and government officials. Making his ultimate flight with BOAC (as Imperial Airways had become the previous year) on 2 July 1940, Bennett was summoned to the Ministry of Aircraft Production in London where he was told by Lord Beaverbrook that he was to be one of the men detailed to form a ferry service for American aircraft deliveries across the Atlantic to Britain. Titled Canadian Pacific Air Services, with Bennett as its appointed Flying Superintendent, the organisation arranged collection of USA-built designs in Canada – America then still being 'neutral' – and duly flew these to Britain.

In August 1941 Bennett, having been superseded in his appointment with the Atlantic ferry organisation by Air Chief Marshal Bowhill, reported to the Air Ministry in London. Having already been told that he was to become a Group Captain in the RAF's Training Command, he was offered the acting rank of Squadron Leader, promptly told the appropriate junior Civil Servant his opinion of such an offer, and was eventually given Wing Commander rank and a posting to a new navigation school at Eastbourne. However, having helped in the initial formation of this school, and seen the first student course inaugurated, Bennett applied for a more active post, and in December 1941 was appointed commander of No. 77 Squadron, based at Leeming, an operational Whitley bomber unit.

Here, as was his invariable and characteristic custom, he set about analysing his unit's operational efforts with a constant view to further efficiency in every aspect; but – again, characteristically – practised what he preached by immediately flying on operations with his crews. His first two sorties were in the capacity of second pilot – to learn the ropes – and in each case he chose a junior Sergeant pilot to accompany. Thereafter he flew with a different crew on each sortie, replacing the skipper in each case in order to assess his crews' efficiency.

His determination to attain total effectiveness in bombing was exemplified during one raid against the Mat-Ford works on the Seine, Paris. It was a moonlight night, with the target clearly visible to Bennett. Unfortunately, his bomb aimer's night vision was not to the same high standard as his pilot's and Bennett eventually spent one and three-quarter hours over the target, circling and running in, before his bomb aimer finally released the bombs – a period in which flak and a persistent

German night fighter made life extremely uncomfortable for Bennett and his crew. After their return to base, more than fifty holes were counted in the Whitley's airframe. . . . On another sortie – a propaganda leaflet 'raid' on Oslo – he spent 10 hours 13 minutes crossing and recrossing the North Sea, but used the occasion to give his crew an overt lesson in the art of precise navigation.

Nevertheless, Bennett's firsthand experiences and observation of the RAF's bombing offensive at that period had convinced him that the bulk of bomber operations were wasted effort, exacerbated by needless high casualty rates among the crews. A year earlier, while still on the Atlantic Ferry, he had been consulted by the Directorate of Operations, RAF regarding the state of bombing operations even then known to be less successful than had been hoped. Bennett's reply had been to point out the relatively low level of navigational expertise of wartime-trained bomber crews, and to suggest the need for a separate formation of expertly-trained crews to act as bombing leaders for main force bombers – the seed of a future Path Finder Force.

In April 1942 Bennett left 77 Squadron to command No. 10 Squadron, also based at Leeming but re-equipped with Halifax heavy bombers. On 27 April Bennett was one of the 32 Halifax pilots who set out from Lossiemouth – drawn from Nos. 10, 35 and 76 Squadrons – to attempt to destroy the German battleship *Tirpitz* in Aasfjord, Norway. Flying Halifax W1041 'B-Baker', with a load of five 1,000 lb special mines, Bennett reached the target area and commenced his run-in, only to be hit repeatedly by the intense flak defence barrage. His tail gunner was wounded, and seconds later the starboard wing erupted in flames.

Passing over the smoke-shrouded *Tirpitz*, Bennett eased his burning bomber round, headed towards the ship as his starboard undercarriage wheel and flaps flopped down and the wing fire spread, dropped the mines, then turned eastwards towards neutral Sweden. Telling his crew to don parachutes and prepare for baling out, Bennett found himself heading towards a mountain range far higher than he could hope to climb with his crippled Halifax and therefore gave the order to abandon aircraft. Remaining at the controls to let his crew get away, he saw his starboard wing finally break away, then jumped fast, pulling his ripcord as soon as he was clear and almost immediately plunging into deep snow. Joining up with his wireless operator, he made his way eventually to Sweden, helped by patriotic Norwegians, and exactly one month after baling out was back at Leeming to resume command of his squadron.

His stay was brief because No. 10 Squadron was about to move from England to North Africa. Bennett, who had been awarded a DSO after his Norwegian venture, was instead ordered to report to the AOC-in-C, Bomber Command, Arthur Harris, who informed Bennett that, despite Harris's personal objections, the Air Staff had ordered him to create a Path Finder Force – the target-locating/marking force which. Bennett had originally suggested in broad terms years before.

Initially the PFF was to comprise one selected squadron from each of Nos. 1, 3, 4 and 5 Groups, Bomber Command, with No. 109 Squadron (Wellingtons and Mosquitos), then engaged in developing the Oboe radar equipment for operations, being 'attached'. Bennett's appointment as commander of the PFF was dated 5 July 1942, with his elevation to Group Captain, and the force came into being officially with effect from 15 August 1942, when its headquarters was established at RAF Wyton, Huntingdonshire. Its four main squadrons and stations on that date were 7 Squadron (Stirlings), 35 Squadron (Halifaxes), 83 Squadron (Lancasters), and 156 Squadron (Wellingtons), based respectively at Oakington, Graveley, Wyton and Warboys. For purely administrative purposes the PFF came under the aegis of No. 3 Group, but Bennett was directly answerable to Arthur Harris. On 8 January 1943, however, the PFF became titled No. 8 Group in its own right, and Bennett was accordingly promoted to Air Commodore and, later, Air Vice-Marshal.

The subsequent history of the Path Finders is now well documented (see Bibliography), but it is seldom fully realised how much the success of the PFF was due to the driving energy and relentless single-mindedness of its wartime commander Don Bennett. To Bennett the prime consideration in *all* matters was the prosecution of the war against Germany to a speedy and successful conclusion – *nothing* was more important. In his untiring pursuit of this aim he was prepared to tackle anyone and any thing which might impede him. Whereas many of the senior officers and government officials he had to deal with were career men in their respective jobs, Bennett was not, thereby giving him an unbiassed view of his task in the RAF. Additionally, being blessed with an intelligence given to few men, and a phenomenal memory for detail, he could never suffer fools gladly; a form of intolerance not calculated to bring him many friends among higher authorities.

His technical knowledge of virtually every facet of flying meant that most of his subordinate PFF crews stood somewhat in awe of him. To quote one PFF navigator, 'The general impression I had was that

Bennett was God himself. It was said that he had written *the* book on navigation – in three parts; one part for beginners, one for advanced students, and one for AVM Bennett because he was the only one who could understand it! It was also said of him that he believed that any-one shot down could and should get back within a month – after all, he had done it! We did not see him too often but everyone loved him and had a grave respect for his ability.'

From the very beginning of the PFF Bennett made it a personal rule to attend one briefing prior to operations and one de-briefing after operations in order to keep his finger on the pulse. In addition he occasionally flew himself to see things at the receiving end. If he decided to pay a visit to any of the stations under his command, he seldom announced this in advance, preferring to arrive unheralded and thereby see things as they really were, apart from not wasting his subordinates' time with pointless parades and 'bull' preparations. His constant search for perfection extended to individual crew members of his force. Though he played no part in their initial selection, leaving that chore to Hamish Mahaddie, his Personnel chief, Bennett personally inter-viewed NCO crew men being recommended for commissioning. Unlike the contemporary fashion for RAF commissioning boards of delving into candidates' social and family backgrounds, Bennett virtually trade-tested each NCO in his particular air crew role – a method which came as something of a shock to many such NCOs, having seldom encountered officers of Bennett's exalted rank with such detailed know-ledge.

If Bennett appeared to be God-like, aloof, even Draconian in his views to his crews, they also knew that – provided they were competent in their allotted tasks – he would never fail to protect them from the grosser idiosyncrasies of the more book-minded RAF authorities whose whole purpose in life, war or no war, appeared to be delighting in adhering meticulously to the letter of every known King's Rule and Regulation in mundane matters. A hard taskmaster to his own, he was equally fierce in his protection of them from outsiders. His many battles with obdurate officialdom – purely in the cause of greater efficiency for 'his' PFF – brought him few friends and no few enemies among RAF and government hierarchies.

At any given moment throughout his PFF reign he had more prac-tical flying experience than the accumulated experience of every other Bomber Command Group commander. Yet, by the end of the war he remained the only Group commander who had served a full term as an Air Officer Commanding (AOC) who was not knighted for his outstanding services. At that time he was the youngest RAF officer to hold the rank of Air Vice-Marshal, but he had been the architect of Bomber Command's ultimate efficiency in its devastation of Hitler's Reich.

CHAPTER FIFTEEN

Basil Embry

'True leadership of any fighting formation, be it a group or a station, could not be conducted with complete success from an office chair, but must spring from physical leadership in the air by the commander . . . an appointed commander who lacked practical up-to-date knowledge of flying could not exercise efficient command' – such was the constant creed of Basil Edward Embry. By contemporary standards and RAF custom, Embry was too old and too senior in rank to participate in operational flying during 1939–45, yet he ignored such precepts and established himself as an outstanding bomber leader, always practising what he preached to his subordinates. Once asked by a senior RAF officer the first quality needed in an officer, Embry replied immediately, 'To be able to fight' – a quality he personified throughout his 35 years of RAF service.

Born at Barnwood, Gloucestershire on 28 February 1902, and mainly educated at Bromsgrove School, Embry had only one ambition from the age of ten – to fly with the RAF. Initially trained at Netheravon, he was commissioned in March 1921 and in the following year joined No. 45 Squadron in Iraq to fly DH9As and Vickers Vernons. In December 1925 he was posted to No. 30 Squadron in Iraq, still flying DH9As, and in the 1926 New Year's Honours List was awarded an Air Force Cross (AFC) for his previous work with 45 Squadron, and promoted to Flight Lieutenant. Returning to England in 1927, he spent two years instructing at Netheravon, then almost three years at the Central Flying School (CFS), before being temporarily grounded in a staff job for two years. To his personal relief, in February 1934 he was again sent overseas to an active flying post, this time to join No. 1 Indian Wing, Kohat on the notorious North West Frontier Province of India (now, Pakistan).

The next two years saw him participating in the almost unceasing active operational flying undertaken by the meagre RAF units attempting to keep the peace along India's northern borders, then in March 1936, with promotion to Squadron Leader, Embry moved to RAF HQ

as a staff officer. In October 1937 he was appointed to command No.
20 Squadron at Peshawar, and in September 1938 was awarded a DSO
for his highly active leadership of that unit. Two months later he
received promotion to Wing Commander, sailed to England in
February 1939, and inherited another desk job, this time at the Air
Ministry.

With the outbreak of war in September 1939, Embry went to his
superior with a forceful plea to be given an active post, resulting in his
appointment as OC No. 21 Squadron at Watton but was immediately
transferred to the command of No. 107 Squadron, based at Wattisham,
a Bristol Blenheim bomber unit which had already begun operations
but suffered casualties. Pausing only to spend two days of intensive
conversion flying on Blenheims, Embry arrived at Wattisham on 14
September to take up his command post. For the next ten days Embry
delved into every facet of his unit's organisation, maintenance, and
other problems, then selected an ex-Halton aircraft apprentice,
Corporal T. A. Whiting (later, Wing Commander, DFC) as his personal
navigator, and Aircraftman 1st Class (AC1) Lang as his air gunner.
On 25 September Embry led two other Blenheims to Germany on a
reconnaissance sortie, was attacked by two German fighters which holed
the Blenheim's petrol tanks, shot chunks out of its wings and fuselage,
and slashed the tyre of one main wheel. Reaching base again, Embry
made a one-wheel landing safely.

For the following six months operations were few and far between
for his Blenheim crews, though he personally flew twelve sorties during
that period, and Embry instituted a series of flying practice exercises
almost daily to keep his men fully occupied and increase their experience. He also instigated various improvements in the squadron's aircraft,
including increased armament and other locally-produced technical
innovations. Yet another facet of Embry's 'all-out' attitude to the war
was an order that all married air crews had to live on the station, an
unpopular yet necessary precaution.

One of 107 Squadron's members then described Embry as a 'little
ball of fire', adding, 'For us the Phoney War never existed, due in large
part to Embry's terrific drive. Battle Orders were issued almost daily
and the squadron was constantly "on operations", although these did
not invariably mean bombs were dropped, because targets were not
always reached or even located. He expected everyone to match his
own fierce energy and enthusiasm – a tall order.'

Certainly, Embry's innate conviction that unit commanders should
literally lead in the air, allied to his personal restless urge to attack the

enemy at every opportunity, meant a hectic life for the crews of his squadron, both air and ground. One example of his stamina occurred when his squadron was detached to Lossiemouth, Scotland on 14 April 1940 to carry out 'support' raids on the German airfields in Norway. That day Embry drove a shooting brake from Wattisham to London for briefing orders, then drove all night from London to Lossiemouth, and at 9 am on 15 April took off at the head of twelve Blenheims to bomb Stavanger airfield, the first of ten raids by 107 Squadron against Stavanger in eight days. His 2½ hours' return flight across the North Sea was made with one damaged engine; forty-eight hours later Embry led twelve of his crews back to Stavanger through atrocious weather conditions and in the teeth of close Luftwaffe opposition which claimed two Blenheim victims.

On return to its normal Wattisham base on 3 May, No. 107 Squadron refurbished its aircraft and quickly worked up to full operational strength again. Then, on 10 May, the German *blitzkrieg* invasion of the Low Countries erupted, and within hours Embry and his crews were in the thick of the desperate battle to stem the German juggernaut advance. Each crew flew two or three sorties daily across the sea to France. On 12 May Embry led his squadron to attack the two bridges crossing the Albert Canal at Maastricht. Deliberately bombing from 4,000 feet to ensure accuracy, the Blenheims ran through a veritable tornado of flak from the ground, and were then jumped by a horde of Messerschmitts, losing seven Blenheims shot down from 107 and its accompanying 110 Squadron, while two other 107 bombers crash-landed back at base, and every Blenheim surviving bore ragged scars of shell and bullet strikes.

This sortie set the pattern for 107's operations over the ensuing weeks, battling continuously against overwhelming odds to protect the retreating British Army on its path to Dunkirk and ultimate evacuation to England, with Basil Embry constantly at the head of his crews in battle. His untiring and inspiring personal example led to the awards of two Bars to his DSO, to add to a DFC already awarded to him the previous October.

Returning from a sortie in the evening of 21 May, Embry was diverted to land at Manston and spent the night sleeping on the floor of a store hut, returning to Wattisham at first light next morning and, after refuelling and re-arming, took off immediately to lead a formation to attack German troops near Arras. Becoming separated from the formation near the target, due to clouds, Embry pressed on alone and received a direct flak hit which blew a gaping hole in his Blenheim's port wing. Barely reaching Hawkinge airfield on return, he brought off a skilful forced landing.

By 26 May the pace of operations had begun to sap even Embry's driving energy, and on return from his last sortie of that day he was told that he was to leave 107 Squadron, be promoted to Group Captain, and take over command of RAF West Raynham station. His protests to be left on operations were to no avail, but next day, with his successor, Wing Commander L. R. Stokes, Embry led 107 Squadron to bomb German troop columns advancing on Dunkirk. Making a steady run-in to release his bombs, despite the flak fury around him, Embry bombed then started to pull away when his Blenheim received a direct hit, killing Lang in the gun turret, and sending the aircraft into an uncontrollable dive. With no alternative left, Embry helped his navigator Whiting to bale out, then managed to escape himself, parachuting down to the battlefield below, behind German lines near St Omer.

Embry's subsequent two months' adventures in Occupied Europe included capture by the Germans, an escape, and subsequent return to England via Spain and Gibraltar, and are well described in the book *Wingless Victory* by Anthony Richardson (Odhams Press, 1950) – a mini-saga of determination and no little courage. Nine weeks and five days after baling out of a crippled Blenheim over France, Basil Embry stepped ashore at Plymouth, a free man again.

After two months' enforced sick leave, Embry was posted to No. 6 Group as Senior Administration Staff Officer (SASO) with the rank of Group Captain, but after only three weeks was offered command of a nightfighter wing in Fighter Command, provided he reverted to Wing Commander – an offer he accepted with alacrity. His wing comprised Nos. 264 and 151 Squadrons, based at Rochford, near Southend, a virtually derelict airfield with bomb-pitted grass 'runways' and no permanent accommodation, still receiving bombing attacks from the Luftwaffe.

The wing was disbanded in December 1940, however, and Embry moved to Wittering to command its sector, including the satellite landing grounds at Collyweston and Kings Cliffe, with four squadrons dispersed among the three airfields. Of these, No. 25 Squadron, based at Wittering, was equipped with Blenheim IF nightfighters, fitted with Airborne Interception (AI) radar, and, typically, Embry began flying sorties with this unit to 'get the gen'. Equally typically, he selected Peter Clapham, a fighter controller declared medically unfit for operational flying, as his regular AI operator, a partnership that was to continue until the end of the war.

Embry remained commander of the Wittering Sector for a year, was then seconded to the Desert Air Force in North Africa as an 'adviser' from October 1941 to March 1942, and resumed command of Wittering Sector on his return to England. In early 1943 he became SASO to No. 10 Group, Fighter Command, but only remained in that post until 27 May, on which date he took over command of No. 2 Group, Bomber Command, a few days before the Group was transferred to the 2nd Tactical Air Force (TAF), then beginning to form as part of the build-up to an eventual Allied invasion of German-occupied Europe.

His appointment meant promotion to Air Vice-Marshal, and his new command was comprised of nine squadrons, each operating either Bostons, Mitchells or Venturas, with a tenth squadron working up on Mitchells; an unwieldy mixture for contemporary standards of bombing operations. With characteristic energy, Embry immediately piloted each type of aircraft to judge its operational worthiness, investigated actual bombing results, visited all units to acquaint himself with the air and ground crews and learn their problems, then issued a clear and precise summary of the future role and intention of No. 2 Group in toto to clarify his personal view of the Group's future.

Following his unshakeable belief in commanders having to give practical leadership in the air, he also issued orders that all station commanders were to fly at least two or three operations with their resident squadrons each month, though not necessarily as the sortie leader, depending upon their accumulated experience. He then set the pace by commencing operations with the squadrons himself, usually in a subordinate position to the formation leader. Owing to his adventures in France, 1940, as an 'escaper', he flew as 'Wing Commander Smith', with appropriate Service identification 'dog-tags' etc.

By October 1943 Embry's strictures had begun to bear excellent fruit. Average bombing error for visual bombing had dropped from some 1,200 yards to less than 200 yards, Mitchell crews had been taught the use of radar devices to aid bombing by Embry's navigator, Clapham, and virtually all staff officers had taken part in operations, including even one padre who flew sorties as an air gunner! By then, too, the group had expanded to twelve squadrons, including five equipped with Mosquitos, with a sixth unit soon to re-equip with De Havilland's masterpiece. On 3 October Embry took part in a 2 Group attack at low level against various transformer stations between Paris and Nantes, and suffered a collision with a large duck on the return leg which damaged his aircraft. Since the future policy for 2 Group would entail much ultra-low level operating, Embry ordered his crews to practise low level cross-country navigational flying all over Britain to sharpen their expertise at minimal altitudes, and also inaugurated a target-modelling section for briefing the crews for future operations.

From November 1943 to early May 1944, No. 2 Group was principally involved in attacking the many V1 robot 'buzz-bomb' sites, coded 'No Ball' by the RAF, and flew some 4,700 individual sorties against these objectives. The Group's casualty toll for this campaign – 41 aircraft shot down and more than 400 others damaged to some degree – was entirely due to the low-level bombers' arch enemy, flak. By early 1944, however, 2 Group's Mosquito squadrons had also achieved a huge reputation for their ability to attack successfully pin-point targets, often single buildings in densely populated towns, with high precision – always from lowest levels. Perhaps the most publicised was Operation Jericho on 18 February 1944 when the Mosquitos bombed Amiens gaol and liberated hundreds of prisoners of the Gestapo, including key members of the Resistance movement. Though planned by Embry in meticulous detail, his intention to lead the raid was thwarted by a direct order *not* to participate.

Nevertheless, Embry did take part in several other equally successful precision attacks. Flying Mosquito PZ222, he led fourteen bombers of 613 Squadron to attack an SS barracks at Egletons, destroying the target in August 1944; flew in the first formation of eighteen Mosquitos, led by Wing Commander Peter Wykeham Barnes, to destroy a Gestapo HQ in Aarhus on 31 October 1944; was No. 3 to Group Captain Bob Bateson, DSO, DFC, who led eighteen Mosquitos to Copenhagen and utterly destroyed Shell House, the local Gestapo HQ; and flew as No. 2 to Bateson on 17 April 1945 to raid the Gestapo HQ at Odense, Denmark.

The successful Odense sortie proved to be Embry's final operational trip of the war. By then he had finally managed to 'ratify' the official recognition by Air Ministry of the air crew status of his usual navigator Peter Clapham. Though legally an administrative (i.e. ground) officer, Clapham by 1945 had flown nearly seventy operational sorties, been awarded a DFC and Bar, yet was not receiving air crew status or pay!

For Basil Embry further honours rolled in in 1945, including the CB and a KBE knighthood. His first peacetime appointment in 1945 was as Director-General of Training, RAF, followed by elevation to AOC-in-C, Fighter Command from April 1949 until April 1953. In July 1953 he was appointed to the NATO organisation to serve as Commander-in-Chief, Allied Air Forces Central Europe (C-in-C, AAFCE), a ponderous label for what in practice meant he was air force commander to the tri-service supreme commander, Marshal of France A. Juin. The following two and a half years were primarily a saga of frustration for Embry, in that he failed to convince the various Allied military and political hierarchy of the need for revision of their contemporary attitudes to the vital importance of air power and its organisation and control within the NATO framework. His blunt, frank, utterly honest criticisms of the existing NATO organisation, in the context of air power and command status, led – perhaps inevitably – to Basil Embry being prematurely retired from the RAF in February 1956.

Basil Embry was, by any standards, one of the most outstanding and inspiring leaders ever to don RAF uniform. If his outspoken impatience with all forms of bureaucracy brought him few admirers within Air Ministry circles, or friends among the RAF adherents to 'by the book' attitudes to running a fighting Service, Embry's devotees among the men he actually led to war are legion. One such is Peter Wykeham, who served under Embry in No. 2 Group in 1944–45, who has described Embry as, '. . . the most energetic and tireless man who had ever occupied the chief office at Bentley Priory', referring to Embry's appointment as AOC-in-C, RAF Fighter Command. Wykeham continued, 'He was an Irishman; both charming and rude, prejudiced and broad-minded, pliable and obstinate, dedicated and human.'*

Above all these things, Basil Edward Embry was a leader.

* *Fighter Command*, Putnam, 1960.

CHAPTER SIXTEEN

Jo Capka

Every man who flew as air crew with the RAF in 1939–45 was a willing volunteer – a simple fact that bears constant repetition. The individual motives which led any man to volunteer for operational flying, however, were not so baldly explainable. Undoubtedly, the sheer youth of most volunteers provided elements of bravado, even 'glamour', to their intention, mixed to varying degrees with the instinctive human defensive reaction of aggression against any threat to their inherited mode of living. A certain proportion of volunteers were certainly motivated by a degree of patriotism, while a minority flew for no greater reason than a desire to fly, akin to a near-adolescent pursuit of adventure.

For one large section of the RAF the motivation was crystal clear – revenge and retribution. The vast majority of the latter section were men from a dozen European countries over-run and occupied by Hitler's hordes, and had witnessed their homes, families, friends cruelly crushed under the heel of Nazi domination. By myriad routes and means, such men had eventually come to England to continue their unceasing struggle against the evil of Nazidom, bringing to their duties a near-fanatical depth of intensity and purpose. One such man was Jo Capka, whose long struggle to regain his birthright of freedom commenced before the war and was destined to last for twenty years.

Jo Capka was a Czech, born in the middle of World War One, who left school at the age of fifteen to serve a two-years' apprenticeship and a further two years' college training as an electrical engineer. Despite this lengthy preparation for a reasonably secure future career, Capka's real ambition was to become a pilot in the Czechoslovakian Air Force, an ambition he soon achieved despite being then under-age and against his mother's wishes. Initially posted to a fighter wing, by the autumn of 1937 Capka was transferred to No. 5 Wing to fly French Bloch 200 bombers, and by May 1938 held the equivalent rank of Sergeant, followed by promotion to an officer's commission shortly after. That same year, however, was a period of anxiety for all Czechs, as the burgeoning ambitions of Hitler to expand his vaunted Third Reich threatened the sanctity of their homeland. In September 1938, having already ordered the invasion and occupation of Austria and the Sudetenland, Hitler openly declared to the British Prime Minister, Neville Chamberlain, that he was prepared to risk world war if his latest demand for *Lebensraum* in Czechoslovakia was not agreed by the other European powers. The result was the notorious Munich Agreement of 29/30 September 1938, in which Britain and France (principally) acceded to Hitler's demand, thereby sacrificing Czechoslovakia in the interests of appeasement and peace. Accordingly, on 15 March 1939, German troops moved into Czechoslovakia, preceded by the Luftwaffe, which occupied the country's various airfields in strength.

Within weeks of the German occupation Capka and many of his colleagues were discharged from their air force, but in June 1939 Capka was among many former Czech air crews who made their way independently to Poland, intending to reform some units under the aegis of the Polish Air Force. Here they were told that this scheme would not be permitted. With the looming clouds of war, it was clear to most that it would merely be a matter of time before Hitler moved against Poland as his next rung up the ladder to world domination. Capka and a few comrades decided to apply to join the French Foreign Legion as a possible step to eventual flying service with the French air services. Enlisted at Marseille, Capka was sent to the legendary Sidi Bel Abbes depot in North Africa where he was immediately inculcated into the harsh discipline, duties, and daily routine of a Legionnaire. In September 1939 came the news that Germany had invaded Poland, and that Britain and France had declared war agaist Germany.

After several fruitless applications to transfer to the French air force Capka was eventually returned to France for flying refresher training at Istres until December 1939, then, promoted to *Caporal-Chef* (roughly, Senior Corporal), he was sent to Avord, south of Paris, for operational training on several ancient bomber designs still in squadron use by the French. In March 1940 he was posted to a forward airfield close to the Belgian frontier, from where he began flying Bloch bombers on operations; after the eruption of Blitzkrieg there followed a series of low-level bombing and strafing attacks against German tank and troop columns. By June 1940 the German advance towards Paris convinced Capka and his friends that there was no immediate future in remaining with the now-impotent

French, and hitch-hiked their way to Bordeaux to join up with various groups of Poles and Czechs intending to sail to England. Finally, on 24 June, Jo Capka stepped onto English soil at Falmouth, Cornwall.

First sent to Cosford for kitting and administrative purposes, Capka and the other Czechs spent several weeks learning essential English phrases while the Air Ministry decided their immediate future employment. This decision was not long in coming. The 500 or so Czechs, air and ground personnel, were to be the nucleus of two Czech squadrons: No. 310 flying fighters and No. 311 flying bombers. Capka was allotted to the bombers. No. 311 (Czech) Squadron was officially formed at Honington, Suffolk on 29 July 1940, commanded initially by Wing Commander (former Colonel) Mares, though at that stage the only available aircraft were three tired Avro Ansons acting as aerial classrooms for the Czech crews.

The obvious need for the Czechs to learn the English language prior to operating under RAF control was a particular problem for navigators, radio operators, and to a slightly lesser extent the maintenance crews, but Capka found, like all other Czech pilots, that even the aircraft were different in certain basic aspects of flying. In Czech aircraft, for example, throttle levers were pulled back to open them, but in RAF aircraft one had to push the levers forward. In the Czech Air Force too the navigator was always captain of the aircraft, whereas in the RAF the first pilot was (then) invariably the skipper. Such difficulties merely increased the Czechs' determination to succeed, each man impatient to begin full operations against Germany.

In August the squadron began receiving their future operational aircraft, Wellingtons, and conversion training commenced immediately under the experienced guidance of several veteran RAF bomber pilots. Perhaps inevitably, casualties occurred during this working-up period, including one pupil pilot whose Wellington suffered a breakdown in one engine during a night exercise. Coming in too low and too fast the bomber demolished the flying control caravan, killing its occupants, then crashed and erupted in flames. The 'real war' was growing nearer.

On the night of 10/11 September 1940, No. 311 (Czech) Squadron flew its first operational sorties when five selected crews were sent off to bomb Brussels, but it was the only operation undertaken from Honington because by the end of that month the Czechs were moved lock, stock and barrel to Honington's satellite at East Wretham; a mud-bogged airfield with wooden hut, still uncompleted, accommoda-

tion for all non-commissioned personnel who had to endure a month
of steady drizzling rain conditions under canvas before thankfully
moving into the finished wooden huts.

By then No. 311 Squadron had become commanded by an Englishman, Squadron Leader P. C. Pickard, DFC, who arrived to take up
his appointment on 29 July, bringing with him as the squadron's
navigation officer his previous navigator J. A. 'Bill' Broadley, DFM.'
Pickard's first appearance on the airfield at Honington was in battle
dress and wearing a high-heeled pair of riding boots, so the Czechs
immediately dubbed him 'Cowboy'. His casual, informal approach
to his task of preparing the Czechs for operations masked a highly
disciplined attitude to the crews in actual flying matters, and Pickard
immediately set up a programme of flying in which he personally
accompanied every pilot to supervise and assess each man.

The language barrier meant that Pickard needed great patience
with his Czechs during the early stages, but even this was stretched
to its limit when one Czech, 'Joe' Snajdr, who had claimed to
have some 2,000 flying hours under his belt, proved 100 per cent
ham-fisted at the controls of a Wellington.

After twenty hours of attempting to 'convert' Snajdr, with no
visible improvement, Pickard blew his top. Snajdr merely grinned,
then said :

'Me not pilot. Me Observer. 2000 hours Observer !'

It should be added that Snajdr eventually made the grade and was
later awarded a DFC.

The day finally dawned when 311 Squadron was let loose against
the enemy in earnest in December 1940. The initial trip was a 'soft'
sortie to bomb Boulogne, and Jo Capka found his name on the battle
order alongside Wellington 'A-Apple'. Once briefed, the crews
assembled in the mess and went through a superstitious 'ritual' which
was to become a preliminary to every operation. Putting a well-worn
record of 'So Deep is the Night' on the Mess gramophone, each
Czech then silently weaved a path around the Mess room in time
with the music. Once this ceremony was completed, the crews left
to go to their aircraft. This was Capka's first sortie into enemy skies
with 311 Squadron, but it proved to be straightforward with no
untoward incidents – though on his return Capka was astonished to
find that his clothing was soaking wet from his perspiration.

In the operations room as the Czech crews filed in for de-briefing
they found the walls lined with crates of bottled beer – an official
welcome organised by Pickard himself. On this, and subsequent

operations, Pickard made it his business to accompany each pilot making his first sortie by climbing on board as a passenger, taking no active part in the control of the Wellingtons, but ever-ready to advise and encourage when necessary. In between such trips Pickard skippered his own aircraft to France and Germany, literally leading his squadron by pure example.

For Capka and his friends, the winter nights of 1940/41 soon became a near-routine operational marathon. Targets included Ostend, Emden, Wilhelmshaven, Essen, Dortmund, Düsseldorf, Cologne, and the Ruhr industrial complex; a nightly vista of flak latticeworks, probing searchlights – Capka's particular *bête-noire* – and casualties. In its first four months of sorties, the squadron lost eight crews who failed to return, apart from the 'normal ration' of crashes due to flying accidents, damage, or other non-operational causes.

For Jo Capka it was a period of constant fear, though he never permitted this to show to the other crew members, adopting a rigid smile as he tackled each new hazard, and acquiring the nickname 'Smiling Jo'. Yet the fear never left him each time he set out on a sortie; a gut-freezing emotion that needed constant control on Capka's part lest he infected other crew men. Yet he returned to the night skies again and again, even volunteering as second pilot to more senior pilots when not specifically detailed for operations.

It was on one such second-dicky trip, flying as 'spare' pilot to Wing Commander Jo Ocelka, that nearly all Capka's nightmares seemed to congregate. The target was Berlin and before reaching it Capka's Wellington was suddenly coned by a dozen searchlights. No flak came up – it had to mean that Luftwaffe nightfighters were close by. Ocelka twisted and jinked the illuminated bomber for what seemed to Capka an age, then finally escaped from the glare.

Carrying on, they ran through two more belts of searchlights and flak before reaching Berlin's suburbs where Capka could see the cauldron of lights, flames, smoke and flak awaiting them. Slightly ahead and below another bomber disappeared into a red-tinged giant smoke-ball as flak found its deadly mark – Capka felt nauseous. Lining up for the bombing run-in, Ocelka flew straight above the Unter den Linden main street through a hail of furious flak and became coned again by the searchlights. Ocelka shoved his Wellington's control column hard forward, diving abruptly with the speed building swiftly to an indicated 300 mph. Levelling out well below 4,000 feet, he then bombed and threaded his way out through the multi-coloured tracer 'necklaces' reaching up for him from the city's defenders below. The return trip was easier, staying below 6,000 feet, dodging searchlights and sporadic flak, and even giving the air gunners a chance to strafe a small ship in the Zuider Zee which had the cheek to fire at them.

A few nights later Capka returned to Germany with his own crew in Wellington KX-A 'Apple' to attack Bremen. Weather conditions were foul, with 8/10ths cloud over the target and flak opposition much heavier than usual which shredded the fabric-skinned fuselage of A-Apple and blew an ugly big hole through its port wing. Capka duly bombed and turned for home, only to receive a signal in plain Czech language 'Quickly home' – meaning that the home base was about to become fogged in.

Crossing the Dutch coast, Capka ran into dense white fog and dropped down to a mere 500 feet height above the sea, but could still see nothing but milky fog all around him. Climbing again to 1,500 feet he burst through the fog layer into bright moonlight to find that the fog blotted out everything below as far as the eye could see. By then the aircraft radio set was out of action, so Capka relied on pure navigation to take him back to base. When over base – according to calculation – his varied attempts to land proved useless until, in near-desperation (knowing he had less than thirty minutes' fuel left in the tanks) he put the bomber down on the first piece of apparently flat countryside he could find.

Landing too fast, the Wellington hit the grass, bounced through a high hedge, hit the earth again and smashed Capka's head forward on to his windscreen, then bellied in for a crash-landing, its klaxon horn shattering the surrounding silence attempting to warn of an un-locked undercarriage. Once out of the crash, Capka and his crew found a nearby farmhouse whose occupant informed them they had crashed near Swinderby, Lincoln.

As the Spring of 1941 stretched gently into early summer, Capka continued to operate frequently against mainly targets in Germany, but with occasional 'one-off' sorties against U-boat pens and the battleships *Scharnhorst* and *Gneisenau* harboured at Brest. Already promoted to Flight Sergeant by then, Capka was awarded a DFM shortly after his first trip to Berlin – the second Czech in the squadron to receive this decoration. On 14 May Pickard left the squadron on posting to No. 9 Squadron, and he was succeeded by Wing Commander Batchelor – promptly nicknamed 'Fousinek' ('Funny Whiskers') by the irrepressible Czechs. On the night Batchelor arrived, Capka set out to bomb Hanover and in mid-Channel was attacked by a Junkers Ju 88 nightfighter. This was quickly shot down by Capka's gunners, but shortly after Capka was forced to fly through an unending cloud bank alive with lightning flashes and freezing ice. Electrical sparks flew from every projection of the Wellington, giving the aircraft an overall glow; then a violent up-current flung the bomber upside down and plunged it into a madly vibrating power-dive.

Capka promptly jettisoned his bomb load, attempting to regain control, and eventually returned to base, shaken but unharmed. By now he was nearing his half-century of operational sorties, and was becoming increasingly apprehensive about completing – and surviving – his first tour of operations. He now began to dread each sortie. His 50th sortie was to Kiel, but on finding the target obscured by thick cloud he flew on to Wilhelmshaven which he bombed quickly and returned to England as fast as possible.

His 52nd sortie, in August, was to Bremen – a target noted for its heavy flak defence. Convinced by then that he would not survive his tour, Capka was fatalistic, but became a semi-tyrant to his faithful crew, giving curt, cryptic orders to each man as the sortie progressed. Over the target his Wellington was coned by the searchlights and flak liberally peppered the bomber, damaging the starboard engine, slashing the tyre of the starboard wheel, and ripping huge chunks out of the fuselage fabric. The return trip, with one good engine and only able to maintain 1,000 feet altitude, ended with a nerve-racking semi-crash landing. When Capka finally left his cockpit his legs were shaking and sweat poured from him. Jo Ocelka greeted him, 'Congratulations, Jo.' 'A piece of cake,' replied Capka with his usual wide, fixed grin – and was then violently sick against the side of his battered aircraft.

Jo Capka flew three more sorties with 311 Squadron and was then declared 'tour-expired' – he had survived after all. Reporting to Czech HQ in London, Capka now sported a DFM, Czech War Cross, and Czech War Medal with two Bars on his tunic breast, and was given a commission, a brief leave, and a posting to an OTU as an instructor at Woolfox Lodge, with a promise of a posting back to 311 Squadron once his instructional 'rest' tour was over. However, in April 1942 the Czech squadron was transferred to Coastal Command, based at Aldergrove, Northern Ireland, and Capka decided that he had no desire for the monotonous role of U-boat hunting and shipping escorts.

Accordingly, in May 1942, he applied to join No. 310 (Czech) Squadron to fly fighters – and was refused. Before he could re-apply, he was detailed along with all other instructors at Woolfox to fly on the first '1,000-bombers' raid against Cologne on the night of 30/31. The thought of taking a sprog crew, in a tired training aircraft, into the hell of a sortie over Germany gave Capka strong misgivings, but the actual trip proved to be one of the quietest in his experience.

His continuing requests to return to operations as a fighter pilot eventually proved fruitful in December 1942 when he joined No. 68 Squadron at Coltishall, Norfolk, a Beaufighter nightfighter unit commanded by Max Aitken, DSO, DFC. He remained with 68 Squadron for the next eighteen months, claiming one Ju 88 victim in April 1944, and converting to Mosquito nightfighters in mid-1944. On 27 June 1944, with Flight Lieutenant 'Willie' Williams, DFC, as his navigator, Jo Capka set out from the unit base at Castle Camps on a general patrol of the Channel and French coastal area. Passing a ragged gaggle of Liberators returning from a mission, Capka spotted a lone Liberator straggling far behind, obviously badly shot-up, with only three engines working.

Closing with the Liberator with the intention of offering some form of aid and protection, Capka's Mosquito was suddenly raked by fire from the bomber's rear turret. The pointblank-range assault shattered the Mosquito's port engine and burst through the cockpit, ripping away Capka's face-mask and tearing out Capka's left eye.

For the next half-hour or so the blinded Capka attempted to keep control of his Mosquito, and finally persuaded Williams to bale out. Unable to follow suit – each time he released his grip on the control column the Mosquito threatened to flip onto its back – Capka, with one hand keeping his right eyelids open, finally brought the crippled aircraft down in a clump of trees in a flapless, 200 mph landing. Thrown out of the wreckage on impact, Capka's survival instinct drove him to get clear immediately as the aircraft exploded in flames, despite his eye injuries leaving him totally blind.

Retrieved by local witnesses to his crash, Jo Capka was taken to Colchester Hospital, then later Ely Hospital, where his burns and wounds were treated. In October 1944 Capka was admitted to the unique East Grinstead 'Guinea Pig' hospital, run by Archibald McIndoe, who used his superb skills to repair Capka's mutilated body in an extended series of treatments which lasted until June 1946. In that month Capka returned to Czechoslovakia to visit his family, then decided to settle there to support his widowed mother. Bringing his wife Rhoda – an ex-WAAF whom he'd married only weeks before his last fated sortie in June 1944 – to Czechoslovakia, Jo Capka rejoined the Czech Air Force as a Captain. Then in early 1948 Czech Communists literally took over control of Czechoslovakia and Capka was one of many ex-RAF men peremptorily dismissed from their positions, then thrown in gaol for alleged 'crimes against the People's Democracy', in June 1948. In February 1949 at a further 'trial' Capka was sentenced to ten years' hard labour in prison. On 19 December 1954 Jo Capka was suddenly released from prison when the new President remitted his remaining sentence, but it took Capka a further two and a half years to persuade the Communist authorities to allow him to leave Czechoslovakia to go to England to rejoin his wife Rhoda, and on 30 May 1957 Capka finally stepped back onto English soil – and freedom.

For nearly twenty years Jo Capka had fought for freedom in various ways, and of all the men and women he met and knew during those fateful years, two men stay particularly uppermost in his mind. One was Sir Archibald McIndoe, the 'Chief Guinea Pig', who restored his body, and the Corporal fitter, Jimmy Brown, who serviced his aircraft on No. 68 Squadron. When Capka finally crashed, Brown had quietly asked the squadron commander to arrange for him to 'donate' one of his (Brown's) eyes to Capka. As Brown expressed it, 'Well, you don't need two eyes to service a kite, and I knew how much flying meant to Flight Lieutenant Capka'. Though gently refused, Jimmy Brown's astonishing and genuine offer restored Jo Capka's faith in the essential goodness of the 'ordinary man'.

CHAPTER SEVENTEEN

'Pick' Pickard

Percy Charles Pickard, DSO and two Bars, DFC, will always be remembered particularly for his leadership – and death – on the precision bombing attack against Amiens prison in February 1944 which saved the lives of more than 250 patriots condemned to death by the Nazi Gestapo for their Resistance activities. His name is also permanently associated with a wartime propaganda film *Target for Tonight*, as skipper of Wellington 'F-Freddie' on which the film script was centred. Yet these were just two examples of the widely varied operational career accomplished by Pickard during the years 1939–44. Whilst these two facets undoubtedly led to his name becoming well-known to the general public, his reputation within RAF circles had few peers and was based upon qualities of leadership, courage and determination in many differing aspects of the aerial conflict.

The youngest of five brothers and sisters, Pickard was born on 16 May 1915 at Handsworth, Sheffield, and was educated at Framlingham College. His academic prowess at the college could hardly be termed brilliant; he preferred physical outdoor activities to book-learning, participating in most sports and becoming an accomplished hand at all forms of riding and shooting. At the age of seventeen he went to Kenya with a schoolfriend, where he spent four years farming and, in November 1935, joined the 3rd Battalion of the King's African Rifle Reserve as a Territorial. A year later he returned to England, applied to join the Army, and was promptly rejected because of his 'lack of academic achievement'. He next applied to join the RAF, was accepted, and in November 1936 began pilot training at Perth, followed by advanced instruction at No. 11 FTS, Wittering, and the award of his wings on 22 May 1937. On 4 September Pilot Officer Pickard arrived at Feltwell, Norfolk to join No. 214 Squadron to fly Handley Page Harrow bombers, and he remained with this unit until August 1938 when his growing reputation as both pilot and navigational expert led to an appointment as pilot and PA (Personal Assistant) to Air Vice-Marshal John Baldwin, AOC Training Command, at Cranwell (later retitled No. 21 Group, Flying Training Command).

On 30 October 1939 Pickard was posted to No. 7 Squadron based at Upper Heyford, flying Avro Ansons and Handley Page Hampdens training crews for Bomber Command's operational squadrons. In April 1940, however, No. 7 Squadron was in effect disbanded when it was amalgamated with No. 76 Squadron to form No. 16 OTU, and Pickard was sent to his old unit, 214 Squadron briefly, then joined No. 99 Squadron, operating Wellingtons from Newmarket Racecourse. For the next three months Pickard and his fellow Wellington crews flew virtually non-stop operational sorties throughout the Norwegian and French campaigns.

On 19 June, skippering Wellington N3200 'O-Orange', Pickard attacked a factory complex in the Ruhr but flak knocked out his starboard engine over the target. Turning for home on his one good remaining engine, Pickard managed to reach the coast and began crossing the North Sea, but was losing height steadily. Finally being forced to ditch, Pickard and his crew spent fourteen hours in their dinghy, baling out sea water with Pickard's shoes, and navigating by means of a button compass from Pickard's tunic which Pickard had been given by his sister Helena, wife of the distinguished actor Sir Cedric Hardwicke. Their path took them clean through a mine field en route (albeit unknowingly . . .) and they were eventually retrieved by an ASR launch.

By late July 1940 Pickard and his crew had flown 31 sorties over Norway, France, Germany and Italy and were due to be rested, but Pickard, and his regular navigator John Alan – 'Bill' – Broadley (later, Flight Lieutenant, DSO, DFC, DFM), were 'seconded' to No. 311 Squadron. Already awarded a DFC for his tour with 99 Squadron, with promotion to Flight Lieutenant, Pickard was given acting Squadron Leader's 'rings' on his sleeve for his latest posting.

No. 311 Squadron had officially formed at Honington on 29 July as the first bomber squadron manned by Czechoslovakian crews who had gathered in Britain to continue their fight against Germany. In August 1940 operational training on Wellingtons commenced, and the first sorties were flown in the following month before the unit moved base to East Wretham. Here training continued apace until December, when the Czechs finally began operations in earnest. Initially, Pickard flew as passenger with Czech pilots undertaking their first sorties – a gesture inspiring confidence in the sprog skippers – but by January 1941 he was captaining his own Wellington over Germany again, leading literally by example. He remained with the Czech squadron for over nine months, but in March and April 1941 was detached to the Crown Film Unit to act as 'Squadron Leader Dickson', skipper of a Wellington 'F-Freddie', in an official documentary film *Target for Tonight*, made at Blackheath Studios. For his work with 311 Squadron Pickard received a DSO in March 1941 while the Czechs gave him their Military Cross, and on 14 May he left the squadron on posting as a Flight commander to No. 9 Squadron.

Yet another Wellington unit, No. 9 Squadron was based then at Honington, Suffolk, and Pickard wasted little time in returning to operations, flying his first with the squadron on the night of 2 June to Düsseldorf, followed by eight more during that month. On 4 July, while en route to Essen, Pickard spotted a Luftwaffe airfield with its flarepath well lit. Unable to resist the temptation he immediately dived and dropped part of his bomb load along the main runway, causing at least one large explosion. His regular navigator was still Bill Broadley, still a Flight Sergeant, but awarded a DFM in August 1941 on leaving No. 9 Squadron.

By early August Pickard had brought his overall operational sorties tally to 65 (officially – though these did not include the various passenger trips flown with 311 (Czech) Squadron) – and was again 'rested'. On 10 August he was posted to No. 3 Group HQ, ostensibly to ferry senior officers and VIPs around the UK, but even here he managed to wangle himself onto two operational sorties – one to France in a Whitley, and a Wellington 'flip' over Holland to deliver a cargo of cigarettes! Pleasant though his spell at Headquarters was, Pickard was soon agitating for a return to operations and on 11 November, with the rank of Wing Commander, he took up his latest appointment as commander of No. 51 Squadron at Dishforth. One week later he was joined yet again by Bill Broadley, now commissioned, who had just completed several months flying with No. 138 (Special Duties) Squadron on clandestine sorties over Europe dropping agents and supplies for Resistance fighters.

No. 51 Squadron, equipped with the cumbersome Whitley V bombers, had been earmarked already for participation in a Combined Services' operation, Operation Biting, and early in 1942 the unit was detached to Andover to begin intensive training. The eventual aim of this operation was to raid a German *Würzburg* radar installation near the French coast village of Bruneval to capture key parts of the radar complex and bring them to England for scientific evaluation. Pickard's squadron had the task of air-dropping a total of 119 para-troops from twelve Whitleys, and on the night of 27/28 February 1942 the operation was carried out with high success. And when the triumphant soldiers landed back at Portsmouth the first to greet them were Pickard and his crews. Pickard's efficient organisation of the aerial aspects brought him an award of a Bar to his DSO.

In July 1942 Pickard and Broadley were parted again – Broadley going to No. 296 Squadron, a glider-towing unit, while Pickard went to 61 Squadron at Syerston – but both met up again at No. 10 OTU briefly, then were jointly posted to No. 161 Squadron at Tempsford in October 1942. Equipped with a motley mixture of Halifaxes, Hudsons, Mosquitos and Lysanders, No. 161 Squadron was engaged in the ultra-secret roles of delivering and retrieving secret agents – 'Joes', as these were dubbed by the RAF – to and from German-occupied countries in Europe; sorties which required meticulous navigation and supreme nerve from the RAF crews. Above all, such sorties necessitated highly developed qualities of individual initiative from the pilots as they flew in enemy skies, by night, unescorted, usually unarmed, and prey to a hundred possible misfortunes.

Pickard flew many such cloak-and-dagger operations during his seven months with 161 Squadron. On 22 November, for example, an otherwise untroubled Lysander 'drop' mission developed into a battle of wits against three determined Luftwaffe nightfighters on the return leg which continued until Pickard was well clear of the enemy coast. On landing back at Tempsford, his Lysander's fuel tank held just five gallons. December 1942 and January 1943 brought appalling wintry weather conditions, nullifying most operations by 161 Squadron; though Pickard's restless soul expressed itself usually by undertaking local flying in a hack DH Tiger Moth, which Pickard then indulged himself by putting the biplane through every known form of aerobatics – his private way of relieving the tensions of operations.

Once committed to an operational sortie, nothing would deter Pickard. In January/February 1943 he flew several trips with one hand in a plaster cast – the result of high jinks in the mess – while on 24/25 February he flew a Hudson to the Tournais area to retrieve seven agents, flying through dense fog which obscured his designated landing zone so thickly that Pickard circled the field for almost two hours before being able to land – and was then bogged down in mud at the end of his landing run. With the help of local villagers and a large horse, the Hudson was bullied back onto slightly firmer ground, then take-off was accomplished in total darkness without benefit of flare-path, slicing through the tree-tops bordering the field. On 26 March a Second Bar to his DSO was promulgated, its citation including such praise as 'outstanding leadership, exceptional ability, and fine fighting qualities'.

By May 1943 Pickard had completed an overall total of more than 100 sorties, while his regular navigator, Broadley, had flown at least 70, resulting in the latter being awarded a DFC and being promoted to Flight Lieutenant on being posted to a staff desk at No. 16 Group headquarters. Pickard too was promoted, to Group Captain, and appointed 'Station Master' (Commander) of RAF Sculthorpe in Norfolk, in July 1943. Elevation to such a command inevitably restricted Pickard's flying initially as he settled in to his (mainly) sedentary duties, but on 1 August he made his first flight in a DH Mosquito to familiarise himself with the 'Wooden Wonder' bomber. In October Pickard became the first commander of No. 140 Wing of the newly-forming 2nd Tactical Air Force (TAF), comprised of three Mosquito VI units; Nos. 21 Squadron RAF, 464 RAAF, and 487 RNZAF Squadrons. The wing's main term of reference was low-level precision bombing, in daylight.

In accordance with the constant creed of Basil Embry, Pickard snatched every opportunity to lead the men he commanded in the air physically, and on 3 October, in Mosquito 'F-Freddie', he led a raid on the Pont Château power station. On the approach to the target the Mosquitos ran head-on into a fierce flak barrage, and Pickard's aircraft received a shattering burst in its starboard engine, which erupted in flames, then seized solid. He released his bombs on target, then set course for Predannack, some 370 miles away, with one good engine. Though he reached the station safely, the aircraft was out of commission for three weeks, but soon after it was repaired Pickard flew it to attack Cleve – and was again riddled with flak, thereby putting Mosquito 'F' back into the hangar for further repairs. By the end of January 1944 Pickard had managed to take part in four more operations in the daylight low-level role, and had by then reunited with Bill Broadley, still a Flight Lieutenant, now wearing a DSO ribbon in front of his DFC and DFM, who was posted in to 21 Squadron on 1 December 1943, but was appointed as Wing Navigation Officer by Pickard in January 1944. By then, too, No. 140 Wing had moved base from Sculthorpe to Hunsdon.

On 8 February 1944 Pickard received a personal visit from Basil

Embry who proceeded to brief him on an imminent, specially requested operation, code-named Renovate (later to be renamed Jericho). Its origin lay in a request from senior members of the French Underground Resistance organisation for the RAF to bomb Amiens Gaol before 19 February, on which date more than 100 inmates – including many Resistance leaders – were due to be executed by the Gestapo. Bombing the gaol might offer the hope of escape, but even if the bombing merely destroyed the gaol the Frenchmen inside had indicated that they'd rather die by RAF bombs than a Gestapo execution squad.

Detailed planning for the operation was masterminded by Embry personally, who intended to actually lead the raid, with Pickard as his appointed deputy leader. The attack was to be mounted in three successive waves of six Mosquitos each, the latter crews being selected by Pickard equally from all three squadrons of his wing. A plaster of Paris model of the Amiens gaol was constructed, scaled precisely to appear to the crews as it would at 500 feet height from four miles away. Timing was crucial. The raid *had* to commence at exactly midday, when most prisoners would be gathered together in the gaol's dining room for a meal, and 'outside' Resistance patriots would be ready to assist all escapers. General and navigation briefings were in the hands of Pickard and Broadley, who were to fly together in Mosquito HX922, EG-F 'Freddie' in the van of the second wave of bombers, and who would decide on the evidence of the first two waves' bombing whether the third wave need bomb.

The order of battle of the three squadrons was decided by Pickard flipping a coin. The 'winners', 487 Squadron, were thus to bomb first in two sections of three to blast holes in the gaol's east walls – these being over three feet thick and twenty feet high. 464 Squadron would then follow in, divide, and open up both ends of the gaol, destroying the German guards' billet in the process; while 21 Squadron's Mosquitos would await Pickard's order to either make good any errors or proceed straight home without bombing if all had gone according to plan. Weather conditions across the whole of Europe in February 1944 were atrocious, with heavy sleet and snow storms blotting out the sky daily, but on 18 February it was decided to go ahead regardless of the conditions.

Basil Embry's intention to lead the raid had been expressly forbidden by his superiors, leaving Pickard with total responsibility for the actual operation. At 0800 hours on 18 February the crews of 21, 464 and 487 Squadrons were called to the briefing room where

they learned for the first time the details and intention of the operation. At the conclusion of his briefing Pickard remarked 'It's a death
or glory job, boys' – words that were to be tragically prophetic in his
case.

At 1100 hours precisely Wing Commander 'Black' Smith, OC the
New Zealand squadron, lifted his Mosquito from the Hudson runway
into the teeth of a blinding snowstorm, followed quickly by seventeen
other bombers and a nineteenth Mosquito detailed to photograph the
results. Within minutes four of the bombers had become lost in the
snow clouds and were forced to abort their sorties, but the remainder
made rendezvous with their Typhoon fighter escorts from No. 198
Squadron over Littlehampton and set course for France, dropping
to sea level to cross the Channel. Crossing the French coast they next
swung north towards Amiens and made their approach along the
ruler-straight Albert-Amiens road, which ran alongside the gaol, at no
more than fifteen feet altitude.

The attack went off like clockwork, with the Mosquitos literally
'hopping' over the outer walls of the prison to deposit their bombs
inside. As soon as each man had bombed he made for England, as per
his briefed orders not to linger in the target area. The two leading
squadrons did their jobs with immaculate precision and Pickard, on
seeing the results, told the third wave to go home in a coded R/T
message.

At that moment groundfire raked one of 464 Squadron's Mosquitos,
MM404, 'T'. Its navigator, Flight Lieutenant R. W. Sampson was
killed instantly, and his pilot Squadron Leader A. I. McRitchie made
a forced landing at some 200 mph in the snow-covered fields near the
gaol.* Pickard saw McRitchie go down and quickly turned to fly
over the crash, presumably to ascertain if the crew had survived – an
instinctive concern for the men he led.

At less than 500 feet height Pickard's Mosquito was attacked from
behind by a Focke Wulf Fw 190 fighter which had just appeared on
the scene. Its first burst of cannon shells severed the Mosquito's tail
section which fell away. The bomber flicked over onto its back, then
within seconds dived straight into the ground near St Gratien,
exploding into flames on impact.

Percy Charles Pickard, DSO, DFC and John Alan Broadley, DSO,
DFC, DFM – Pick and Bill – aged 28 and 22 respectively had made
their last flight together.

---

* McRitchie, astonishingly, survived the crash to become a prisoner of war.

Their deaths had not been in vain. Of the 400 or so prisoners who originally escaped from Amiens Gaol that day, 258 retained their freedom, including several key Resistance patriots due to be shot next day. Perhaps inevitably some prisoners died in the actual bombing, but it is known that of the 102 who died that day a large proportion were shot by a prison guard's machine gun as they attempted to escape.

CHAPTER EIGHTEEN

Ron Middleton

In every bomber aircraft, irrespective of actual rank, the first pilot
was the captain, or skipper, to whom the remaining crew members
looked for final decisions in every facet of operations. He in turn
assumed ultimate responsibility not only for the aircraft and successful
completion of all given duties, but, more significantly, the lives of his
crew. Such heavy responsibilities were borne readily upon the
shoulders of young skippers, many of whom had not even reached the
contemporary legal definition of adult of 21 years' age. Equally, such
readily accepted moral obligation often meant that the skipper needed
to call on extraordinary depths of raw courage and, too often, left
him with a straight choice of preserving his own life or sacrificing his
own slim chances of survival in order to preserve the lives of his
faithful crew. In the climate of common peril of operations, the tight-
knit bond between all members of a bomber crew often surpassed the
natural ties of any blood relationships – each man recognising from
the outset that only total cohesion as a skilled team could offer a
hedge against death in the night skies. Only by such a wholly mutual
co-operation might they survive.

Rawdon Hume Middleton – 'Ron' to his intimate friends – was a
bomber captain. Born in 1916 at Waverley, New South Wales in
Australia, he was the son of a sheep farmer and, on completing his
early education, became a jackeroo – riding the farm managed by
his father at Yarrabandi and generally assisting in shepherding the
stock. Tall (nearly six feet in height), rangy in body, with deep brown
eyes, Middleton excelled in several outdoor sporting activities, but
more usually shunned any extrovert antics which most youngsters of
his age tended to undertake. His natural reserve often led others to
assume that he was introspective in character, and indeed for most
of his life Middleton appeared unsociable in company, even
melancholic.

With the outbreak of war in Europe, however, he decided he
wanted to join the struggle against Nazi Germany and eventually
enlisted in the Royal Australian Air Force (RAAF) in October 1940

to undergo pilot training. After initial instruction at No. 5 EFTS, Narromine, he went to Canada for further training from February 1941, and eventually gained his wings, and promotion to Sergeant, on 6 June 1941. Arriving in Britain in September that year, Middleton received his final training at No. 23 Operational Training Unit (OTU) from October to December 1941, then, with further promotion to Flight Sergeant, joined his first operational unit, No. 7 Squadron RAF, based then at Oakington, flying the giant Short Stirling bombers.

Middleton's stay with 7 Squadron was brief, being posted to No. 149 Squadron in February 1942, another Stirling unit, based at Lakenheath, Suffolk. Here he commenced his operational tour, initially as a second pilot, with trips over Germany. As a pilot he was painstakingly thorough in all matters, though by no means regarded as more than average in ability overall as yet. To his crew he at first seemed sombre, almost depressive, but a particular sortie on the night of 6/7 April changed this near-gloomy reputation. The target that night was Essen, which he duly bombed, then began the return flight. Still acting as second pilot, Middleton was reflecting on the actual bombing results when, without pre-warning his Stirling was attacked by a Messerschmitt Bf 110 nightfighter. A flurry of accurate cannon shells ripped chunks out of the bomber's starboard wing, shattered one engine, and ruptured the aircraft hydraulic system. Finally escaping from the nightfighter's attentions, the crippled Stirling managed to regain its base, but as it touched down on landing the undercarriage collapsed and the bomber bellied onto the concrete runway at high speed.

Having survived this ordeal, Middleton appeared to have accepted it as his true blooding on operations, and his general demeanour immediately became more cheerful and optimistic, and decidedly more sociable. It was as if his perfectly natural fear of how he might react if faced with a distinct possibility of death had been assuaged – he had survived. On the last night of July 1942 he flew to Düsseldorf, flying Stirling W7566, 'C-Charlie' for his eleventh operational sortie, but this time was captain of his own crew for the first time.

On 25 August, with a total of fifteen ops in his log book, Middleton, and his crew, were transferred to No. 7 Squadron. This unit had now become one of the four 'founder-member' squadrons of the recently created Path Finder Force (PFF), commanded by Don Bennett, intended as the future specialised marking force for Bomber Command's main bomber streams over Germany. Just three nights later Middleton and his crew set out on their next operation, ostensibly to raid Nuremburg. The trip turned out to be something of a fiasco. Poor navigation resulted in Middleton eventually arriving some 100 miles away from his briefed target, flying over Munich. Dropping down to a mere few hundred feet altitude, Middleton allowed his gunners to strafe the city – though unbeknown to the crew the German Führer, Adolf Hitler was actually passing through Munich at that moment!

Returning to England, Middleton soon found that the unscheduled diversion to Munich had eaten up precious fuel, and on approaching the Kent coastline with his petrol gauges almost registering a Nil state he put the labouring Stirling down on Manston airfield. As the bomber flattened out for touchdown all four engines cut abruptly, starved of fuel. With no power control it ploughed its way spectacularly through a gaggle of parked Spitfires and eventually shuddered to a halt by crashing into the station armoury, losing both wings in the process.

Next day Wing Commander 'Hamish' Mahaddie from 7 Squadron fetched Middleton and his crew back to Oakington, where he gave the taciturn Australian a straight choice. If he would agree to replace his navigator, he could continue operating with the PFF, otherwise the whole crew would be posted out. Middleton refused pointblank to split up his crew; consequently on 2 September they returned to 149 Squadron to complete their tour with the main force.

On 14 September he set out on his next sortie – a bombing raid on Wilhelmshaven – but was forced to return early with engine problems; but by the end of the month had completed four more sorties, including two 'Gardening' trips, sowing sea mines in the Bay of Biscay zone. His 23rd op came on 13 October when, in Stirling W7619, he bombed Kiel, but due to flak damage had to make the whole return trip with two engines fully feathered. On 23 October Middleton made his first 'ice-cream' run – flying over the Alps to raid Genoa, Italy in BF392, and he landed back at Manston with near-empty petrol tanks and with only three engines giving full power. He returned to Genoa on the night of 7 November, made another Gardening sortie on 10 November, then returned to Italy to attack Turin on 20 November – his 28th operational sortie. By then Middleton's air gunners had each flown at least 30 trips and were, technically, tour-expired. Nevertheless, each volunteered to stay with their Aussie skipper while he made two more sorties to complete his own tour of operations.

On 28 November 1942 Ron Middleton and his crew were briefed

for their next sortie, yet another long slog across occupied-Europe and over the towering Alps to bomb the Fiat factories at Turin; just one of 182 bombers detailed for this operation. Allocated Stirling BF372, OJ-H, an aircraft Middleton had only piloted once before, his crew comprised seven other men. His second pilot was Flight Sergeant Les Hyder, an ex-Glasgow student on his fifth operation, and his navigator now was Flying Officer George Royde. The wireless operator was Pilot Officer Norman Skinner, a 31-year-old former journalist from Scarborough, whilst the flight engineer was a 19-year-old ex-Halton Aircraft Apprentice, Sergeant Jimmy Jeffery, a Dorset man. The trio of air gunners were all veterans. Up in the nose turret was Sergeant John Mackie, a tough Scot from Clackmannanshire with 30 sorties under his belt; in the mid-upper sat Doug Cameron, another Scot and ex-gamekeeper with vast operational experience; while in the rear turret was Sergeant Harold Gough, ex-garage mechanic and, like Skinner, a native of Scarborough, now about to fly his 33rd op.

Their particular Stirling for this trip, 'H-Harry', was hardly the best-liked kite on the squadron, having been a constant source of technical headaches for both air and, especially, ground crews. Now, weighed down with a full 8,000 lb bomb load and the maximum fuel needed for the long haul to Italy, it would need all Middleton's experience and skill to get it to and back from the target.

At 6.14 p.m. that evening Ron Middleton lifted his bomber from Lakenheath's long runway and began patiently coaxing the over-burdened Stirling to its highest possible ceiling for the long flight across Europe. Within the hour it became all too apparent that 'H-Harry' was going to maintain its reputation as a dog by guzzling fuel excessively. Moreover the automatic pilot, George, was found to be inoperative. Reaching 12,000 feet height, Middleton realised that this would be the most he could hope to get from his aircraft, and therefore had a check taken of fuel states. Jeffery told him they could still make the round trip, but with only a minimal margin for safety. Middleton decided to press on, but warned his navigator that he'd need to navigate *through* – not over – the Alps, some peaks of which towered to 15,000 feet or higher.

With no moonlight that night, Middleton found himself approaching the French Alpine range virtually blind, with only occasional snow-covered tips to guide him. Unforecast head winds en route had also reduced the fuel states to even thinner margins of safety. Tension among the crew steadily increased as their skipper meticulously threaded his path through the menacing mountain tops. Finally, as he found himself running into yet another apparently dead end with a mountain blocking his forward path, Middleton in frustration ordered the bomb doors to be opened in readiness, should he need to jettison the bomb load. Almost immediately the front gunner, Mackie, yelled, 'It's there . . . look . . . to starboard !'

Through a gap in the peaks Middleton saw the lights of Turin, with cascades of pyrotechnic flares descending from the preceding marker Lancasters. A quick check on fuel states, then Middleton announced, 'Right, we're going down' and began weaving gently downwards towards his objective.

As 'H-Harry' emerged from the mountains it was instantly engaged by the Italian ground defences. Shells punched a ragged hole in the port wing and splashed shards of red-hot metal along the fuselage. Continuing his dive, Middleton levelled out at about 2,000 feet over the edge of the city and began his bombing run, with Hyder helping at the controls to hold the bucking bomber rock-steady for the final drop. Seconds later the Stirling was hit again – a direct hit in front of the pilots' windscreen, between the two pilots' seats. Hyder received hits in both legs and the side of his head, while Skinner was wounded in a leg. The windscreen was blasted apart, exposing both pilots to a roaring icy slipstream which created havoc inside the cockpit.

In his captain's seat Middleton was grievously injured. One sliver of metal tore through the right side of his face, taking out the right eye and leaving the bones of his right temple and cheek exposed, while in the same instant other shards punctured his side, chest and legs. Saying 'I'm hit', Middleton doubled up under the shock of the multiple impact and fell forward over his controls. The Stirling dropped its nose and started a headlong dive, still being hit by groundfire as it plunged into the lower belt of flak bursts. Hyder, dazed and in pain from his injuries, instinctively hauled back on the stiffening controls and managed to recover from the dive at a mere 800 feet.

As the Stirling commenced slowly to climb again, Middleton recovered consciousness, realised the situation, then said to Hyder, 'Hang on'. Reaching 1,500 feet again, the bomb load was released to lighten the aircraft, and then Middleton ordered Hyder back into the fuselage to have his wounds dressed on the rest bunk. Skinner meanwhile remained at his wireless set, not mentioning his leg injury, while Gough in the tail turret kept up a barrage of bullets at the ground until further flak hits rendered his turret hydraulics useless.

John Mackie now climbed out of his turret and stood by his skipper, helping him to set a compass course out of the flak zone; and back in the mid-fuselage Doug Cameron helped Hyder to dress the latter's leg wounds. Once this was done Hyder insisted on returning forward to the cockpit, groping his way with his flying suit blood-spattered, and more blood bubbling from the outer fringe of his leather face-mask. Back in the cockpit a 150 mph freezing gale was howling through the shattered windscreen, battering the huddled figure of Middleton, yet the Australian remained conscious and began organising the return flight.

He had several alternatives to consider. He could fly to neutral Switzerland where his crew would be interned, but would have their wounds treated quickly. He could set course for North Africa rather than face crossing the treacherous Alps again, though it would mean a lengthy trip crossing the Mediterranean – an unattractive prospect. Or he could try to reach England again – at least four hours' flying, assuming nothing further happened to the aircraft en route. He made up his mind quickly, telling the crew, 'I'm going to try to make our coast.'

Getting a course for home from his navigator, Middleton then ordered the rear crew men to lighten aircraft, and Royde, Jeffery, Skinner, Cameron and Gough set to with a will – chopping away any 'unnecessary' parts of the internal structure, and beginning to dump overboard ammunition belts, oxygen bottles, flares, camera, seats, rest bunk, fire extinguishers, even the sextant. Royde then plugged in to the intercomm and asked his pilot, 'Shall we jettison the guns, skipper?' The crew heard Middleton reply in a noticeably weak voice, 'OK George, carry on, but try not to talk to me. It hurts too much when I answer.' By then the moon had risen, bathing the Alps clearly in blue-white light clearly.

Refusing the offer of a drink of coffee, Middleton remained almost motionless in his seat, staring with his remaining eye through the gaping hole in his windscreen at the moonlit mountain peaks ahead and around him, and edging the Stirling gently northwards. Beside him stood Mackie, helping, comforting; while in the other seat Les Hyder fought off recurring waves of faintness and surging pain.

Finally leaving the threatening mountain range behind them, the crew settled down for the flight across France as the Stirling droned on over the sleeping countryside below. Their skipper remained immobile in his seat, guiding his aircraft surely despite the agonies of his shattered body and continuing loss of blood from his horrifying wounds. Then, over southern France, the bomber was suddenly coned by several searchlights. Gathering strength from some unplumbed depths, Middleton eased the Stirling into quick evasive manoeuvres and managed to escape from the probing lights. This effort simply increased his pain. Growing weaker from blood loss, unceasing pain, and waves of secondary shock and almost blind sitting in the teeth of the slipstream's icy blast, Ron Middleton remained silent – his mind now filled with just one purpose, to get his crew home again.

Reaching the Channel coast of France the Stirling yet again came under fire, this time from some German coastal defence guns, but Middleton again took evasive action until, through a red mist of pain, he could dimly see the English Channel slipping away beneath him. He asked Jeffery for a fuel state. 'No more than five minutes' flying time, skipper', came the reply. The crew began to prepare for ditching in the Channel, but Middleton was still determined to offer his crew every chance of survival and pulled the aircraft up to 2,500 feet, crossed over Dymchurch to a point about two miles inland, then turned onto a course parallel to the coastline. Only then did he give the order to bale out.

Hyder, by now semi-conscious and suffering badly from his injuries and exposure, was helped to the escape hatch by Mackie, who put the pilot's hand on his parachute D-handle, then pushed him out. Royde, Cameron and Gough followed Hyder, then Norman Skinner jumped into the void below, Middleton turned the nose of the Stirling out to sea again – obviously trying to avoid crashing on any civilian housing below.

Aboard the doomed bomber, Mackie and Jeffery delayed leaving their dying skipper, but finally took to their parachutes. Their bodies were only recovered the following afternoon by a naval rescue launch. There was no further sign of the Stirling or its captain; both had dived into the sea at approximately 3 am on 29 November, a few miles off the shore near Dymchurch.

On 13 January 1943 the *London Gazette* announced a posthumous award of a Victoria Cross to Ron Middleton; while, never known by the courageous Australian, official notification had been received on his squadron of Middleton's promotion to commissioned rank as a Pilot Officer, effective from 14 November 1942 – two weeks before his ultimate sortie. The surviving members of his crew each received a DFC or DFM, these being gazetted on 27 January. Then, on 1 February 1943, the body of Ron Middleton was discovered, washed ashore on Shakespeare Beach, Dover by the Channel tides. Taken to

Mildenhall, the body was given a warrior's funeral, lying on a cata-
falque in the tiny airfield chapel overnight with fellow air crew men
mounting the all-night vigil. Next morning, 5 February 1943, Rawdon
Hume Middleton, VC, RAAF was buried with full military ceremony
in St John Church, Beck Row, Mildenhall.

The citation for Middleton's VC award was unusually lengthy and
detailed, yet possibly the summary of the Australian's supreme self-
sacrifice was best described by an official RAF spokesman who said
of him : '. . . lt does not seem possible that even death could have
had the heart to seek out and destroy such tenacious, valiant and
enduring courage. No man will ever know what force uplifted that
tortured body in its last struggle for the lives and liberty of a faithful
crew'.

Or perhaps the simpler phrase from Chapter 15 of St John's
Gospel : 'Greater love hath no man than this, that he lay down his
life for his friends. . . .'

Guy Gibson

In direct contrast to the great majority of bomber men during 1939–45 two pilots in particular received wide public acclaim and international media publicity, albeit totally unsought by either man – Group Captain G. L. Cheshire, vc, om, dso, dfc, and a pilot of whom MRAF Sir Arthur Harris once said; '. . . as great a warrior as these Islands ever bred', Wing Commander Guy Penrose Gibson, vc, dso, dfc. Although known to the lay public, even today, principally for his outstanding leadership of 617 Squadron's near-legendary attacks on a cluster of German dams on the night of 16/17 May 1943, it is seldom emphasised that Gibson flew a total of 177 operational sorties before his death in action – 76 of these in bombers, and the remainder in fighters. Moreover, he flew operations from the first day of the war until his ultimate sortie almost exactly five years later, with only relatively few 'rests' from operations along the way. Gibson's constant wish to remain on operations earned him the soubriquet 'flying fool' in some RAF quarters; a description meant as a compliment to his unceasing desire to fly with the firstline crews carrying the war to Germany.

Born on 12 August 1918, Guy Gibson's first attempt to join the RAF in 1935 was initially rejected, but his innate characteristic stubborn determination to succeed in any matter refused to accept this initial reaction from RAF officialdom, and he persisted, with the result that on 16 November 1936 he commenced pilot training and eventually gained his wings in September 1937, and was posted to 83 Squadron, a bomber unit based then at Scampton, flying Hawker Hind biplanes. On 31 October 1938 his unit received its first Handley Page Hampden (L4048) and by 9 January 1939 was fully re-equipped with their new bombers to a 12-aircraft establishment. With the announcement of war with Germany on Sunday, 3 September 1939, Gibson was one of six Hampden skippers from 83 Squadron who left Scampton at 6.15 pm that evening, briefed to bomb the entrance to the Kiel Canal. Flying Hampden L4070, OL-C, Gibson, like the other five pilots, had no success in locating the target, and all six jettisoned their bomb loads in the North Sea before landing at Scampton at 10.30 pm. For the

next seven months, however, 83 Squadron flew no war sorties apart
from several sea patrols during a detachment to Lossiemouth, Scotland
in early 1940. Thus it was not until 11 April 1940 that Gibson undertook his second true operational trip to Europe – a sea-mining sortie –
but by September that year he had completed a further 27 sorties, and
had been awarded a DFC. This, his first tour of operations, had had its
'moments'. On May 17 Gibson in L4070 was one of five Hampden
captains from 83 Squadron who bombed Hamburg, and Gibson flew
low enough to hit a balloon cable which wrapped itself around one of
the Hampden's propellers – a 'souvenir' he brought back to base. On
the night of 1/2 July Gibson was carrying a 2000lb SAP bomb in his
Hampden's bomb bay when he attempted to attack Kiel, releasing this
– Bomber Command's first drop 'in anger' of this particular store – by
'accident' into the heart of the city. On the night of August 24/25,
while on a sortie over enemy territory, he temporarily 'remustered' to
fighter pilot by calmly attacking a Dornier bomber flying below him,
and shot it down in flames.

Having completed an operational tour of 42 sorties, Gibson was
posted to 14 OTU on 26 September 1940 for instructor duties, moving
to 16 OTU on October 11; but this restless urge to return to operational
life led to a further posting on 13 November 1940 to 29 Squadron at
Digby, where as a Flight Lieutenant, he became commander of the
unit's A Flight. His latest squadron was a nightfighter unit, flying the
recently-introduced Bristol Beaufighter, on which type the squadron
was in the process of 'working-up' for eventual night defensive operations, moving to Wellingore, and eventually West Malling for this
purpose. Gibson's first operational patrol in a Beaufighter came on
10 December 1940, but it was not until the night of 12 March 1941
that he finally claimed a victim by destroying a German bomber near
Skegness, flying Beaufighter R2246 with Sergeant R. H. James as his
Observer. Two nights later, flying Beaufighter R2250, Gibson destroyed
a Heinkel 111, but on April 8, when about to land at the end of a
fruitless sortie, he was strafed by a Junkers 88 'intruder' and crashed
with a wounded Observer, though without injury to himself. On April
23 he claimed a German bomber as 'Damaged' only, not seeing his
opponent's actual fate, but on May 7 there was no doubt of the result,
when another German bomber exploded in mid-air as Gibson's cannon
shells ripped into its belly. Three nights later he managed to damage
one enemy aircraft; while on July 6 he 'trapped' a Heinkel 111 near
Sheerness and again watched an opponent explode in mid-air at some
5500 feet height. On October 21 he made his last combat claim – two

Junkers Ju 87s damaged near Dover; and flew his ultimate Beaufighter sortie with 29 Squadron on 15 December 1941. By then he had received a Bar to his DFC, and been promoted to Squadron Leader; and with effect from 1 January 1942 he became the Chief Flying Instructor (CFI) at 51 OTU, Cranfield. Throughout his lengthy sojourn with 29 Squadron he had flown 99 operational sorties, destroyed three enemy aircraft, probably destroyed a fourth, and at least damaged four others.

Gibson's second spell as an instructor lasted little more than three months before he had 'wangled' himself back onto the operational scene, being appointed as commander of 106 Squadron at Coningsby from 13 April 1942. His new squadron was equipped with Avro Manchesters at that time but was about to receive Lancasters, and for several months flew a mixture of both types of bomber on sorties. Gibson wasted little time settling in to his new job, and on April 22 flew Manchester L7418 on a mine-laying trip to the Baltic; followed three nights later by a bombing attack against Rostock. Two more Manchester sorties in May were followed by a brief trip in Lancaster R5845 for type experience, a month away from the squadron in hospital and on sick leave, and on July 8 he flew his first Lancaster operation, bombing Wilhelmshaven from 10,000 feet with five 2000lb bombs. On July 11, for a change, he made a low-level daylight attack on Danzig harbour, bombing from a mere 1000 feet, and a week later flew another daylight sortie, this time to Essen. By the end of August Gibson had flown six more sorties the last of which, on August 27 in Lancaster W4118,Y, was to Gdnyia to bomb three German warships. Haze over the harbour area meant Gibson having to make 12 bombing runs before actually releasing his six 1000lb bombs against the *Gneisenau,* narrowly missing his objective, but an inkling of Gibson's characteristic determination to carry out his task to the utmost of his ability. Indeed, his bomb load resulted in 'Overdue' action being taken back at base before Gibson finally returned.

On the night of September 1/2 Gibson was at the helm of Lancaster R5551, 'V', with an 8000lb HC blast bomb tucked in the 'pot belly' modified bomb-bay, which he proceeded to drop on Saarhuis accurately – though the target intended had been Saarbrucken, and had been mis-identified by the PFF marker aircraft preceding the main bomber force. It was Gibson's 56th operational bombing sortie and, including his trips with 29 Squadron, his 155th sortie in three years of war; amounting to slightly more than 500 operational flying hours to date, or more than half his overall flying hours since the start of hostilities. He flew just two more sorties in September – to Bremen and Wismar – and then began a series of daylight formation practice flights at low level in preparation for a 'special' operation. The 'special op' turned out to be a daylight, low-level attack by 87 Lancasters, drawn from nine squadrons, against the Schneider works at Le Creusot, with seven other Lancasters concentrating on a transformer and switching station at Montchanin – the latter being Gibson's specific objective which he bombed from 500 feet, collected a few bullet holes in his Lancaster W4118,'Y', with its Mickey Mouse cartoon insigne and title *Admiral Prune,* but returned safely after ten and a half hours airborne.

On the night of October 22/23 the bombers' Italian 'season' opened – coinciding with the start of the Battle of Alamein, Egypt – with Gibson's *Admiral Prune* dropping 4000lb of high explosive and a shower of incendiaries onto Genoa; followed on October 24 with a daylight foray against Milan, another night raid on Genoa on November 7/8, and two night attacks on Turin on November 18/19 and 28/29; the last of these being the occasion for Gibson to deliver the first 8000lb HC blast bomb to be dropped on Italian soil. In January 1943, however, 106 Squadron returned to its more usual target, Germany, and on January 16/17, flying Lancaster R5611,'W', Gibson carried an 8000lb HC bomb to Berlin, with the BBC radio broadcaster Richard Dimbleby aboard. It proved to be an eventful sortie, as described by Flying Officer Frank Russell, Gibson's navigator* : 'We set off with Dimbleby in the flight engineer's seat, and I did the F'E's job to save a body. The crew was Ian McNair on the bomb-sight (a Rhodesian, later killed), Gibson, myself, Hutchinson, Brian Oliver (our mid-upper) and Johnny Wickins in the tail.† We went out high, and over the Baltic Brian's suit-heating went off so that he was freezing. Hutch went back to try and fix it by checking the slip-rings at the pivot of the turret. Brian then reported the heat coming on again, but Hutch didn't reappear (this all took some time, of course). I went to find Hutch and found him flaked out on the floor and freezing cold – he had had no oxygen. I went back to my seat to report, got a portable oxygen bottle, and took it to Hutch, only to find it wouldn't fit on his face-mask tube (I was similarly deprived). So I had to drag him back to his seat where he could get warmth and oxygen – which took quite some time as he was heavy, the floor was slippy, and I had to keep dodging back for a breath of oxygen. Eventually I got him to where his oxygen pipe could be plugged in and then left him. By then my DR (*navigation*) was screwed up and we had overshot

---

* Later, Wing Commander, DFC

† Plus Sub-Lt Mottrie, RNVR . . . *Author*

our turning point near Stettin, but I recovered and we found the target early enough. The defensive area was very extensive, and the night was dark. Gibson was determined not to throw our bomb away, especially as Dimbleby was present, and the result was that we did two dummy runs and were in the defences for a very long time. Poor Dimbleby was sick on the floor during this period, while Hutch recovered to a certain extent but was useless for the rest of the flight, and was put to bed for a couple of days on return. Dimbleby went back to London by car and did a broadcast on the eight o'clock news, which was Tannoyed round Syerston. It was my last trip on 106, and the crew broke up.'

Gibson, who had been awarded a DSO in November 1942, continued leading 106 Squadron into 'battle', flying three more sorties in February 1943 – to Milan, Nuremburg and Cologne – then on March 11 set out for Stuttgart for the final trip of his long tour with 106. On the outward leg one engine became defective, but Gibson pressed on and bombed the target. Two weeks later he was awarded a Bar to his DSO – a second recognition of his inspiring leadership during his eleven months in command of 106 Squadron; while the Stuttgart sortie had been his 170th of the war. Thus, at the age of 24 Gibson was a Wing Commander, with four gallantry awards, and a veteran of three and a half years' almost continuous operational experience. His reputation in bomber circles was well established by then – tough, somewhat brash on occasion, outspoken if the need arose, and epitomising the popular conception of the 'press-on' type of leader; yet fiercely loyal to his chosen friends, and dedicated wholly to the ultimate goal of obliterating the Nazi dream of global mastery. To many men, on first acquaintance, Gibson demanded high standards in all things, and has been described variously by men who flew with him as a 'fire-eater', 'pure bulldog', and 'explosive in temperament'. He was, indeed, all of these things, but asked no man to do anything which he was not prepared to do himself if need be. As a pilot he was a skilled professional in every facet, and expected others to match his dedication to 'the job'. He never suffered fools gladly and, if necessary in his view, could be something of a martinet in pure disciplinary matters. Yet, almost paradoxically, a well-camouflaged inner streak of 'humanity' occasionally surfaced; as on the occasion of a nine-year old cousin's birthday, merely one week before the famous Dams' raid, when he found time to buy and send her a gold and enamel brooch of pilot's wings as a present.

After the Stuttgart sortie on 11 March 1943, Gibson and his crew were due for some leave, and Gibson himself had already been told that he would be 'rested' from operations for a spell. To his dismay, however, he was notified that his leave was cancelled, and he was to report to No. 5 Group HQ to see the AOC. At the interview with AVM Ralph Cochrane, Gibson was asked if he would volunteer for one more 'special' operation. A little reluctantly, Gibson agreed, and was then told that he was to form a new squadron for this, as yet 'mystery' sortie, but could hand-pick his crews, air and ground. The result was the formation of 617 Squadron, at Scampton, with effect (officially) from 21 March 1943. Though Gibson had yet to be told the exact nature of the objective, he was ordered to train his Lancaster crews in ultra low-level flying, and to raise bombing and navigation standards to the highest possible states.

In the event, Gibson learned his target – the Möhne, Eder, Sorpe, Ennepe, Lister and Schwelme dams in Germany; several of which supplied hydro-electric power to the huge industrial complex of the Ruhr. A force of 20 specially modified Lanacsters was mooted, each carrying a specifically designed cylindrical 'mine' weighing 950lb (6600lb explosive content), which by its nature would need to be released at *exactly* 60 feet height above the dam water, at a range of 400-450 yards from the dam superstructure wall, and at a speed not exceeding 250 mph – and at night. Such precision parameters were without precedent in Bomber Command history; thus Gibson and his crews needed to invent their own means of achieving such precise limitations. Finally, at 9.30 in the evening of 16 May 1943 a total of 19 Lancasters from 617 Squadron, in three waves, began taking off from Scampton. Leading one wave of nine Lancasters was Gibson in ED932/G,AJ-G, who was to master-mind the whole operation and whose primary target was the Möhne dam. The subsequent events of the raid are now more than fully recorded in various published books, including Gibson's personal account in *Enemy Coast Ahead* (Joseph, 1946). Of the 19 Lancasters despatched, eight failed to return, while three others failed to complete their sorties. The Möhne and Sorpe dams were breached. Guy Gibson was awarded a Victoria Cross.

Immediately after the raid the surviving crews of 617 Squadron were taken off operations while replacement crews and aircraft were arranged, and Gibson managed to fly one more sortie on August 2 before being officially 'rested'. For the following year he was to be given various desk jobs, despite constant requests for a return to operations, all of which were firmly refused. Even so he managed to 'scrounge' an occasional sortie – four in all – but these merely intensified his efforts to rejoin the 'sharp end'. Finally, the AOC-in-C, Bomber Command, Arthur Harris relented to the extent of granting Gibson 'just one more sortie'. The raid selected was an attack by 220 Lancasters and 10 Mosquitos against the industrial centres of Rheydt and Munchen Glad-bach on the night of 19 September 1944. For this operation Gibson was to act as Master Bomber, flying Mosquito B.XX,KB267,'E' of 627 Squadron, with the veteran Squadron Leader Jimmy Warwick, DFC as his navigator. The actual raid progressed well, with the main force dropping some 652 tons of bombs on targets. Five bombers were lost; four Lancasters and Gibson's Mosquito, AZ-E. After the last Lancaster had bombed, Gibson's voice was heard at 2153 hours saying, 'Nice work, chaps. Now beat it home'. At 2238 hours a ground witness saw his Mosquito 'circling over Steenbergen, Holland, then heard its engines 'splutter then stop', and watched the aircraft become 'an arc of flames curving to earth'. The Mosquito exploded into the ground, throwing the crew clear, though both men were beyond recognition. The sole identifiable item in the wreckage found by the Germans was a letter addressed to Warwick, and accordingly both men's remains were buried in a single grave, marked by one cross bearing only Warwick's name. After the war the Imperial War Graves Committee identified Guy Gibson as the other crew member, and two official standard headstones replaced the single cross in Steenbergen Cemetery.

CHAPTER TWENTY

Len Cheshire

Serving from the first to the last days of the Second World War, Geoffrey Leonard Cheshire completed 103 operational bombing sorties, and was awarded a Victoria Cross, Distinguished Service Order and two Bars, and a Distinguished Flying Cross – such are the bald facts in summary of Cheshire's remarkable wartime record. Yet of the 32 airmen awarded a VC during the years 1939–45, he was the only man to receive that supreme honour for an extended period of sustained courage and outstanding effort, as opposed to any specific, singular act of superb valour – in itself a hint of the innate character of Cheshire. Like Guy Gibson, Cheshire was accorded much contemporary media publicity, but there the resemblance ended, because in terms of general character these two men were opposites in many ways. Squadron Leader Dave Shannon, DSO, DFC, who served under the command of both men in 617 Squadron gave as his opinion; 'They were both first class pilots and leaders of men, though individually as different as chalk and cheese. Both were fantastic leaders by example; Guy with the bulldog approach and Leonard a little more refined and with the persuasiveness of a Pied Piper. They never expected anything of anybody that they could not or would not do themselves.'

Born in Chester on 7 September 1917, Cheshire was the son of a professor of law and bursar at Exeter College, Oxford, and was educated at Dragon School, Oxford and Stowe before becoming an undergraduate at Merton College, Oxford reading for a law degree, from October 1936. If the genetics theory of 'kindred spirits' has any real basis, it might be bolstered to some degree in Cheshire's case, because while still a pupil at Chatham House, Stowe, three of his closest school friends were later to gain great distinction for individual courage – Jack Randle, awarded a posthumous VC in Assam, Jock Anderson, another posthumous VC while serving with the Argylls, and Peter Higgs who served with 111 Squadron RAF and died in action as one of the 'Few' of the Battle of Britain. At Oxford Leonard Cheshire was little different from any other 19-years old undergraduate, and pursued the normal hedonistic pleasures of adolescence, having, in his own words, '. . . little aim in life other than my own pleasure and profit, both of which I pursued with relentless determination.' In 1937 he became interested in flying, joined the university's Air Squadron (OUAS), and on completion of pilot training was commissioned in the RAF Volunteer Reserve (RAFVR) on 16 November 1937, then returned to his studies.

Mobilised on the outbreak of war, and after a spell of RAF instruction, Cheshire was awarded his RAF wings on 15 December 1939, then proceeded as a Flying Officer to 10 OTU, Abingdon and Jurby, and on 6 June 1940 joined his first operational unit, 102 Squadron, based then at Driffield and flying the ungainly Whitley bombers. His introduction to operations came three nights later when he flew as second pilot to a New Zealander, Pilot Officer P. H. Long, DFC over Abbeville. After several more sorties Cheshire soon recognised how little he really knew of the many responsibilities he was about to assume as a bomber captain; a sobering thought which led him to start 'learning his trade' methodically, by consulting his ground and air crews on technical and procedural methods, and thoroughly familiarising himself with virtually every facet of his Whitley. For the next five months sortie followed sortie, each adding some aspect of solid experience, but on the night of 12/13 November 1940 his coolness and courage received their first real testing. Piloting Whitley P5005, 'N-Nuts', his target was an oil refinery at Wesseling, near Cologne. Over the objective cloud obscured the refinery and, after circuiting the spot for almost an hour attempting to see his target, Cheshire decided to bomb the alternative, railway yards in Cologne. During that 50 minutes circling Wesseling his aircraft had survived intense flak opposition without undue damage, but as it settled on its bombing run into the railway yards with bomb doors open, and about to release an illuminating flare, flak scored a direct hit shredding the Whitley and detonating the flare still in the bomb bay. A ten-feet chunk of the side fuselage was ripped open, the rear fuselage filled with flames and smoke, and Cheshire had to fight to retain his control. Continuing his bomb run, he released the bombs, then swung away and took stock of the damage. His wireless operator Henry Davidson had been blinded by the explosion but refused to leave his post, continuing to signal to base; while the other crew men fought the flames and eventually extinguished the fire. Nosing northwards into a head-on 80mph wind, Cheshire brought the crippled Whitley back to base. His cool control earned him the immediate award of a DSO – an unusual award for so junior an officer – while the stoic Davidson received a DFM for his fortitude.

By January 1941 Cheshire had completed his first tour of operations, but immediately volunteered for a second tour, and was posted to 35 Squadron at Linton-on-Ouse. The first unit to operate Handley Page Halifax 'heavies', 35 Squadron had reformed in November 1940, and flew its first Halifax sorties in March 1941. In the latter month Cheshire was awarded a DFC, while in April he was promoted to Flight Lieutenant. From April to July 1941 he was detached from the squadron for ferrying duties to and from Canada, but resumed operations with 35 Squadron, being further promoted to Squadron Leader in October 1941, and completing his second tour of 'ops' by early 1942. His 'rest' consisted of a posting to 1652 HCU at Marston Moor as an instructor, though during the following four months he managed to fly four more operational sorties, including the first of the famous '1000-bomber' raids, against Cologne. By August 1942, however, Cheshire had returned to full operational flying, with 76 Squadron, another Halifax bomber unit, and was appointed commanding officer with the rank of Wing Commander. By then he had been awarded a Bar to his DSO, he remained with 76, bombing such targets as Mainz, Karlsruhe, Duisburg, Mannheim, Lorient and Wilhelmshaven, until finally leaving the squadron in March 1943 on promotion to Group Captain – at the age of 25 – and an appointment as commander of the Marston Moor RAF station.

At Marston Moor Cheshire found himself floundering in the totally unfamiliar 'sea' of myriad administrative and organisational aspects of a training station; duties in which he had no previous experience or in-depth knowledge. Typically, however, he set about his new role in his highly individual manner, introducing several fresh methods of improving aircraft maintenance *et al* – many of these being highly unorthodox in RAF terms. Nevertheless, the appointment was not entirely to his liking and it was with no small personal relief that when he was offered an opportunity to return to operations in September 1943 – albeit with reversion to Wing Commander rank – he accepted eagerly. His new post was to be as commander of 617 Squadron, based by then at Woodhall Spa, and tasked with 'specialist' operations only by higher command. On taking up his command, however, he was privately disturbed by higher authority's insistence that he train 617's crews in high level bombing technique. Throughout his long operational career Cheshire had been a firm advocate of low-level attacks, thereby improving accuracy. Biding his time for almost four months, while obeying orders by getting his 617 crews to practise high-level bombing, Cheshire seized the first real opportunity to demonstrate his belief in low-level attacks on the night of 8/9 February 1944. The target was to be the

Gnome-Rhone factory and under no circumstances to bomb nearby French workers' homes. Cheshire, flying a Lancaster, proceeded to mark the factory with incendiaries with absolute accuracy from a mere 200 feet, and the rest of the squadron, bombing from some 10-12,000 feet placed their bombs precisely on his 'markers'.

Having overtly demonstrated his point, Cheshire was permitted to use a Mosquito for future marking roles, and on April 4 flew Mosquito VI, ML976 'N' to Toulouse as the spearhead of a successful operation. It was one of several specifically-detailed targets attacked by the 617 'specialists' during the spring of 1944, and others included Clermont-Ferrand's Michelin factory, Bergerac, Angoulême, Ricamarie, and the squadron's 'hoodoo' objective, the Antheor Viaduct in Italy. Cheshire's penchant for low-level target-marking was probably most vindicated on the night of 24/25 April 1944 when 617 Squadron was required to provide a four-Mosquito marking force for a 260-bomber main force attacking Munich, Germany's fourth largest city and virtually the focal point of the Nazi cult. Munich was known to be heavily defended – at least 200 flak guns, apart from searchlights and the ever-present Luft-waffe's *Nachtjäger* force – and various feint and spoof aircraft 'raids' were detailed to help confuse the enemy defences; eleven Mosquitos of 627 Squadron flying ahead to drop *Window* anti-radar foil over the target approaches, while six Lancasters of 617 carrried out a feint attack on Milan, dropping flares and markers as if preparing for a full-scale raid.

Piloting Mosquito NS993, Cheshire, and his three companions Dave Shannon, Gerry Fawke, and Kearns, could only count on a maximum of 15 minutes' reserve of fuel for the whole operation, and therefore set a direct course to Munich, crossing the heavily defended Augsburg area en route and coming under continuous heavy flak opposition from there on. On reaching Munich Cheshire saw the advance Lancasters high above him commence dropping illuminating flares but was then expertly coned by German searchlights – he was the centre of near-blinding illumination from all sides. Putting the Mosquito into a full power drive, Cheshire flattened out at some 700 feet and ran across the aiming point releasing his red markers with pinpoint accuracy. The other three Mosquitos followed suit, placing their markers with pre-cision, followed by Lancasters reinforcing the illumined point. Thousands of feet higher the main force began to bomb. Cheshire now circled the city at 1,000 feet, seemingly oblivious to the furious flak bursting all around him and the cascade of bombs tumbling down from the Lancasters above. His Mosquito bucked several times as shards of

flak damaged it, but as Cheshire finally decided he had to leave –
fuel gauges indicated no margin for more dallying over Munich – he
discovered that disengaging was no simple matter, and spent a full
12 minutes jinking and avoiding flak and lights before he was able
to leave the target zone. Arriving back at Manston with near-dry petrol
tanks, he almost became the victim of a roving German intruder.
Switching off all lights, Cheshire put the Mosquito down and landed
in total darkness.

Leading every squadron raid thereafter, Cheshire brought the 'art'
of preliminary target-marking to a high peak of efficiency. Three days
after D-Day (June 6) Cheshire led a sortie designed to knock out the
Saumur Tunnel athwart the main German resupply railway line from
southern France to the Normandy beaches. He released his markers no
more than 40 yards from the south-western end of the tunnel, and the
main force of 19 Lancasters from 617 Squadron (which included the
American 'Nick' Knilans and Scot Bill Reid, vc) dropped 12,000lb HE/
DP 'Tallboy' bombs dead on target, demolishing the tunnel. On June
14 Cheshire was again in the lead when 617 made a daylight attack
against E-boat pens in Le Havre, and though his aircraft was hit by
flak early in the proceedings, Cheshire continued to fly over the target
area until he was satisfied that his crews had accomplished their task.
From late June until September 1944 RAF Bomber Command concentrated much of its effort in destroying a new menace – the German
A4 (more commonly, V2) rocket missile sites. For 617's operations
against such spot targets Cheshire now often flew a fast Mustang
fighter to mark the target. His first flight in a Mustang was in some ways
typical of the man. The objective was a V- site at Siracourt, and though
Cheshire hadn't flown a single-seat aircraft for years – and had *never*
flown a Mustang – he quietly familiarised himself with the cockpit
instruments on the ground, then climbed in and took off for Siracourt.
On completing his marking he returned safely, landing the unfamiliar
fighter in the dark.

The Siracourt operation had taken place on June 25, and eleven days
later Leonard Cheshire flew his final operational sortie with 617
Squadron – a devastatingly accurate attack on another V-site at
Marquise. Shortly after he was told by AVM Cochrane that he was
being taken off operations permanently. On 8 September 1944 the
London Gazette announced the award of a Victoria Cross to Cheshire.
Its citation, after summarising his war career, ended with the words:
'In four years of fighting against the bitterest opposition he has main-
tained a record of outstanding personal achievement, placing himself

invariably in the forefront of the battle. What he did in the Munich operation* was typical of the careful planning, brilliant execution, and contempt for danger which has established for Wing Commander Cheshire a reputation second to none in Bomber Command.' The expression 'contempt for danger', however, possibly needs some explanation. It is certainly not a description that Cheshire would ever have used in respect of himself. The opinion of a distinguished Harley Street neurologist, Sir Charles Symonds – whom Cheshire had consulted in late 1943 to plead that *lack* of operational flying was causing him an anxiety neurosis – was perhaps nearer the truth. In Symonds' view; 'Cheshire, though an acutely sensitive and introspective man, seemed completely immune from apprehension . . . he had the heart of a lion and the incisive brain of the practical planner, so that risks appeared to him as impersonal obstacles made to be overcome. He had the foresight courage gives with none of the fearfulness beforehand. Cheshire has always seemed to me, despite his frail appearance and his reflective nature, a man rarely if ever beset by natural fear. He was born fearless – or as nearly so as makes no difference.'†

Yet another side to Cheshire's true character was glimpsed when he was summoned to Bomber Command HQ, where Arthur Harris was the first to inform him of his VC award. Cheshire's overweening self-confidence – evidenced throughout his young life – was for once decidedly shaken by this announcement – indeed, he was stunned, bewildered. In terms of his still-adolescent susceptibility to rewards and acclaim, the award was flattering and pleasing, but his well-buried natural humility could not accept such an honour as really deserved. Even so, the clinically practical side of his nature seized the opportunity to request of Harris a more interesting appointment than the staff desk job at Group HQ to which he had been assigned on leaving 617 Squadron weeks before. The result of his request was a posting to Calcutta, India to join HQ Eastern Air Command, as a Group Captain on the tactical planning staff, and he left the UK on 10 September 1944. By the end of the year he was in Washington, USA on the British Joint Staff Mission, and on 24 July 1945 had returned to Guam in the Pacific theatre. On 9 August 1945 Cheshire was aboard the Boeing B-29 'observer' aircraft accompanying another B-29 which dropped the second atom bomb on Japanese soil – devastating Nagasaki. On return to Britain soon after, Cheshire gave a full report of his observa-

---

* Referring to the operation on 24/25 April 1944.

† Quote from *No Passing Glory* by A. Boyle; Collins, 1955.

tions of the Nagasaki sortie to the newly-elected Prime Minister, Clement Attlee; then in January 1946 was discharged from the RAF at his own request.

Leonard Cheshire's postwar activities, culminating in the founding of the Cheshire Homes Foundation, are now known on an international scale; a continuing zealous – and entirely sefless – crusade to succour the needy and to relieve suffering. He is the first to point out that this global organisation resulted from, and is maintained by a small army of equally dedicated men and women. Yet Cheshire remains the principal inspiration, the 'leader' – just as he had been throughout his remarkable flying years.

CHAPTER TWENTY-ONE

Vignettes

For every bomber crew member awarded a Victoria Cross for selfless sacrifice or Distinguished Service Order for inspirational leadership, many hundreds of others might be mentioned who performed acts of astonishing courage or paid the ultimate sacrifice, yet went un-honoured to their graves. Deeds 'above and beyond the call of duty', if not common, were at least never rare. And what of the many thousands of bomber crews who died in the night skies over enemy lands? How many of those men performed acts of outstanding valour during the closing minutes of their young lives – unwitnessed, except by other crew members destined to share a horrifying death alongside them? Posthumous decorations in the RAF were restricted to the Victoria Cross, or the brass oak leaf of a 'Mentioned in Despatches' – all other awards were for the still-living. Of the 32 VCs awarded to airmen during 1939–45, 25 went to men flying in bombers – and sixteen of the latter were posthumous awards.

The whole subject of awards and decorations is a contentious one, particularly so within Service circles. It can be argued that any Serviceman is bound simply to carry out his sworn duty in *every* circumstance – or in layman's language, 'That's what he's paid for'. Nevertheless, there has always been an accepted norm of just what limits can be expected of the average man when performing his 'duty'. Thus it follows that any act of effort, endurance, and/or sheer bravery above that unwritten stratum of devotion to duty should be specially marked and honoured.

'Gongs' – the RAF soubriquet for medals – were quite naturally a source of private satisfaction for most recipients; a sort of prize for deeds well done, akin to Speech Day prizes during not-so-far-away schooldays, for the majority. To a tiny minority, however, such awards were status symbols, outwardly visible pronouncements of the wearer's experience and/or courage – a harmless vanity, though one likely to permanently stigmatise the boastful owner as merely a gong-hunter thereafter, with social consequences. Yet another aspect of gallantry decorations concerned the official standards considered necessary before any award recommendation would be forwarded through channels for eventual approval. Such standards varied considerably almost year by year as the war got rougher, and almost always depended initially upon individual unit commanders' views and opinions, even motives, for recommending specific men for any particular medal or cross.

Whether medals should *ever* be awarded to fighting Servicemen remains a matter of individual debate; even so, certain gongs have come to be regarded by most Servicemen as higher or better than others, whatever the official designations. For example, throughout 1939–45 a total of 19,247 awards of the Distinguished Flying Cross (DFC) were approved for commissioned and warrant officers; yet the so-termed equivalent award of the Distinguished Flying Medal (DFM), for *non*-commissioned air crew personnel, was generally given more respect within the RAF community.

Only one decoration was universally acknowledged as the supreme honour – the Victoria Cross (VC). The little bronze cross stood in a class of its own in Service regard, far above the ruck of *all* others. Its rarity may be judged by the simple fact that of the 1,352 VCs ever awarded since its inception in 1856, only 51 have been awarded to airmen – and 25 of these were posthumous decorations.

How did such awards come to be made? What sort of men earned decorations for devotion to duty? There is no single answer to such questions. The air crews of Bomber Command were of every type, from dozens of different countries of origin, with social backgrounds varying from Cockney barrow-boy to wealthy aristocrat, sheep farmer to garage mechanic, professional airman to bush pilot, university don to elementary schoolboy – the widest, deepest possible cross-section of male humanity. They came in all sizes, shapes and ages. Some had joined simply to grasp a unique opportunity to fly; others were pursuing personal vendettas against the Germans who had killed their wives, children or other relatives in bombing attacks on their homelands; a few (relatively) simply wanted to get into the war despite the neutrality of their own countries of birth. They shared in common a uniform, a trade of battle, and a determination to survive. And a tight-knit bond of comradeship within each crew, flight and squadron which was often closer than a blood relationship. They also faced common hazards, and a varying form of death or mutilation, each time they set out on an operational flight.

Perhaps the greatest single fear among all air crews was fire. Flying in an aircraft containing thousands of gallons of highly inflammable fuel and more thousands of pounds of high explosive – mostly unprotected by armour plating – the chances of merely one sliver of red-hot flak or penetrating cannon shell avoiding hitting any vital pipeline were hair-thin. Once ignited, any outbreak of fire, particularly fuel fire, usually spread with lightning swiftness, accelerated by the torch-like effect of a 200-250 mph slipstream. A complete bomber could be consumed by fire in mere seconds at worst, even if a fuel tank or bomb failed to detonate in the soaring temperatures. Captains of any bomber set on fire needed to make split-second decisions if they were to save their crews from cremation – and by unwritten tradition a skipper was always *last t*o abandon his aircraft. It was just such a decision that had to be made by the veteran captain of Halifax DT488, 'S-Sugar' of 35 Squadron on the night of 18/19 November 1942 as he approached the southern Alps on the return leg of a bombing raid against Turin, Italy.

Wing Commander (then) Basil Vernon Robinson, DSO, DFC was a pre-war pilot, born in Gateshead in 1912 and initially commissioned in the RAF in 1933. He quickly distinguished himself playing Rugby as a wing three-quarter for the RAF and his home county XVs, and by April 1938 had been promoted to Flight Lieutenant. By 1941 he had risen to Squadron Leader and been awarded a DFC in July of that year during an operational tour with 78 Squadron, flying lumbering Whitleys over France and Germany. An ebullient character, with a distinctly unorthodox approach to certain RAF customs and procedures, his trademark was a generously proportioned ginger bushy moustache. On leaving 78 Squadron, Robinson joined 35 Squadron in late 1941, based at Linton-on-Ouse in Yorkshire, to fly Halifaxes. Indeed, 35 Squadron had been the first operational unit with the Halifax, and in August 1942 was to become one of the four 'founder-member' squadrons of the newly-created Path Finder Force (PFF).

The mode of Bomber Command operations at this stage included unescorted, long range daylight sorties to certain key objectives, particularly against German naval units and installations. One such priority target was Brest harbour, the contemporary haven for the Atlantic raiders *Scharnhorst* and *Gneisenau*, and on 18 December 1941 Basil Robinson was among the 47 bombers which set out to bomb these battleships.

In a clear, sunny, cloudless sky the mixed force of eighteen Short Stirlings, eighteen Halifaxes, and nine Avro Manchesters began their bombing from some 17,000 feet, just within a fearsome box barrage of flak gunfire, and under constant attack by German fighters which calmly penetrated the flak zone in their eagerness to close with the mini-armada of Allied heavy bombers. The sky above Brest quickly became a sprawling mêlée of individual combats and raining bombs set against a carpet of black smoke-bursts of continuing flak, and in the event four Stirlings, one Halifax and one Manchester were lost; the remaining bombers returned with varying degrees of battle damage, at least one Stirling crashing on landing back in England. The bombing appeared to have been successful, several Messerschmitt Bf 109 fighters had been claimed by the air gunners, and shortly after a total of ten decorations were awarded to various participating air crew, including Basil Robinson who received a DSO.

In March 1942 Wing Commander Jimmy Marks, DSO, DFC failed to return from an operation and his appointment as commander of 35 Squadron passed to Basil Robinson. As such Robinson continued to lead his squadron from the front; undertaking a series of sorties alongside his crews. On the night of 18/19 November 1942 the target was Turin involving a long haul across France and the Alps. Piloting Halifax 'S-Sugar', Robinson's outward trip was uneventful and he duly reached Turin and bombed, then turned for home. Unbeknown to the crew one of the marker flares had hung-up and was still in the bomb bay, and as the Alps loomed into view the Halifax fuselage was suddenly filled with acrid smoke as the flare ignited in the belly. Robinson quickly realised the cause and ordered the bomb bay doors to be opened, hoping the flare was loose enough to drop away, but the exposed flames merely spread to the port wing and increased in intensity. Taking in the situation swiftly, Robinson ordered his crew to bale out immediately and each man left the apparently doomed Halifax in quick succession. Still at his controls, Robinson quickly prepared himself to get out – then the fire went out!

Robinson checked round – it was true, the fire had just stopped. He checked to see if any of his crew was still aboard, only to be greeted with utter silence on the intercom. He was alone, in a damaged Halifax, and about 700 miles from base; a prospect of four solid hours of piloting an aircraft without benefit of navigator, flight engineer, radio operator, or even air gunners for defence if he met nightfighters. The thought of baling out flicked through his mind – at least he'd be safe – but he rejected it as quickly, then settled into his bucket seat for the solo mini-marathon flight ahead.

Crossing the Alps and then droning on over France, Robinson was lucky not to run into any roving Luftwaffe *Nachtjäger* – perhaps the fact that he *was* alone saved him in this respect – but on reaching England he had no means of calculating an accurate route to his own airfield. Without a radio to warn those below, he put the Halifax down on the first aerodrome he could find, Colerne in Wiltshire, switching on all lights he could reach in order to indicate his presence and intention. Rolling to a stop, he climbed out to meet the ground staff awaiting him – and derived an embarrassed amusement at the looks on their faces when they realised that no other crew men were aboard. His lone flight brought Robinson a Bar to his DFC.

On 1 May 1943 Robinson was promoted to Group Captain and appointed commander of RAF Graveley. Station commanders were severely restricted by higher authority from undertaking operations, being rationed to two or three sorties per month at most. Robinson, typically, selected particularly tough targets for his few trips, and on the night of 23/24 August 1943 the tough target was Berlin – the 'Big City'. He personally briefed Graveley's crews, then took a scratch crew out in a Halifax of his old unit, 35 Squadron. Of the 719 bombers despatched to Berlin that night – 117 of these PFF aircraft – 56 failed to return, including two 'Station Masters', Group Captain A. H. Willetts from Oakington, and Group Captain Basil Vernon Robinson, DSO, DFC, AFC.

Six nights before Basil Robinson undertook his ultimate, fated sortie, a force of 597 four-engined heavies set out on a special operation – to destroy the German 'flying bomb' research and experimental station at Peenemünde on the Baltic coast. Apart from its singular nature, the raid introduced the role of Master of Ceremonies, or Master Bomber as the job was more familiarly titled later. The post was self-explanatory – a chosen, well experienced bomber pilot who would arrive over the target before the PFF marker aircraft, assess conditions, guide in the initial marking and illuminating aircraft, then remain in the target area throughout the main force's actual attack, correcting faulty marking or bombing continuously by personal radio instructions, and generally supervising the whole conduct of the assault. Deliberately to remain in the target zone for any period up to an hour or even longer on occasion, subjected to constant danger from flak, nightfighters, even possible air collision, required a special type of stoic determination and no small courage.

The role of MC had in essence first been applied by Wing Commander Guy Gibson during the famed 617 'Dam-busting' operation in May 1943, but the Peenemünde operation amounted to the first regular use of the role for a major bombing attack. Master Bomber for the Peenemünde raid was Group Captain John Searby, commander of 83 Squadron, PFF, a pilot well-versed in heavy bomber operations, who had first rehearsed the Master Bomber role during a raid against Turin on 7 August 1943.

John Searby had been born in April 1913 at Whittlesey in Cambridgeshire, and joined the RAF as a Halton Aircraft Apprentice in 1929. By 1935 he had gained his pilot's wings as a Sergeant, and after service with Nos. 104, 106 and 108 Squadrons, was commissioned at the outbreak of war in 1939, sent on the Specialist 'N' (Navigation) course, then became an instructor at a Bristol Blenheim bomber OTU. His next posting was to Ferry Command on the North Atlantic route and later, as a Flight Lieutenant, he opened the South Atlantic run. A brief spell in 1941 as a staff officer was followed by promotion to Squadron Leader and an appointment as a Group Navigation Officer; then in 1942 he joined No. 106 Squadron as a Flight commander to fly Manchesters and Lancasters on his first full tour of operations.

Commanded by Wing Commander Guy Gibson, DSO, DFC (later, VC), 106 Squadron then was based at Coningsby in mid-1942, moving base to Syerston in September, and in the forefront of Bomber Command's nightly offensive, but also contributed ten Lancasters to the daring daylight attack on Le Creusot in October 1942. In March 1943 Searby was awarded a DFC, then succeeded Guy Gibson in command of 106 Squadron, before being further promoted to Group Captain and appointed CO of No. 83 Squadron, PFF at Wyton on 9 May 1943.

The Peenemünde operation was specially mounted, a 'one-off' target which, the air crews were told at briefing, 'If you don't knock it out tonight, it'll be laid on again tomorrow night and every night until the job's done'; a chilling thought to the more experienced crews. It was also to be a precision attack, concentrating on the destruction of specific buildings, as opposed to the more normal area attack methods then in use. Accordingly, three aiming points were to be marked and bombed, instead of merely one.

Secrecy about the operation was paramount and, apart from one or two hierarchy, only Searby and his 'master' crew knew the target prior to the actual briefing, being shown a model of the objective on the day before by Air Vice-Marshal Don Bennett, the 'boss' of PFF. In all, 43 squadrons were to provide the main heavy bomber force, in three waves, while eight Mosquitos of 139 Squadron were to precede that bomber stream and carry out a spoof attack on Berlin in the hope of drawing off the Luftwaffe's nightfighters. Searby's allotted position as Master Bomber was backed by two Deputy Masters, Wing Commanders Johnny Fauquier, the hardbitten veteran commanding 405 (Canadian) Squadron, and J. H. White of 156 Squadron. The main force finally comprised over 500 Lancasters and Halifaxes, plus Stirlings from 100 Group and other units.

All crews were briefed during the afternoon of 17 August, though the *reason* for the raid – hopefully to halt the development and production of V1 and V2 missiles – was not disclosed even then. By 8 pm the crews were ready to board their aircraft, and John Searby, at the controls of Lancaster JA928 'W-William', was first away, some five minutes ahead of the main force to give him time to study the target before ordering in the spearhead PFF marker aircraft.

The night was a full moon and as the bombers reached the English coast each dropped down to no more than 200 feet above the sea to prevent German early warning radar spotting the incoming aircraft. The first clashes with the Luftwaffe occurred near the enemy coast, but not by the bombers. Five Messerschmitt Bf 110s of IV/NJG 1 were ordered to intercept a group of low-flying 'bombers' off the Frisians and, led by Oberleutnant Schnaufer, found these to be Beaufighters of 141 Squadron, led by Wing Commander John Braham. The meeting resulted in three Bf 110s going down in flames.

As this combat was taking place, the first bombers were heading inland across Denmark, and alert warnings began to be sent to the various Luftwaffe nightfighter bases, resulting in a total of 213 *Nachtjäger* getting airborne. Meanwhile 139 Squadron's feint attack on Berlin, though recognised by Luftwaffe J Korps, as a spoof, achieved its objective as far as the Berlin defenders were concerned. Alerting the *Wildesau* ('Wild Boar') fighters of JG300, *without* notifying other outlying Luftwaffe central controllers, the Berlin control effectively massed the bulk of nightfighters over Berlin – 100 miles away from Peenemünde and the main bomber stream. Confusion was added to confusion as the first 100 or so nightfighters reached the capital and began circling to await the arrival of the RAF, causing a few trigger-happy flak gunners to commence firing blindly into the night skies, until eventually all 89 flak batteries were blazing away at the 'phantom' raiders.

While all this initial chaos reigned over Berlin, Searby had reached Peenemünde, scanned the target to clearly identify aiming points, then patiently waited for a few minutes until the leading PFF aircraft arrived to illuminate Peenemünde with their flares first, then put down yellow and green ground markers for the main force to bomb on. As the attack began to develop, the frustrated nightfighters still circuiting Berlin realised their controllers' error. The single-engined fighters by then had little alternative but to land with emptying fuel tanks, but a few twin-engined fighters, with more fuel reserves, set course immediately for Peenemünde. The clear moonlight gave perfect visibility for the fighter crews, and within twenty minutes of the bombing beginning the leading nightfighters began to reach the bombers. As the final wave of bombers commenced their own attack the fighters plunged through the aircraft stream, hacking at each target to come within range. Several bombers were destroyed in the first onslaught but the bulk of the bomber stream were by then on the first legs of their return flights, racing hard for the Danish coast and the relative safety of the North Sea.

Searby, meantime, continued to orbit the target, directing, correcting, concentrating the final bombing of Peenemünde, which by then was almost obscured by the smoke and fires of the previous bombing waves. To ensure accuracy, Searby orbited much lower than the main force, running a constant risk of being hit by the steady rain of 4,000 lb 'Cookies' and other explosive stores dropping all around him. Then, at 1 pm, having been over the target for almost an hour, John Searby tucked into the tail-end of the retreating main force aircraft heading for home. Below, the target was now totally obscured by smoke. Within minutes Lancaster 'W-William' came under attack by a nightfighter, but Searby's gunners managed to damage it, causing it to disappear. Dropping down to minimum height over the Baltic Sea, Searby and his crew could see that a running battle between the returning bombers and nightfighters was being fiercely fought higher up, as bomber after bomber succumbed to pointblank range cannon assaults.

Finally, at 0431 hours on 18 August, John Searby landed back at Wyton – seven hours and 39 minutes after original take-off. The losses amounted to 40 heavy bombers and one Mosquito missing, with a further 32 damaged by flak, fighters or bad landings – 287 air crew men who had failed to return. Unbeknown to the bomber men, the Luftwaffe had lost twelve night fighters in action that night, nine of these in aerial combat. In less than two hours' concentrated aerial clashes almost 300 men had died.

One week later John Searby was awarded an immediate DSO for his leadership of the raid. He remained with 83 Squadron on operations until 2 November 1943 when he handed over his command to Wing Commander Ray Hilton, DSO, DFC and became station commander of RAF Upwood. In July 1944 he went to Bomber Command

Headquarters as Command Navigation Officer, remaining in this post until the end of the war. His postwar career saw him eventually retire as an Air Commodore.

The qualities which added up to a 'born leader' have always been difficult to define in cold print. Moreover, the qualities looked for by 'subordinates' varied considerably. At the lowest level of the initial formation of an air crew for bombers at the OTU stage of training, a high proportion of individual crew members tried to link up with the quiet, seemingly steady type of pilot-skipper, preferably a married man of slightly older age than themselves. Their reasoning was pragmatic – a captain with a wife and children would *want* to survive, hence their own chances of survival seemed greater. Wishful thinking, perhaps, but only too real to youngsters about to place their unfulfilled lives in jeopardy. Other men looked for something specific in their new boss – previous experience perhaps or a certain look about him which suggested strength of will.

The lay image of the steel-jawed, aggressive pilot who knew no fear belonged almost wholly to cheap fiction and Hollywood invention. Some outstanding air leaders, men like Basil Embry, were unstoppable bundles of unceasing energy and action; men whose very presence emanated an aura of determination and utter self-confidence in all matters. Yet such men were the exception in Bomber Command. Many acknowledged bomber barons, held in the highest regard by their fellow men, were outwardly the very antithesis of such obvious, natural courage. To give merely one prominent example of such quiet, instinctive leaders, Wing Commander John Fulton, DSO, DFC, AFC – or 'Moose' as he was invariably known.

Fulton, a Canadian born in Kamloops, British Columbia, had learned to fly initially in 1931 at the tender age of eighteen, and in 1934 came to England to join the RAF, being awarded his wings and a commission in March 1935. In September that year he joined his first squadron, No. 10, based at Boscombe Down, Wiltshire, to fly the huge biplane Handley Page Heyford bombers – the beginning of a seven-years' association with heavy bombers. He eventually commenced operations in June 1940 and soon began to display an inward determination to overcome all odds, exemplified during one sortie in September to Brussels when his starboard engine failed on the outward flight. All attempts to re-start the recalcitrant motor apparently failed, so Fulton reluctantly turned back. Shortly after the stubborn engine restarted and Fulton immediately turned and resumed his intended sortie, reached Brussels, then made two bombing runs over the city's railway junction with excellent results. By the end of his first operational tour Fulton was a Squadron Leader and in October 1940 was awarded a DFC.

His rest period in 1941 was spent on experimental and development flying at Farnborough, work which brought him the further award of an Air Force Cross (AFC) in the 1942 New Year's Honours List, but just prior to this decoration Fulton, now a Wing Commander, had returned to the sharp end of bombing operations. At Mildenhall in Suffolk on 15 December 1941, No. 3 Group, Bomber Command acquired its first Canadian unit, No. 419 Squadron RCAF, when the latter – the third RCAF heavy bomber unit to be inaugurated in the UK – came into existence. Its equipment comprised Wellington bombers, the first two aircraft arriving on the squadron three weeks later, and on 11 January 1942 the unit despatched its first operational sorties – Wellingtons Z1145, VR-A (Pilot Officer T. G. Cottier) and X9748, VR-B, piloted by the squadron's first appointed commander, John Fulton.

His arrival on the squadron was inauspicious, quietly assuming command and immediately tackling the myriad problems of preparing his unit for operations as quickly as possible. The bulk of the crews were fellow Canadians, who regarded Fulton with some awe and no small puzzlement at first. His DFC ribbon denoted experience and guts, while the AFC ribbon next to it implied outstanding flying skills. Yet the man's appearance gave no obvious display of such qualities. Chubby-faced, with a shock of red hair, shy on first acquaintance, even apt to blush on occasion – he looked more like the average successful business executive in the City.

Any lingering doubts about the boss's capabilities were short-lived when operations commenced. Fulton could always be found among his crews when any particularly rough target appeared on the battle order. Even so, he seldom, if ever, used his rank and status to obtain the best aircraft or even the best crew. On the night of 30/31 May 1942 the first-ever '1,000-bomber' raid – against Cologne on this night – was ordered. No. 419's contribution initially was sixteen Wellingtons, all the serviceable Mk III Wimpys available, but each had its own crew allotted.

Fulton, determined not to miss this historic sortie, nevertheless refused to replace any of his young skippers and instead got his ground staff to produce a clapped-out Wellington Mk 1c, used as a training hack on the station. It had no GEE radar aids, and would be some

50 mph slower than the Mk IIIs, but Fulton, recruiting a scratch crew together, earmarked it as 'his', then went to Cologne. Always trailing well behind the other 419 Squadron Wellingtons, Fulton reached the target, bombed from barely 17,000 feet, then came home without incident. On another specifically ordered operation against U-boat pens at Hamburg – a particularly dicey trip – Fulton was emphatically ordered by Group HQ *not* to fly; but when the detailed crews arrived at their dispersal they found Fulton already there, fully kitted up and ready to go.

One sortie which demonstrated Fulton's inner strength occurred on the night of 28/29 April 1942. The target was Kiel – 419's first 'visit' to this port – and Fulton led his men to the objective, bombed, and began the home run; only to be attacked by a Messerschmitt Bf 110 nightfighter just as he left the enemy coastline. The Bf 110's fire was deadly accurate, shattering the Wellington's rear gun turret and wounding its occupant, Flight Lieutenant O'Callaghan, slicing through the hydraulics system thereby causing the bomber's under-carriage to flop down and the bomb bay doors to drop open, wrecked most instruments, blew a chunk out of the port propeller, and sieved the fabric-covered fuselage in a hundred places. Flying at only 1,500 feet at that moment, Fulton felt the mounting vibration from the port engine, quickly feathered the broken propeller, then dropped down to a mere twenty feet above the North Sea.

By then the nightfighter had vanished, so Fulton took a chance and restarted the port engine. The vibration began to build again, threatening the wing structure, but the added power gave Fulton the opportunity to gain some height. Meanwhile his observer, Sergeant E. S. 'Red' Alexander, though himself wounded in the arm, went back to the rear turret, hacked the rear doors off the turret with a fire-axe, then extricated the injured gunner. Once satisfied that the gunner was being cared for, 'Red' went up front again and helped Fulton navigate the crippled Wimpy back to base. On arrival over Mildenhall, Fulton realised that his undercarriage and flaps were unreliable and therefore brought his aircraft in for a supremely skilful belly-landing. Examination of the riddled Wellington next day revealed the extent of the damage – how Fulton had managed to keep it airborne remained a mystery to the other crews. Shortly after Alexander received a DFM for his part in the sortie, while John Fulton was awarded a DSO.

Continuing to lead 419's crews to Germany during the short summer nights of 1942, Fulton was at their head on the night of

28/29 July, attacking Hamburg. Weather conditions were foul, with severe icing and dense clouds, while the flak and nightfighter defences were particularly heavy. One 419 Squadron Wellington failed to return next morning – the aircraft skippered by John Fulton. The last fix placed him some ten miles west of one of the Frisian Islands, and his last message to base read, 'Fighters . . . wounded . . . 500' – then silence.

Some weeks before his death John Fulton had been at a ceremonial occasion in London when the Lord Mayor had presented 419 Squadron with 'Bruce the Moose', a stuffed, mounted moose's head, as the unit's official mascot. Fulton thereafter became nicknamed 'Moose' himself, and it is an indication of the high regard and deep respect in which Fulton was held by his squadron that after his death No. 419 Squadron RCAF included the title ('Moose') after its number in all future references; a tribute which became a permanent epitaph when, in June 1944, HM King George VI authorised the squadron's official badge. Its central motif is an attacking moose, and the squadron was legally adopted by John Fulton's birthplace, Kamloops, BC, Canada.

The losses of such brilliant bomber captains as John Fulton so early in the war were tragic enough in themselves, but in the broader view deprived the RAF of many potentially great future senior commanders, both in the war and indeed the subsequent peace years. In September 1939 the RAF had in the ranks of its air crews a host of junior officers and senior NCOs who had committed themselves to fulltime careers in the Service. Such men had been nurtured and shaped for their RAF futures via the Service's own nurseries – Trenchard's aircraft apprentice scheme and the Cranwell Cadet College – and at the outbreak of war represented the spine of the RAF; the core which had to bear the initial brunt of operations – and casualties – until wartime recruitment had trained and produced the swelling numbers of crews that would later share the responsibilities of prosecuting the aerial offensive against the Third Reich and its Axis partners.

Inevitably, many of those early crew members were destined to suffer a high casualty rate – relatively, they were too few in number to provide total coverage in the myriad campaigns and responsibilities undertaken by the RAF in 1939–40. Thus many individuals who displayed outstanding prowess during those years did not live to share their vital skills and experience with the incoming tyro air crews. Such men flashed across the screen of operational flying all too briefly before paying the ultimate price for their courage and determination; performing unpublicised acts of valour and splendid example, then being slowly forgotten as the tempo of the air war increased and enlarged.

One of those many potentially great leaders was James Anderson Pitcairn-Hill – 'Jamie' to his many friends and associates. Born in Prinlaws, Fife, Jamie decided early in life that his future could only be with the RAF, and he joined the Service as an aircraft apprentice at Halton in September 1932. Tall, strong, and gifted athletically, his academic abilities were equally well above the average, and on completing his apprenticeship in August 1935 he was one of the few granted a direct cadetship to the RAF College, Cranwell. His two years' Cranwell training was spent in the company of many cadets later to carve out highly distinguished RAF careers, including such men as Peter Wykeham-Barnes and Leslie Mavor, both of whom became Air Marshals.

Eventually graduating in July 1937 and receiving a permanent commission as a Pilot Officer, Pitcairn-Hill's first posting was to No. 83 Squadron, based at Turnhouse – a bomber unit equipped then with biplane Hawker Hinds, commanded by Squadron Leader L. S. Snaith, AFC. The peacetime routine of air exercises, public displays, and tactical practices provided 83's crews with plentiful air experience, while on 14 March 1938 the squadron *en bloc* moved south to take up permanent residence at Scampton, just north of Lincoln. Little more than six months later the unit began re-equipment with the type of aircraft it was destined to fly initially in the imminent European war, the Hampden; the first example, L4048, being collected on 31 October 1938, and full unit complement being achieved by 9 January 1939.

On 21 August 1939 Wing Commander R. B. Jordan replaced Leonard Snaith as 83's CO. His arrival coincided with a welter of activity as the squadron prepared to mobilise for the 'real thing', and on the first day of the war, Sunday, 3 September, six Hampdens of 83 Squadron took off on the first operational sorties – an optimistically-briefed task of 'attacking the German Fleet'. . . . In the event, the 'German Fleet' was not located and the Hampdens ditched their bomb loads in the North Sea during the return flight. This initial panic operation was the first of only four operations flown by 83 Squadron for the rest of the year; in the interim the crews returned to a frustrating series of training exercises, though even these were finally curtailed in January 1940 due to the severity of that winter's weather conditions. Pitcairn-Hill, by then a Flight Lieutenant, participated in the unit's detachment to Lossiemouth in February 1940 – a month which produced fourteen sorties only – but returned with the squadron to Scampton on 20 March to resume night flying exercises and stand-bys for leaflet raids which, in the event, failed to materialise.

If 83 Squadron's first six months of war had, like so many other RAF units, been somewhat 'phoney war', April 1940 saw it commence operations on an ever-escalating scale. The German invasion of Norway provided the basis for a total of 45 sorties that month, with Pitcairn-Hill and his fellow crews undertaking their first trips in anger against enemy targets. In May came an increase to 75 sorties, including the squadron's first forays against targets inside Germany itself; while June 1940 saw the Hampden crews tot up a total of 142 sorties as the Nazi 'blitzkrieg' assault on the Low Countries and France swept on. Pitcairn-Hill's part in these soon established him as one of the unit's most determined pilots, pressing home his attacks against all opposition without apparent regard for his personal safety, and on 9 July the award of a DFC was promulgated. July 1940 continued the pace of the Hampdens' offensive, pounding German land and and naval objectives. On 11 July the target was Ludwigshaven, when Pitcairn-Hill in Hampden L4094 ran through a particularly accurate flak barrage as he deliberately bombed from low altitude, then brought his riddled aircraft back to base.

On the night of 12/13 August 1940 Pitcairn-Hill, by now an acting Squadron Leader, piloted Hampden P4402 in the lead of a specially-ordered operation – to breach the vital Dortmund-Ems Canal. Eleven Hampdens – six from 49 Squadron and five from 83 Squadron – were despatched; five of these carrying special canister-'mine' bombs detailed for the actual attack on the canal aqueduct carrying the canal over the river Ems, north of Munster, while the other Hampdens carried out diversionary raids nearby. Alongside each canal bank the Germans had installed a deadly row of flak sites and searchlight batteries, and shortly after 11 pm, in the clear light of a half-moon, Jamie Pitcairn-Hill took his Hampden down to 100 feet and began his bombing run through the straight lane of flak guns, the first of the five aircraft attacks. His aircraft immediately became the focus of an unceasing barrage, with searchlights attempting to blind his forward view, but in spite of a succession of shells tearing chunks out of his aircraft and buffeting him, Jamie pressed home his attack and dropped his canister into the canal before banking out of the danger zone and limping home.

Behind him, the next two Hampdens attempting to follow suit were blasted out of the sky, the next had one engine shattered but managed to get back to England, while the fifth, Hampden P4403, piloted by Flight Lieutenant Roderick Learoyd of 49 Squadron, completed his run by breaching the waterway, then returning to Scampton in such a damaged state that he was forced to wait circling the airfield until dawn gave him sufficient light to make a safe landing. Shortly after this raid, Learoyd was awarded a Victoria Cross, while Pitcairn-Hill received a DSO for his leadership and example on the sortie.

In September 1940, with the Battle of Britain reaching its peak of intensity, Bomber Command began concentrating on destroying the concentration of German invasion barges being gathered into a string of French and Dutch ports along the English Channel. 83 Squadron's biggest nightly force – 15 Hampdens – that month set out on the night of 15 September to bomb barges gathered at Antwerp, and before the evening was over one of the unit's youngest air gunners, John Hannah, had won a Victoria Cross for staying with his pilot in a burning Hampden. Three nights later nine more Hampdens set out from Scampton to bomb some French docks, among them Jamie Pitcairn-Hill in Hampden P1183. Over the target, at low altitude, his aircraft was seen to explode – a direct hit by flak. Squadron Leader Pitcairn-Hill, DSO, DFC and his crew Pilot Officers Linsdell, Rendell, and Sergeant McCarthy failed to return. . . .

If many of the acknowledged bomber barons achieved such a recognition through sheer leadership and eventual senior rank, no few became minor legends among bomber crews by the sheer forcefulness of their characters – men who ran up long operational tallies, but were also outstanding personalities and invaluable factors for maintaining morale among the younger crews when things were going badly. Take the example of Squadron Leader T. W. – 'Tommy' – Blair, DSO, DFC & Bar. Tommy was a navigator – virtually the doyen of PFF navigators eventually – who flew nearly 100 sorties over Germany, spread over three tours; yet claimed that he only survived because of a lack of imagination. Those who flew alongside Blair thought differently – to them Tommy was the epitome of the 'press-on' type; tough, efficient, yet unfailingly displaying an extrovert gaiety and joviality which was always infectious. At squadron parties at the Ferryboat Inn, Tommy Blair would always be leading the festivities, tankard in hand and his deep 'earthquake' voice resounding around the bar; yet any day his name appeared on the night's battle order Blair drank just one half-pint of light ale with his lunch. Powerfully built, with the quicksilver lightness of movement of the natural athlete, Tommy Blair exuded confidence; yet found private peace when relaxing in the mess ante-room after any raid by listening to the gentle music of a fellow officer playing the mess piano.

Blair's first tour was on Hampdens and Manchesters in 1941 – a period which Blair later described as 'gentlemanly – we bombed how and when we liked, and were left very much to our own devices'. By late 1942, and his second tour, however, he was flying Lancasters and 'things got far more serious'. It could be said Tommy had been lucky on his first tour – not once had his aircraft been damaged. The second tour proved 'more dangerous', though Blair always returned and came to be regarded as almost a good luck charm by the crews he flew with. During 1943–44, Blair, who rose to Squadron Leader in this period, flew with 83 Squadron on some of the unit's hardest operations, when the air crew casualty rate rose alarmingly. Strangely, such casualties seldom affected Blair due (he claimed) to his lack of imagination – to Tommy the missing crews had merely been posted elsewhere and would probably be met again sometime in the future. Whether in fact Tommy truly *believed* this remains a moot point; in private his deeply camouflaged sensitivity occasionally brought personal grief to the surface. When, for instance, he heard of the death of Wing Commander Guy Gibson, VC, a man whom Blair had always regarded with particular admiration, Tommy Blair, the squadron's tough guy, retired to his room and wept.

If Tommy Blair's presence aboard any bomber boosted the crew's morale, so did that of Sammy. Sammy was Blair's pet cocker spaniel dog, floppy, sad-eyed, with a lugubrious expression ever associated with the breed. Sammy flew on 50 sorties with Tommy, visiting the Ruhr twenty times, and Berlin four times, and was usually to be found curled up under the wireless operator's table – near the aircraft heater – asleep, despite all hell being roused outside by flak *et al*. Only when the aircraft had its undercarriage lowered for landing did Sammy usually become active, making his way forward to the bomb aimer's perspex nose panel to cast a critical eye over the skipper's landing technique. Bureaucracy had forbidden the carriage of animals, pets, or unauthorised passengers in RAF aircraft – but men voluntarily facing extreme peril are seldom impressed by 'pen-pushing' dictates.

They gave Tommy Blair a DFC in June 1943, a DSO in the following month, and a Bar to his DFC in October 1944 when he had finally been taken off operations. On the day after his final sortie Blair was summoned to Bomber Command HQ for an interview, but when he returned to his station he heard that his crew, with a fresh navigator, had been all killed in an air collision over a target.

This news, more than anything else which had happened to Blair throughout his lengthy operational career, cut deeply into Tommy's soul; but an incident which occurred only days after peace had been officially declared in early 1945 remained in Blair's memory most clearly until his last days. Operation Exodus – the air repatriation of British prisoners of war from Germany – commenced in April 1945, and on one airfield batches of RAF air crew ex-PoWs, mostly ex-bomber men, had been embarked in various Lancasters for the trip to England. On take-off, several Lancasters crashed, killing all aboard – this was Tommy Blair's most poignant recollection, this hurt him the most.

For most tyro crews arriving on their first operational squadron, the prospect of finally going to war was – at best – worrying. How would each man stand up to the crucial test of his courage when he first ventured into enemy skies? Would he be able to accept the risks and carry on? Worst of all, would he let the rest of his crew down when it came to a crunch? And, at the back of every man's mind was the thought – will I survive? Fresh crews arriving from OTUs to join No. 35 Squadron at Graveley in late 1943 to mid-1944 were rapidly brought down to earth on their first acquaintance with their unit commander. Ushered into the Wing Commander's office, they saw at his desk a young 23-year-old pilot, with the ribbons of the DSO and DFC below his wings, but suspended above his head was an axe! Once introductions had been made, the Wing Commander calmly pointed upwards and told them, 'That's what you'll get here – the bip chop', followed by an explosive laugh so infectious that the new men immediately relaxed. It was a harmless, near-childish joke, but Wing Commander Sydney Patrick Daniels – 'Pat' – knew only too well what was needed to get his crews up to scratch; he was a veteran of bomber operations serving on his third tour.

Born in 1921, Pat Daniels joined the RAF at the age of eighteen and in September 1940 commenced his first tour of ops with No. 58 Squadron, flying Whitley Vs from Linton-on-Ouse to Germany, bombing targets as far afield as Zeebrugge, Berlin, Cologne, Emden, Mannheim and Brest, the last target resulting in a crash-landing back

at base in early May 1941. In the following month, as a Flight
Lieutenant, he was awarded a DFC, then rested at the end of his tour.
In 1942 Pat Daniels, now a Squadron Leader, joined 83 Squadron
at Wyton to start his second tour, this time as one of the first group
of Pathfinders in the newly-created PFF, and in December that year
undertook the role of Master Bomber for an intended raid against
Munich, though in the event the raid was cancelled due to severe
weather conditions, and it fell to Guy Gibson, vc, then later John
Searby, formally to introduce the Master Bomber role on an actual
operation.

Daniels' period with 83 Squadron saw him leading many of the
unit's heaviest attacks against German objectives, acting as marker
or deputy Master Bomber on many occasions. His press-on spirit was
always evident, though he often achieved results by unofficial tactics,
ignoring on occasion the recommended altitudes, etc, when his past
experience dictated more practical methods. The 'chop rate' on 83
Squadron at that period was dauntingly high yet crew morale
remained good; aided by men like Pat Daniels who played as hard as
he worked. In November 1942 he was awarded a Bar to his DFC,
and in March 1943, at the close of his second tour, added a DSO to
his ribbons for 'exceptional leadership and outstanding determination'.

It took Daniels just six months to get back into operations when, in
November 1943 he was appointed Wing Commander to succeed Wing
Commander D. F. E. C. 'Dixie' Dean, DFC (later, DSO) as commander of No. 35 Squadron, PFF at Graveley. His squadron operated
Halifaxes, and Pat Daniels took up the reins of command at a
particularly active period; in December 1943 alone the unit lost 37
air crew members over Germany. As might have been expected of
Pat, he was soon on the battle orders, leading his men up-front, often
as Master Bomber for the main force's raids. On the night of 30/31
March 1944 Daniels piloted one of his newest crews to Nuremburg
– his 77th operational sortie of the war – but on the outward flight
soon realised that if he stayed with the main stream of bombers
flying at the briefed height his chances of returning were not going
to be too healthy. In crystal-clear moonlight conditions, the main
stream began to come under constant attack from a horde of German
nightfighters, and as Daniels looked down from several thousands of
feet higher altitude to which his instinct had driven him to climb, he
could see the results as bomber after bomber succumbed to fighter
onslaught. Daniels returned from the disaster of that Nuremburg raid,
in which Bomber Command suffered its heaviest loss figures for any

single operation of the war, but as he said later, 'I thought it was getting a bit dangerous and it was time I packed it in'. . . .

Dangerous or not, however, Pat Daniels remained with 35 Squadron for another four months of operations. His vast experience and coolness under fire continued to see him appointed as Master Bomber for certain precision bombing attacks; as on 7 July when he master-minded an attack by 457 Halifaxes and Lancasters on Caen, to obliterate the strong German ground resistance to the Allied armies in the Normandy beach-head zones. It was a task requring absolute precision and direction because forward Allied infantry positions lay less than 2,000 yards from the target area. In the course of almost forty minutes, the main force concentrated 2,363 tons of high explosive bombs on the German positions, reducing these to rubble and so dazing the German troops there that these offered little resistance to advancing Allied infantry next day.

Daniels finally retired from the operational scene on 25 July 1944 when he handed command of 35 Squadron back to newly-promoted Group Captain Dixie Dean, and shortly after Pat received the award of a Bar to his DSO. The *London Gazette* citation for this, promulgated in October 1944, read in part : 'He has pressed home his attacks with the greatest determination and his coolness and courage in the face of enemy fire have been most inspiring. He is a highly efficient squadron commander whose sterling qualities have impressed all.'

If the majority of acknowledged bomber barons achieved their deserved reputations almost entirely on operations with the frontline squadrons of Bomber Command, a relative handful of those men not only flew 'normal' operations but also spent long periods on developing and testing certain vital equipment and aircraft intended to improve the quality and ultimate success of firstline bombing. It was hush-hush, highly secret work, necessitating rare skills and unusual expertise; unpublicised, unglamorous, rarely rewarded by honours and decorations, yet a foundation for the eventual supremacy of the Allied bombing offensive against Germany. The crews involved in such back room experimentation and trials possessed particular qualities of determination, allied with flying skill, technical understanding, and no little foresight – men like Harry Emlyn Bufton – 'Hal'.

There were two Bufton brothers, the elder being Sydney Osborne Bufton, born in 1908, who entered the RAF, and was then commissioned in December 1927. By 1937 'Syd' had risen to Squadron

Leader and in July 1940 was CO of No. 10 Squadron. Receiving a
DFC in November that year, Syd next commanded No. 76 Squadron;
then with the rank of Group Captain he commanded RAF Pockling-
ton, before moving to the Air Ministry to become Deputy Director of
Bomber Operations. He eventually retired from the RAF as Air
Vice-Marshal, CB, DFC in October 1961.

The younger Bufton brother, Hal, was born in May 1916 and
joined the RAF as a cadet at Cranwell in 1934. Commissioned in
December 1936, Hal's first posting was to No. 214 Squadron at
Scampton to fly the new Handley Page Harrow bombers then beginning to re-equip the squadron. By the outbreak of war Hal was a
Flight Lieutenant, and in mid-1940 was appointed a flight commander on the 'secret' BAT & DU (Blind Approach Technical &
Development Unit) at Boscombe Down, Wiltshire, the RAF's main
experimental station then. Virtually under the personal control of the
Prime Minister himself, the BATDU had the highest priority for any
needed equipment to accomplish its prime concern with discovering
the means and methods of guided night bombing then being used over
Britain by the Luftwaffe; especially the so-termed *Knickebein*
(literally, 'Crooked Leg') radio beam navigational aid. The BATDU
was also in close partnership with the civilian-manned TRE (Tele-
communications Research Establishment) at Swanage; a boffin
scientific research centre investigating the improvement and possible
future airborne use of what would later become generically titled
radar.

Hal Bufton spent many months with the BATDU (later to be
retitled WIDU – Wireless Investigation Development Unit – and even
later to become the nucleus of the reformed No. 109 Squadron). His
job included discovering the technical details of *Knickebein*, then
testing and inaugurating tactics to defeat this German beam system.
It meant many hours of plodding around the night skies in tired
Ansons and Whitleys, proving his theories, but achieved workable
results. By early 1941, however, Hal Bufton managed to be posted to
operations, being posted to No. 9 Squadron at Honington, Suffolk to
fly Wellingtons. In February 1941 Hal set out to bomb an Italian
target but was forced to ditch in the Mediterranean. He was rescued
by a Spanish fisherman, with whom he stayed for two months before
finally returning to his squadron a month later and resuming
operations.

Just three months later, on 26 August, while skippering Wellington
W5703 in a raid on Cologne, he was shot down again! His luck

still held out and he evaded capture by the Germans, being gradually fed down the escapers' line by patriots to Gibraltar, and arriving back in England again in time to celebrate Christmas 1941 in more congenial surroundings.

On 10 July 1942, as a Wing Commander, he was appointed commander of No. 109 Squadron – virtually a return to his old BATDU/WIDU Flight. By now 109 was a full squadron, based at Stradishall but moving to Wyton on 6 August. Its equipment when Bufton arrived was Wellingtons, though in August 1942 the unit began receiving Mosquitos and by December was completely Mosquito-equipped. Its role, too, was almost a continuation of Bufton's former radio/radar investigation-cum-testing trials – in 109's case, proving and introducing the Oboe radar blind-bombing system to Bomber Command operations. From August 1942 it became completely associated with the new PFF, though technically part of the PFF's initial paper strength.

For the closing months of 1942 the squadron steadily built up to operational strength in crews and Mosquitos, training hard to perfect their Oboe techniques; then on 20 December, though still having only six trained crews and eight Mosquitos, 109 Squadron flew the first Oboe operation, attacking a coking plant at Lutterade in east Holland. By January 1943 four more crews became fully operational, and on 15 February four crews bombed a German officer-cadet school at St Trond in Belgium, obtaining direct hits on target. These, and other, 'small' sorties were in the nature of proving trials for Oboe, but on the night of 5/6 March 1943 the device was given its first real blooding.

The target was Essen – Bomber Command's No. 1 'choice' objective – and a force of 442 heavy bombers in the main force were preceded by eight Oboe Mosquitos, backed up by eight Lancasters of 83 Squadron,* to mark the aiming point. The result was a more accurate and destructive attack than any previous assault on Essen – it was the opening round of the so-termed Battle of the Ruhr. Of the eight Oboe Mosquitos, led by Hal Bufton, three had failures in the Oboe equipment(including to his chagrin, Bufton's) while one put its red target indicators down more than two miles astray; but the remaining four gave precise marking for the 'backers-up' to supplement with their green TIs, resulting in a high proportion of the following main force bombing accurately. This Essen success set the

* Including Lancaster ED601, skippered by R. A. 'Wimpy' Wellington whose navigator was Tommy Blair.

future pattern for Oboe spearheading of major raids; vindicating the long and difficult proving months undergone by Hal Bufton and his few crews from 109 Squadron.

In early 1943 Hal Bufton received the awards of an AFC and a DFC within weeks of each other, tardy recognition of several years' patient, skilled flying. He remained with 109 for the rest of 1943, still operating and continuously testing fresh methods of improving the accuracy and range of Oboe; but on 6 March 1944, with promotion to Group Captain, he was given command of RAF Bourn, then received a DSO for outstanding leadership in past operations. Here he remained until the end of the war, then stayed in the RAF until retirement in March 1961. Hal Bufton, DSO, OBE, DFC, AFC, Oboe pioneer, died in Canada in September 1972.

CHAPTER TWENTY-TWO

Greater Love hath no Man. . . .

Self-preservation is among man's highest primal instincts, a natural inherited selfishness stamped on the consciousness of the human character as the base-rock of ultimate survival of the species. How then does one explain the myriad occasions when man in battle deliberately sacrificed themselves in order that others might live? Indeed, what force drove men voluntarily to place unfulfilled lives on the brink of constant jeopardy in defence of their homeland? Patriotism may have played a large part; most fighting men of the 1939-45 war had grown up in an era when 'King and Country' had been a meaningful concept. Duty – that much-abused abstract – had been another inherited facet of youthful upbringing in the early years of the present century; an imposed code of obligated conduct accepted by youth from its elders as a natural self-discipline. Certainly, in the context of operational air crews, there was no question of mere mindless obedience to orders; the very nature of air crew duties of all types demanded men with intelligence, above-average education, and individual initiative. Such men are not given to blind obedience to mere authority; rather they are bound to their duties and fellow crew members by a self-imposed discipline, a willingness and high determination having no roots in bureaucratic rules and regulations.

The bonds of comradeship between members of any bomber crew were almost invariably fiercely knit. Such cohesion of minds and purpose was – if nothing else – vital for the common desire to survive. Yet as sortie followed sortie that link often became even deeper, as the unsuspected depths of each man's quality became evident. It was a spirit invariably carried forward when veterans of a first operational tour undertook further tours with fresh crews, thereby forming a near-tradition.

Pure strategists of the air war might have regarded losses of aircraft and crews as cold data in statistical surveys, but to every air crew man the war was a matter of people – men with whom they shared common dangers in the air, and the reliefs of off-duty relaxations. To wake one morning in a hut filled with men and boys with whom one had shared so many experiences, then return next morning after a sortie to find several empty beds – the occupants of which only hours before had been joking, laughing, planning the next night off – was an almost unbearable experience, and perhaps added even more necessity to the unbidden desire to stay close to one's own crew.

The unnumbered occasions of members of a particular air crew placing the safety of other members above their own lives are now almost legendary. This was especially true of bomber skippers, several of whom were awarded posthumous Victoria Crosses for deliberately staying at the controls of crippled aircraft in order to give their crews a slim chance to live by abandoning the aircraft first. Other posthumous VCs went to men like Ron Middleton and Arthur Aaron who, mortally wounded with no hope of survival, spent their dying moments concentrated on getting their crews to safety. On rare occasions such deliberate acts of selflessness resulted in pilots' escaping death.

One particular example of 'daring and winning' happened on the early morning of 21 December 1943 at Graveley airfield. A Toronto-born Canadian pilot, Squadron Leader Julian Sale, had piloted Halifax HX328 to Frankfurt the previous evening as a Primary Visual Marker for the 600-plus main force. Over the target thick clouds at low heights obscured Sale's view of the intended aiming point and he made five circuits at succeedingly lower altitudes attempting to identify the target to no avail. Releasing his high explosive bomb load, he retained his target indicators and returned to Graveley. On reaching base, and as he circled the field prior to landing, one of the TIs in the bomb bay detonated, setting the rear turret and a wing on fire. Climbing away from the airfield in a full-boost climb to 2,000 feet, Sale levelled out and ordered his crew to bale out. He then trimmed the Haifax to stay (hopefully) in level flight as he prepared to take to his parachute and follow his crew -- only to find Flight Lieutenant Bob Lamb, his mid-upper gunner, standing by the pilot's seat holding a burned out parachute pack. Sale immediately forgot his own intended escape, radioed Graveley to clear the runway for an emergency landing, and flew the blazing Halifax down quickly, taking it at full speed as far as possible away from the main buildings. As the burning aircraft slowed down, Sale and Lamb leapt out, still in full flying gear, and raced as fast as possible away from the bomber. Just 200 yards were covered before the Halifax exploded and burned out, flinging both men onto the ground by blast, but both then stood up uninjured.

Julian Sale's luck had been stretched over a long period of operations. On 1 May 1943 he had been shot down on a sortie, but evaded capture, returned to England, and became commander of 35 Squadron's A Flight before the 20/21 December sortie already described. In the interim he was awarded a DSO and Bar, and a DFC, but on 19 February 1944, during the outward leg of a raid against Leipzig, Julian Sale's luck run out. Attacked from below by a Wunstorf-based Junkers Ju 88 nightfighter, Sale was wounded and one of his Halifax's fuel tanks erupted in flames. Ordering his crew to take to their parachutes, the wounded Sale managed to follow suit shortly after. Tragically, his wounds proved fatal and he died on 20 March 1944 in captivity.

If the tradition for a skipper to place his crew's lives before his own was constantly exemplified by many experienced pilots, it was not confined to the old hands. Flying Officer H. G. Payne – 'Lofty', due to his large physical size – had been a farmer before he joined the RAAF from his hometown of Nungarin, West Australia. On 25 April 1945 – two months before his 25th birthday – Lofty Payne was skippering a Lancaster of No. 460 Squadron RAAF out of Binbrook on only his seventh operational trip. The target was Hitler's private mountain retreat at Berchtesgaden, a daylight attack for which a force of 359 Lancasters had initially been despatched.

Payne was one of the last to make his bombing run, and only seconds after releasing the bomb load his aircraft was hit by nine direct flak hits right in the belly. The bomb bay doors were blown away, both port engines erupted in flames and the starboard inner motor was shattered, instrument panels were smashed, and the fuselage and wings were punctured in dozens of places. Seconds after that the only remaining good engine became useless, leaving Payne with a burning, broken, 65,000 lb 'glider' to control.

To the north, some forty miles away, were the forward American infantry lines, and Payne edged his Lancaster round hoping to glide to these, but he quickly realised that the fuel tanks had also been ruptured as raw fuel began flooding the fuselage floor. It would need just one spark to convert the Lancaster to a cremation chamber, so Payne ordered his crew to abandon ship through the nose hatch in order to check them all out safely. He next began to unstrap himself from his seat in order to be ready to follow them, but found the last man, his rear gunner, was trailing a petrol-soaked, already spilled 'chute – its release ring had accidentally hooked on some projection as the gunner paddled through the fuselage to the nose end. Payne told him to find the normal spare 'chute quickly, but when the gunner came forward again it was to report that the spare had not been put aboard prior to take-off. Payne now had two choices – to bale out safely himself, or take the slimmest of chances for survival by trying to ride the burning Lancaster down and crash-land to give both men a faint hope of living.

For Payne, though, there was only one choice in his mind. He climbed back into his seat and began letting down from some 15,000 feet, ever-conscious of the burning port outer engine which was spreading its flames slowly towards the inboard fuel tank in the wing. In the fuselage the pool of loose fuel too was getting deeper, filling the interior with vapours which would need little to ignite them and blow the Lancaster to oblivion. Reaching a height of 500 feet, Payne care-fully turned the bomber into wind prior to landing, only to be con-fronted by some high tension overhead wires. Now close to stalling, the Lancaster dipped just under these wires – so close that they sliced off the tops of the aircraft's tail fins – then bellied in for a heart-stopping crashlanding. For these few seconds Payne's fortunes were good – despite the impact, the friction-heat as the bomber ploughed across a large field, and a six-inches deep fuselage pool of naked fuel, there was no fire or explosion. Payne and his gunner evacuated the wreck smartly, but were almost immediately arrested by a bunch of very young Hitler Youth soldiers nervously holding lethal sub-machine guns. Taken into captivity shortly after by older Germans, Payne spent a few weeks as a prisoner of war before the Allied victory in Europe led to his repatriation to England. He received no award for his action on, rather appropriately, Anzac Day, April 25th, but Payne's private reward was knowing he'd saved his crew – it was all he needed.

Two New Zealand pilots faced with the same basic choice – to live themselves, or try to succour their faithful crews – were Flight Lieutenant N. A. D. Stokes, an ex-clerk from Christchurch, and Flying Officer I. E. Blance, an ex-cinema projectionist from New Plymouth. Both attempted to save their crews – and both died. The occasion was a raid on Stuttgart on 29 July 1944. On the outward trip Stokes' Lancaster was attacked by a Luftwaffe nightfighter, its cannon shells killing the rear gunner instantly and traversing the length of the fuselage, smashing equipment and putting the crew intercomm out of action. The Lancaster fell away in an uncontrolled dive, with a fire in the bomb bay threatening to spread and filling the fuselage with acrid smoke fumes.

Stokes and his second pilot struggled with the damaged controls attempting to bring the bomber's nose up onto an even keel. It took every ounce of their combined muscle-power, with legs braced against the instrument panel, but they succeeded in levelling out at low altitude. Still losing height steadily, with the bomb bay fire intensifying, apart from the increased attentions of flak and searchlight batteries, the Lancaster was obviously unable to remain airborne much longer, so Stokes ordered his crew out. Remaining at his controls to maintain the Lancaster's steady descent, Stokes was still in his seat when, only a minute later, the bomber exploded into the earth.

For Blance the trip to the target had been without incident. Having duly bombed the target, he was on course for England when a nightfighter homed in on him and attacked. Its first burst of shells put all four engines out of commission, setting fire to the bomber, and raked the fuselage from end to end, killing the mid-upper gunner and wireless operator, and wounding the navigator. Its second run-in took it straight through a concentrated burst of fire from the rear gunner, and it spun away to eventually crash. Fully ablaze and almost out of control the stricken Lancaster plunged towards the ground, yet Blance managed to hold it steady enough for three crew men to take to their parachutes before the bomber dived into the ground, crashing within half a mile of its recent Luftwaffe opponent. Only seven months earlier Blance had celebrated his entry to legal adulthood – his twenty-first birthday.

If inexperience was allied naturally to slender odds for survival of any first operational tour, it did not follow that long experience guaranteed avoidance of the Grim Reaper. Squadron Leader H. F. Slade, DSO, DFC, an Australian veteran skipper of No. 156 Squadron PFF, was one of 307 heavy bombers and Mosquitos' pilots who set out to bomb Hamburg on the night of 28/29 July 1944. For Slade it was the ultimate trip of his third tour of ops, and his thoughts included anticipation of the 'tour-ex' party awaiting him back at Upwood when he returned. On reaching the target he commenced the longish run-in to bomb, but was hit by flak which among other damage riddled his aileron controls. Holding the Lancaster as steady as possible, Slade continued his run-in, heard his bomb aimer call 'Bombs gone', then felt the aircraft 'fall out of my hands', slowly spiralling downwards out of control. Slade warned his crew to stand by for bale-out, but finally managed to regain a modicum of control over the diving bomber.

With the physical help of his navigator and flight engineer, Slade gingerly edged the Lancaster out of the flak zone and set course for base. His aileron control was no better than ten per cent, leaving him no possibility of taking evasive action in the event of meeting any nightfighter or further flak belts en route to the coast. The journey home became an unceasing concentration on delicate balancing of fuel weights, while every second was spent trying to prevent the Lancaster steepening its constant shallow nose-down attitude – any moment's loss of that physical and mental effort would have seen the aircraft fall away instantly to the sea below. Eventually reaching Woodbridge, Slade gathered his last dregs of strength and willpower and slid the Lancaster in for a crash-landing, wrecking the aircraft but without injury to any of his crew. The Reaper had been denied seven more lives.

To newly-commissioned Pilot Officer A. J. Cockerill, a Halifax captain with No. 462 Squadron RAAF, the ops detailed for the night of 14/15 October 1944 appeared to promise something big. The target was to be Duisburg, and many of the squadron's crews had already visited that city during daylight on that day, the 14th, and were now going back again for an immediate second crack. No. 462 Squadron had detailed thirteen Halifax crews for the second (night) raid, including Cockerill; one small part of a total force of 1,065 bombers due to devastate Duisburg that night. The daytime raid had been, in the words of one participating pilot, 'hairy, with Jerry fighters roaming all around', and fifteen bombers had been lost. The follow-up night foray proved much quieter in terms of opposition from nightfighters but equally dangerous in terms of flak opposition. For Cockerill the flak began early, zeroing in on his Halifax as this was coned accurately by searchlights even before Cockerill had begun his bombing run. The first flak burst shredded the forward fuselage wounding Cockerill in his left eye, knocking him unconscious on impact.

The Halifax immediately dropped its nose and began to dive at a steep angle, but Cockerill regained his senses, pulled it out of its descent, then despite his wound resumed his run-in to bomb. Once the bomb load had gone Cockerill refused a morphia injection – he knew that only he could pilot the aircraft back, and that he would need a clear mind. Setting course, in constant pain and steadily growing weaker from blood loss, Cockerill remained at the controls throughout the return flight.

Shortly after leaving the target the Halifax was suddenly illuminated from above by a string of fighter flares, increasing the tension aboard, but fortunately no nightfighter appeared. Then one engine started pluming flames and took time before being extinguished. By the time Cockerill was approaching the Kent coast he was virtually blind and unable to read his instruments, but called up a crew member to stand by him and shout out necessary readings as he prepared to bring his aircraft in to land at the nearest airfield, Manston. Cockerill succeeded in bringing off a smooth emergency landing, without injury to his crew – then collapsed over his controls. Cockerill survived the war – yet another bomber captain who had placed the lives of his crew before his personal safety. He was awarded an immediate DSO for doing so.

Myriad other examples could be given of the skippers' code of 'bring 'em back alive'; supreme acts of selfless concern for the men who collectively and individually placed their complete trust – and lives – in the care of *their* pilot even when a situation seemed utterly hopeless. This unity of trust and confidence often led to crews completing one tour of operations and willingly volunteering for an immediate second tour with their own skipper – on occasion the pilot personally 'volunteered' his crew to do this *without* consulting them first! For some men the operational aspects of flying were the only worthwhile part of their service; being on ops for such men became almost the *only* way of life – it got into the blood, ever-beckoning, ever-satisfying. Leonard Cheshire and Guy Gibson, both VCs, even persuaded higher authorities that unless they were returned to operations, they might develop virtual neuroses. Too often this seemingly irrational urge to constantly fly operationally led to tragic cases of individual bomber barons with already outstanding careers undertaking 'just one more op' – and paying the supreme penalty. Guy Gibson, vc, was one such case, being killed on the night of 19 September 1944 when acting as Master Bomber for a main force attack against Rheydt and München Gladbach. Gibson had spent months in a desk-job, pleading to be allowed to return to operations, and the AOC-in-C, Bomber Command, Butch Harris, had (against his personal judgment) relented to the extent of 'just one more' sortie.

Other 'hard-luck' cases come to mind readily, veteran bomber pilots who had completed two and three times the normal ration of sorties, yet were impelled to fly one more. Danny Everett was one such compulsive case. Starting his career as a Sergeant pilot, D. B. 'Danny' Everett rose to Squadron Leader and was awarded a triple DFC during three operational tours, amounting to 98 sorties. At that point Danny was *ordered* off operations and posted to a safe staff job, testing new aircraft at PFF Group maintenance units. On 7 March 1945 – only eight weeks before VE Day and the cessation of the European conflict – Everett heard that his old unit, 35 Squadron, was operating that night, and that there was 'a spare kite available'. Without informing his immediate superiors, Danny scrounged together a scratch crew and took off behind the rest of 35 Squadron's Lancasters in the spare kite – he never returned.

For Wing Commander W. G. Lockhart – 'Guy' – who was eventually the recipient of a DSO, DFC & Bar, and *Croix de Guerre*, there was never to be a full period of his flying career when he was not undertaking operations of some kind, *any* kind, such was his dedication to pursuing the fight against Germany to the bitter end. His first taste of operations early in the war was as a fighter pilot, but by 1942 he was engaged in the secret sorties of No. 161 Squadron at Tempsford, flying Lysanders and other types of modified aircraft to convey or retrieve secret agents to or from German-occupied territories in Europe.

It was a task demanding superlative skills, judgment, and raw courage; deliberately landing in enemy territory by night, unescorted, prey not only to the obvious dangers of Luftwaffe flak, searchlights, and roving nightfighters, but even the constant possibility of being betrayed by traitors, or simply crashing on primitive grass fields, unlit and unfamiliar in near-total darkness on every sortie or drop. The skills and courage applied to this role by Guy Lockhart were officially recognised by the awards of a DFC, then a DSO, in mid-1942.

Returning to more conventional operations,Lockhart was appointed as commander of No. 692 Squadron at the close of 1943. The squadron formed officially at Graveley on 1 January 1944 with Mosquito bombers as part of the PFF's Light Night Striking Force (LNSF) and soon began ranging far and wide over Germany, bombing Berlin and similar key targets, often carrying single 4,000 lb HC 'Cookies'. Lockhart's personal hatred of the Nazi regime often motivated him to press home attacks in circumstances which might have deterred other pilots, as on the occasion when one engine of his Mosquito failed on the outward leg of a sortie to Berlin. Feathering the propeller of the offending motor, Lockhart carried on to his target and bombed. On other sorties the Mosquito crews of 692 Squadron, unarmed and unescorted, flew spoof raids to decoy the Luftwaffe nightfighters away from actual main force objectives; as on the night of 5 January 1944 when a few crews ostensibly marked Berlin, while the main force attacked Stettin. It meant running the considerable risk of flak and fighter interception, but after the raid the Mosquito crews learned that their feint had worked beautifully; nearly all nightfighters had been called to Berlin, while the main raid had suffered negligible interference from the Luftwaffe.

On 22 March 1944 No. 7 Squadron (Lancasters) at Oakington lost its commanding officer, Group Captain K. Rampling, DSO, DFC on operations, and Guy Lockhart was appointed to fill the vacancy. Just five weeks later Lockhart set out on a sortie, with a crew gathered together from several senior squadron officers, and failed to return. Several months after his death the *London Gazette* promulgated a late citation for a Bar to Guy Lockhart's DFC. Perhaps no finer assessment of Guy Lockhart can be found than that made by the PFF's commander, Air Vice-Marshal Don Bennett, who said of him;* 'I never, throughout the entire war, met anybody so fanatically courageous and "press-on" at all times and in all circumstances. Virtually nothing would stop him . . . his determination passed all bounds.'

If the team spirit of air crews was most plainly evident among the heavy bomber units, it was transformed into virtual brotherhood in the Mosquito squadrons, where a pilot and his navigator sat almost shoulder to shoulder in the cramped, claustrophobic panoply of the aircraft's tiny cockpit. Squadron Leader W. W. – 'Bill' – Blessing was a 'Mozzie' pilot, an Australian ex-salesman born in Glen Innes, New South Wales in October 1912, who came to England to fly with the RAF during the early part of the war. Bill first saw operational service with No. 13 Squadron, but in October 1942, as a Flight Lieutenant, he joined No. 105 Squadron at Marham, Norfolk; the first unit to operate Mosquito bombers. Bill had only recently learned that his brother, Sergeant W. G. Blessing, had been killed providing air escort to a Malta convoy on 15 June 1942 – a private grief which added to his incentive to help defeat Germany.

For the following nine months Bill Blessing took part in most of 105's daylight sorties, usually with Flying Officer Muirhead, DFM as his navigator. Awarded a DFC in early 1943, Blessing was promoted to Squadron Leader to command 105's A Flight, and flew as the second wave leader to Wing Commander Reg Reynolds, DSO, DFC in a daring attack against the Schott glass works at Jena and its allied

* *Pathfinder* by AVM D. C. T. Bennett; F. Muller, 1958.

Zeiss optical factory. The raid took place in the evening of 27 May 1943 – the deepest penetration sortie undertaken by the squadron by that date – and Blessing received a DSO for his part in the operation.

In mid-1943 the Mosquitos commenced regular night sorties when 105 Squadron was transferred to the aegis of No. 8 PFF Group from June 1943, and in the following month commenced Oboe – guided marking duties ahead of main force bomber streams raiding Europe. By early 1944 the squadron began receiving modified 'fat-belly' Mosquitos, capable of carrying the 4,000 lb HC 'Cookie' blast bomb and dropped its first 'Cookie' on Duisburg on 7 March. The next three months saw the squadron involved in the pre-invasion softening-up offensive undertaken by Bomber Command; attacking French and German communications' systems and taking out key targets likely to impede the projected Allied invasion of Normandy. By 6 June – D-Day – 105 Squadron was operating by day and by night, round the clock, despatching sixteen, twenty or even twenty-five sorties on each occasion; a pace which was maintained during the crucial first few weeks of the Allied landings.

On the evening of 7 July the squadron despatched ten Mosquitos to mark Caen for a main force of 467 'heavies', with Bill Blessing and his navigator Pilot Officer D. T. Burke, in Mosquito ML964, 'J', detailed as a primary marker. As Blessing began his run-in he was intercepted by a Luftwaffe fighter whose fire was accurate, severely damaging the Mosquito. Blessing's first thought was for his companion and he ordered Burke to bale out – seconds after the navigator had left, the Mosquito fell into an uncontrollable spin and broke up.

Epilogue

The foregoing chapters have offered merely a glimpse of a tiny selection of bomber barons and other equally outstanding individuals of RAF Bomber Command during the fateful war years of 1939–45. Had space been available many, many more such men might have been worthily included; men such as Group Captains Johnny Fauquier, R. J. Lane, G. H. Womersley, K. J. 'Slim' Somerville, George Grant, S. W. B. Menaul, R. W. Cox, J. A. Ingham, R. W. P. 'Fatty' Collings, T. L. Bingham-Hall, John Woodroffe. Or Wing Commanders Ray Hilton, Roy Elliott, Alan Craig, 'Tubby' Baker. Or Flying Officer G. Wilson, who won a DSO, DFC and DFM before his death in action on 6 September 1944. The list is long. If each of those men were indeed individuals, then each in his own manner displayed some, if not most, of the sterling qualities inherent in widely varying degrees in every man who flew, however, briefly, as air crew in a bomber then.

Certain individuals have since come to be dubbed heroes – an appellation solely created by sensation-conscious media or adolescent idealism – but few, if any, ever regarded themselves in such romantic terms. In the main they were essentially ordinary men, mostly in the first hot flush of adulthood, inexorably caught up in the human race's latest attempt to commit genocide, who volunteered to do their bit for their mother country. Being human, and not immortal, they possessed all the human frailties and weaknesses, yet when the test of fire was upon them the vast majority gave abundant evidence of those rarer human qualities – endurance, courage, and a selfless spirit seldom encountered in the present-day world.

The aftermath of the bomber men's war was principally one of great loss. Some 56,000 such men died, either on actual operations or in preparation for them, men who – like the many thousands of other men and women who did not live to witness the eventual 'peace' – represented the very finest of their generation. One can only theorise on the genetic impairment their loss did to our present society. Even those who survived the 'the valley of the shadow' were permanently transformed, having been witness to scenes and deeds which would remain imprinted upon their memories for the rest of their lives. As in all wars, many thousands were not only mentally scarred but faced a bleak future of physical handicap; young men at the peak of blossoming manhood condemned to a lifetime of pain and/or deprived ability. Boys like the 19-year-old Brunon Godlewski, an American-born son of Polish immigrants, who came to England voluntarily to fly as an air gunner with the Free Polish Air Force. On the night of 5 March 1943, flying in a Wellington of No. 305 (Polish) Squadron attacking Essen, he received severe wounds from a German nightfighter, having both arms almost severed. Authority rewarded him with the highest Polish decorations for valour, a British DFM, an American DFC and Medal of the Purple Heart – and two crude 'tin' hands.

Others suffered horrific burning and mutilation, to be restored to a normality by the skills and utter dedication of men like 'Archie' McIndoe, the eminent plastic surgeon, and his staff at East Grinstead, home of the Guinea Pig Club. Whether crippled or whole, the survivors had been catapulted from innocent youth to veteran maturity in a fraction of the more normal leisurely transformation process; then returned to civilian mundanity abruptly to re-adjust their as yet unfulfilled future lives.

Nothwithstanding the double traumas of the hell of operations, and resulting permanent physical impairment, a high proportion of those men put aside bitterness, recrimination and self-pity and forged successful and fully satisfying lives in Civvy Street – in itself an overt exemplification of the spirit of determination and sheer guts displayed by almost all bomber (and other) air crews throughout the war. If any doubt still remains in their private thoughts in reflective moments it is the simple query, 'Was it all worth it?' Or in other words, was such a scale of sacrifice justified in the context of the post-bellum society which evolved after 1945? The answer can only come from the conscience of each nation, each individual, presently enjoying a freedom they might never have known had the Nazi dream of global subjugation become reality. Possibly, Rubert Brooke's tribute to the dead is the most succinct:

> These laid the world away; poured out the red
> Sweet wine of youth; gave up the years to be
> Of work and joy, and that unhoped serene,
> That men call age; and those who would have been,
> Their sons, they gave, their immortality.

Acknowledgments

The author acknowledges most gratefully the help and co-operation of the following: The late Squadron Leader S. Clayton, DSO, DFC, DFM; the late Air Commodore Sir Hughie Edwards, VC, KCMG, CB, DSO, OBE, DFC; E. Hine, Esq of the Imperial War Museum Photographic Library; Major H. C. Knilans, DSO, DFC; R. W. Mack, Esq of the RAF Museum, Hendon; Group Captain T. G. Mahaddie, DSO, DFC, AFC, C Eng, AFRAeS; H. Meades, Esq; Wing Commander J. R. G. Ralston, DSO, AFC, DFM; Dr S. Z. Ross, DD; M. J. Scadden of the MOD, RNZAF; W. E. Sutton, Esq; G. R. Whitten, Esq; the late Group Captain D T. Witt, DSO, DFC, DFM. And never least, Dave Gray of Walkers Studios, Scarborough for his customary magic in producing superb prints for use in illustration.

Select Bibliography

Anderson, W., *Pathfinders*; Jarrolds, 1946.

Bell, E. D., *110 Squadron*; Air Britain, 1969.

Bennett, D. C. T., *Pathfinder*; Muller, 1958.

Bowyer, C., *Mosquito at War*; Ian Allan, 1972.

Bowyer, C., *Path Finders at War*; Ian Allan, 1977.

Bowyer, C., *For Valour* – The Air VCs; Kimber, 1978.

Bowyer, C., *Bomber Group at War*; Ian Allan, 1981.

Bowyer, C., *Wellington at War*; Ian Allan, 1982.

Bowyer, M. J. F., *2 Group*; Faber & Faber, 1974.

Capka, J., *Red Sky at Night*, Blond, 1958.

Cumming, M., *Pathfinder Cranswick*; Kimber, 1962.

Embry, B. E., *Mission Completed*; Methuen, 1957.

Firkins, P., *Strike & Return*; Australia (460 Sqn).

Hamilton, A., *Wings of Night*; Kimber, 1977.

Kostenuk, S./Griffin, J., *RCAF Squadrons*; Canadian War Museum, 1977.

Lucas, F. J., *Popeye Lucas*, Queenstown; Reed, 1968.

Mason, T., *Leads the Field* (12 Sqn); Private, 1960.

Mason, T., *9 Squadron*; Beaumont Aviation, 1965.

Moyes, P. J. R., *Bomber Squadrons*; Macdonald, 1964.

Musgrove, G., *Pathfinder Force*; Macdonald & Jane's, 1976.

Northway, B. (Ed), *107 Squadron History*; Private, 1964.

Ransome, D., *105 Squadron History*; Air Britain, 1968.

Reilly, R., *The Sixth Floor*; Frewin, 1969.

Robeson, N. J., *History of XV Squadron*; Private, 1975.

Robertson, B., *Lancaster*; Harleyford, 1964.

Saward, D., *The Bomber's Eye*; Cassell, 1959.

Sharp, M./Bowyer, M. J. F., *Mosquito*; Faber & Faber, 1967.

West, R. J. (Ed), *7 Squadron History*; Private, 1974.

White, A., *44 Squadron History*; Private, 1977.

Wooldridge, J. de L., *Low Attack*; Sampson & Low, 1944.

Wynn, H. (Ed), *Fighter Pilot*; Kimber, 1976.

Index

Index